Professional Translators in Nineteenth-Century France

This book shines a light on the practices and professional identities of translators in nineteenth-century France, speaking to the translatorial turn in translation studies which spotlights translators as active agents in the international circulation of texts.

The volume charts the sociocultural, legal, and economic developments which paved the way for the development of the professional translation industry in France in the period following the French Revolution through to the First World War. Drawing on archival material from French publishers, institutional archives, and translators' own discourses, and applying historiographical methodologies, Pickford explores the working conditions of professional translators during this time and the subsequent professional identities which emerged from the collective practice of translation across publishing, business, and government. In its diachronic approach to translators' practices and identities, the book aims to recover the collective contributions of these translators and, in turn, paves the way for a new approach to "translator history from below".

The volume will appeal to students and scholars in translation studies, particularly those with an interest in literary translation, translation history, and translator practices.

Susan Pickford is Head of the English unit at the Faculty of Translation and Interpreting, University of Geneva, Switzerland.

Routledge Research on Translation and Interpreting History
Edited by Christopher Rundle, Pekka Kujamäki and Michaela Wolf

This series showcases cutting-edge research in English on the interdisciplinary dialogue between translation and interpreting studies and historical perspectives. Building off the emergence of translation and interpreting history as a subdiscipline of the field in its own right, the series features interdisciplinary work spanning a range of cultural and geographical contexts which engages in the treatment of translation and translation practice as social and historical events.

Languages in the Crossfire
Interpreters in the Spanish Civil War (1936–1939)
Jesús Baigorri-Jalón
Translated by Holly Mikkelson

Queering Translation History
Shakespeare's Sonnets in Czech and Slovak Transformations
Eva Spišiaková

Retracing the History of Literary Translation in Poland
People, Politics, Poetics
Edited by Magda Heydel and Zofia Ziemann

The Renaissance of Women Translators in 19th-Century Greece
Vasiliki Misiou

Professional Translators in Nineteenth-Century France
Susan Pickford

For more information about this series, please visit https://www.routledge.com/Routledge-Research-on-Translation-and-Interpreting-History/book-series/RRTIH

Professional Translators in Nineteenth-Century France

Susan Pickford

NEW YORK AND LONDON

First published 2025
by Routledge
605 Third Avenue, New York, NY 10158

and by Routledge
4 Park Square, Milton Park, Abingdon, Oxon, OX14 4RN

Routledge is an imprint of the Taylor & Francis Group, an informa business

© 2025 Susan Pickford

The right of Susan Pickford to be identified as author of this work has been asserted in accordance with sections 77 and 78 of the Copyright, Designs and Patents Act 1988.

All rights reserved. No part of this book may be reprinted or reproduced or utilised in any form or by any electronic, mechanical, or other means, now known or hereafter invented, including photocopying and recording, or in any information storage or retrieval system, without permission in writing from the publishers.

Trademark notice: Product or corporate names may be trademarks or registered trademarks, and are used only for identification and explanation without intent to infringe.

Library of Congress Cataloging-in-Publication Data
Names: Pickford, Susan, author.
Title: Professional translators in nineteenth-century France / Susan Pickford.
Description: New York, NY: Routledge, 2025. |
Series: Routledge research
on translation and interpreting history |
Includes bibliographical references and index. |
Identifiers: LCCN 2024030642 | ISBN 9781032001791 (hardback) |
ISBN 9781032001821 (paperback) | ISBN 9781003173090 (ebook)
Subjects: LCSH: Translators–France–History–19th century. |
Translating and interpreting–France–History–19th century.
Classification: LCC P306.8.F8 P53 2025 |
DDC 418/.02094409034–dc23/eng/20240819
LC record available at https://lccn.loc.gov/2024030642

ISBN: 9781032001791 (hbk)
ISBN: 9781032001821 (pbk)
ISBN: 9781003173090 (ebk)

DOI: 10.4324/9781003173090

Typeset in Sabon
by Deanta Global Publishing Services, Chennai, India

Contents

	List of Figures	*vi*
	Introduction	1
1	The Emergence of a Mass Market for Translation	12
2	Tracing an Emergent Discourse of Translatorial Labour	43
3	Tracing Translators in Publishers' Archives	65
4	Developing a Legal Framework for the Nineteenth-Century French Literary Translation Market	85
5	The Economic Lives of Nineteenth-Century Women Translators	109
6	The Life and Career of Auguste-Jean-Baptiste Defauconprêt, Inventor of the "Lingual Steam Engine"	131
	Coda	166
	Appendix: Translators and Transactions in the Institut mémoires de l'édition contemporaine archives	*171*
	Bibliography	*201*
	Index	*222*

Figures

1.1 An invoice issued on 2 October 1810 by the translator
J.C. von Asten in Aix-la-Chapelle. Image courtesy of
the *Archives nationales*, Pierrefitte-sur-Seine   34

1.2 The price list from the advertising brochure for
Léopold Courrouve dit Pold's *Athénée polyglotte*
translation and business services agency. Image
courtesy of the Newberry Library   40

2.1 Auguste-Jean-Baptiste Defauconprêt's call for
subscribers opening the French translation of
Walladmor, 1825. Image courtesy of the Bibliothèque
nationale de France   63

3.1a and 3.1b Translation contract between Charles Lever
and Charles Lahure, September 1857. Images courtesy
of Archives Hachette/IMEC   68

3.2 Pre-prepared form signed by Charles Berthoud
to acknowledge payment for translating Ouida's
Guilderoi, 5 May 1892. Image courtesy of Archives
Hachette/IMEC   82

4.1 François Rignoux's list of errors and omissions in
Defauconprêt's translation of *Ivanhoe*, presented to
the court to counter accusations of plagiarism. Image
courtesy of the Bibliothèque nationale de France   93

4.2 *Bureau de la propriété littéraire* registration ensuring
the exclusive right to translate Benjamin Disraeli's
Lothair, 2 June 1870. Image courtesy of Archives
Hachette/IMEC   97

4.3 Prospectus for Charles Bernard Derosne's cross-
Channel literary property agency, 5 February 1865.
Image courtesy of the Bibliothèque nationale de France   98

5.1 Official record of Louise Swanton-Belloc's literary
stipend, noting her death in 1881. Image courtesy of
the *Archives nationales*, Pierrefitte-sur-Seine   119

5.2	Police report into the Belloc family finances, 19 December 1856. Image courtesy of the *Archives nationales*, Pierrefitte-sur-Seine	121
5.3	Hetzel account book for 1866, showing details of translation payments to Emma Allouard. Image courtesy of Archives Hetzel/IMEC	127
6.1	Photographic portraits of Auguste-Jean-Baptiste Defauconprêt (bottom left) and his son Charles-Auguste Defauconprêt (bottom right), *Portraits d'écrivains et hommes de lettres de la seconde moitié du XIXe siècle* vol. 2. Image courtesy of the Bibliothèque nationale de France	133

Introduction

As I began writing this book in late 2021, TikTokers were hotly debating the quality of the English subtitles on Netflix's highly successful Korean drama *Squid Game*. Podcaster Youngmi Mayer's video on the topic has to date garnered an astonishing 2.9 million likes and 51,600 comments, taking translation viral.[1] Experienced subtitlers soon weighed in on Youngmi Mayer's critique of the *Squid Game* subtitles, pointing to her apparent lack of knowledge of the constraints inherent in subtitling practice and challenging working conditions in the modern subtitling industry.[2] A few months prior, the controversy over who should translate Amanda Gorman's poem *The Hill We Climb* into Dutch had spilled over the confines of literary translation circles to attract international media attention. Critics of the decision to entrust the translation of Gorman's poem to the non-binary Dutch novelist Marieke Lucas Rijneveld pointed out that they had no prior translation experience and had indeed spoken in public before about their lack of expertise in English (Collectif 2020; Kotze 2021).

In fact, translation had quite a media moment in 2021. As I began teaching my first classes at the University of Geneva in early September, the renowned literary translator Jennifer Croft was busy launching a campaign to give into-English literary translators cover credit. The campaign led by Croft, best known for winning the International Man Booker Prize in 2018 for her translation from the Polish of Olga Tokarczuk's *Flights*, met with some success: Pan Macmillan became the first major publisher to announce they would now do so. Croft's campaign for translator visibility, echoed in *The Guardian* article "Why Translators Should Be Named on Book Covers" on 10 September 2021, was an impassioned plea for recognition of literary translators. Translators, she compellingly argued, choose

---

1 https://www.tiktok.com/@youngmimayer/video/7013820557414141189?lang=en (accessed 5 May 2023).
2 https://www.nbcnews.com/news/asian-america/translators-experts-weigh-squid-game-subtitle-debate-rcna2568 (accessed 5 May 2023).

DOI: 10.4324/9781003173090-1

2 Professional Translators in Nineteenth-Century France

every word in the books they write; they are not "ninjas", but "guides" for readers and "advocates" for books. As such, they should be hailed for their creativity and be given equal billing to authors (Crofts 2021).

A month later, on 7 October, Crofts spoke out again. This time, she posted a tweet denouncing the expectation of unpaid labour in the literary translation sector, quoting a publisher who had asked her to volunteer her expertise for free. The tweet garnered over 4,400 likes and numerous responses, unanimous in their support of her position and comparing the position of literary translators as economic actors with professions and trades such as neurosurgery, baking, law, plumbing, and medicine.[3] In September, she had called for professional recognition within the creative economy for herself and her fellow translators; by October, the unnamed publisher was once again relegating her to amateur status in the expectation that she would be keen to volunteer her labour unpaid.

Translation does not often hit the headlines, but when it does, as this small cluster of viral translation debates demonstrates, questions of quality and visibility are brought to the fore. One largely unspoken issue behind such debates is the boundary between amateur and professional translation practice – a distinction brought into sharp relief by Croft's two experiences within the space of a month, which highlighted the fuzzy nature of this boundary and of professional translatorial identities.

Being a translator is not like being a doctor or a barrister. There are no barriers to entry, no binding codes of professional conduct, and no mechanisms for expelling members who fail to uphold professional standards. In most cases, translation is not a regulated profession (sworn translators being the major exception). The threshold and criteria for laying claim to professional status in translation are therefore by no means clear-cut. Svahn, Ruokonen, and Salmi (2018) explore how the boundaries around the profession are constructed, negotiated, and experienced, outlining various recent steps towards professionalisation in university training and accreditation. However, they conclude, the process of professionalisation is incomplete: translation remains a semi-profession with ill-defined, porous boundaries. Many people who would not call themselves translators do in fact translate in their daily lives; conversely, some people who *do* call themselves translators work rarely or work unpaid. There is a propensity for literary translators in particular to label themselves as such when the practice represents a small fraction of their working time and income. Croft's article in *The Guardian* equating literary translators with authors placed the former firmly within the exceptional economy of the arts and creative industries, in which unpaid labour is widely recognised

---

3 https://twitter.com/jenniferlcroft/status/1446089657759027206 (accessed 5 May 2023).

Introduction 3

as endemic (Brook, O'Brien and Taylor 2020). Yet her later tweet and its responses seemed on the contrary to suggest that literary translation was more akin to other economic sectors in which practitioners not only expect to be paid as a matter of course but measure their billable output down to the minute. While the two stances seem somewhat at odds with each other, the latter is commensurate with recent calls by leading business translators such as Chris Durban, Judy Jenner, and Michael Schubert to shift from a word-based billing model to hourly or lump-sum payments as a means of equating translation with a high-end professional service.[4] This range of stances taken by regular practitioners of translation points to a labile definition of translation as a professional practice, depending to a large extent on the market sector in which it is conducted (see for instance Dam and Koskinen 2016).

If issues of professional translatorial identity are complicated to unravel in the present, attempting to do so in the past no doubt seems like a fool's errand. Yet there are good reasons to apply a historical lens to the question of professionalism in translation. First and foremost, there are no issues of client confidentiality, no non-disclosure agreements, no awkwardness relating to my own positionality as a practising translator. Taking a historical perspective lets me avoid perhaps intrusive conversations with colleagues about their experiences, their careers, their income. Second is the sheer thrill of the chase. Uncovering tenuous connecting threads between people long dead, when the scholar's searchlight serendipitously falls on a long-forgotten node in a long-lost network, is one of the great joys of research, movingly described by Mary Bardet:

> Increasingly entrenched in theory and rhetorical arguments, we forget to emphasise the thrill of tracking down forgotten stories, the pure excitement of uncovering the lives of neglected players, and the joy of finally being able to connect up seemingly unrelated dots.
>
> (Bardet 2021: 41)

Accordingly, this book sets out to explore how translators lived and worked, what their careers looked like, in nineteenth-century France. Anyone familiar with today's translation market will readily be able to gauge the extent to which the patterns and structures laid bare in the following chapters hold true today.

* * *

4 https://twitter.com/Degermanizer/status/1445177732422201345 (accessed 5 May 2023).

4 Professional Translators in Nineteenth-Century France

> Ne méritent-ils pas enfin une place dans l'histoire, ces serviteurs modestes de la France, qui ont défendu sa politique comme on défend un drapeau, et qui sont tombés plutôt que de la trahir? Ne valent-ils pas qu'on parle d'eux, ces vieillards blanchis sous le harnais administratif …?
>
> (Masson 1877: xi)

> [Do they not deserve a place in history at long last, these modest servants of France, who defended its policy like one defends a flag, and who fell rather than betray it? Are they not worthy of being spoken of, these old men grown hoary-headed under the administrative yoke …?][5]

In these impassioned terms, the late-nineteenth-century historian Frédéric Masson (1847–1923) spoke out in favour of what was not yet termed history from below. His history of the French Foreign Ministry in the revolutionary period includes painstakingly compiled records of personnel from the ministry's various incarnations across the period. Among the hoary-headed servants of revolutionary France he counted were the members of the *bureaux de traduction*: men from France, Ireland, and Italy who spent their days disseminating legal texts and revolutionary propaganda in both regional and foreign languages, giving language lessons and trawling the European press for intelligence relevant to French affairs (Masson 1877; Schreiber 2015; Kleinman 2005). Translating decrees and reports into German, Italian, and English was vital revolutionary work, "soit pour les faire pénétrer dans les camps ennemis soit pour en répandre la connaissance chez les peuples dont nos armées occupent les territoires" [either to take them into enemy camps, or to spread knowledge of them among peoples whose territories are occupied by our armies] (AN C/356, quoted in Schreiber 2015: 148).

Masson offers a partial response to Judith Woodsworth's questions on the transmission of revolutionary-era cultural values, "Who actually translated? How were the translators recruited?" His work likewise goes some way to shedding light on her hypothesis that "The translations were probably carried out by teams working in *ad hoc* translation bureaus" (2012: 203). Translation bureaus, yes; ad hoc, no. These were officially appointed government services with opening and closing hours and professional standards.

We know this from material held in the French national archives. We know that some translation bureau staff were recruited after writing to the Comité de Salut Public: a Venetian by the name of Vianelli was employed

---

5 Unless otherwise stated, all translations are by the author throughout.

on the basis of an application letter dated 17 messidor an II [5 July 1794].
We know they had fixed hours, since a decree dated 14 brumaire an III [4
November 1794] stipulated "les heures de sortie des employés du bureau
des traducteurs" [the time translation bureau staff were allowed to leave];
we know that they were held to certain professional standards, because
a certain Pierre-Louis Beaufort was dismissed in May 1795 for "inexact-
itudes dans son service" [lack of punctuality] (Masson 1877: 343). We
know the *Convention nationale* translators ran their own printing press,
anchoring them in the wider communication circuit (Schreiber 2015: 148;
Darnton 1982).

Yet much remains to be learned about the working practices of such
translation service staff. What did they earn? Did they have regular
breaks? Did they have to hit productivity targets? What tools did they
have at their disposal? Did they take their work home with them? Did they
see themselves as mere cogs in the revolutionary machine, or as linguists,
or language service providers, or translators? Did they see themselves as
professionals?

As outlined in the opening pages of this book, issues of professional
translational identity and workflow have begun to preoccupy translation
studies scholars working on the here and now, applying innovative interdisciplinary approaches such as translator self-image (Dam and Zethsen
2010; Singer Contreras 2022), ergonomics (Ehrensberger-Dow and
Hunziker Heeb 2016), and workplace studies (Risku, Rogl and Milosevic
2020; Moorkens 2020; Walker 2023) to individual translators, translation agencies, and language service providers (LSPs), building up a detailed
picture of what professional translation looks like in modern society. This
is necessary work, but insufficient. Without the diachronic angle, we lose
perspective (Grbić and Kujamäki 2018). The more we know about how
the LSP sector worked historically – long before it would have called itself
by that name – the more we can discern long-term patterns and trends and
the more this information can cross over into the industry to inform discussions around best practice. As translation studies matures as a field of
research, it has recently developed a series of highly specialised offshoots,
beginning with translator studies (Chesterman 2009) and subdividing into
literary translation studies (Large 2021), literary translator studies (Kaindl
2021), and translation industry studies (Walker 2022). Perhaps this book,
in its later chapters, can claim to inaugurate the new field of literary translation industry studies. Yet however we label this new research, and despite
the flourishing study of historiographical methodologies (Rizzi, Lang and
Pym 2019; Richter 2020; Rundle 2021; *Chronotopos* 2019–ongoing), little
work to date has sought to combine industry strands of research with a historical perspective. Furthermore, ironically, what work has been done fails
in some instances to circulate far beyond its original sphere of reception

6 *Professional Translators in Nineteenth-Century France*

for want of an English translation. Jennifer Willenberg's remarkable 2008 study of the distribution of English print in eighteenth-century Germany, *Distribution und Übersetzung englischen Schrifttums im Deutschland des 18. Jahrhunderts*, is a case in point: available only in German, it has been quoted almost exclusively in other German-language research.

The sparsity of historically informed industry research is perhaps understandable: trying to apply modern workplace studies approaches to translation history seems almost doomed to fail. As Anthony Pym remarked in his landmark 2008 essay "Humanizing Translation History", it is not easy to "unearth the obscure": it is challenging "to find out about translators as people, with their own life stories and evolving ideologies". Those who left the most traces tended to be those who "found fame wearing a different hat, as authors, political figures, polemicists, and so on" (Pym 2009: 32). Paradoxically, this has led to an over-focus on the most amateur practitioners, sociologically speaking, to the detriment of those most heavily invested in the translation field in professional terms. As a result, there are significant gaps in our knowledge of translation practices past, including the "daily practice" of working translators (Santoyo 2006; O'Sullivan 2012).

Even digging deep into the archives, actively seeking to foreground the everyday experiences of unsung translators is a challenge. Yet it is an important undertaking, to avoid the false sense of professional homogeneity that risks arising if the diversities of translator communities remain hidden (Atefmehr and Farahzad 2021). By the very nature of the archive, some translators and some categories of information are relatively easy to recover (Gomez 2017; Pickford 2021). Other sources can only be recovered with great difficulty, if at all. As a result, while most translators may be invisible to some extent, some are nonetheless more invisible than others, and some aspects of their working practice most invisible of all. History has often overlooked the men, and occasionally women, who earned a living from their language skills in centuries past, oiling the wheels of international trade and diplomacy.

Yet, as Masson demonstrates, we do catch occasional glimpses of their work obliquely, in archives and memoirs: enough to apply "method of clue" analysis to reveal the gaps in our knowledge and challenge the view of a monolithic past (Atefmehr and Farahzad 2021). Genealogy websites prove a surprisingly useful tool, building increasingly complete family trees and fleshing out social structures for figures once lost to history. Patiently, we are able to piece together snippets gleaned here and there to build up a picture – sometimes sparse, sometimes surprisingly complete – of the working lives of translators past, their place in society, their networks. Pleasingly, one such set of connections came to light while writing these opening paragraphs: as a young man in the 1860s, Frédéric Masson studied at the Collège Sainte-Barbe in Paris under the headship of Charles-Auguste Defauconprêt, one of the translators whose life and career are explored in depth in a later chapter. Another of the translators whose career Masson documented, the Irishman Nicholas Madgett, was a friend and associate of John Hurford Stone, who printed translations by Defauconprêt's better-known father Auguste-Jean-Baptiste. Translation in nineteenth-century France was sometimes a small world.

And by (sometimes laboriously) cross-referencing a range of sources we can, occasionally, arrive at more or less confident answers to some of the questions outlined above: how and when translators worked, how fast, and for how much money. Combining close reading of translated texts with the dictionaries then available on the market can tell us what difficulties they encountered. Cross-referencing publication dates announced in publishers' announcements on either side of the English Channel can point us to information on productivity. Translation contracts and publishers' sales ledgers give data on translator income. Where there is a will, there is – sometimes – a way.

Due to the nature of archives, much of the surviving material used for this book relates to one particular sector of the translation industry: book publishing. While this sector looms disproportionately large in translation studies research as a whole compared to its economic significance within the wider language services industry, this is at least partly due to the relative accessibility of sources; furthermore, broadly speaking, the literary translation scholar runs less risk than elsewhere of running into issues of data confidentiality, research ethics, or commercial sensitivities. This book did not set out to explore the publishing sector *per se*, but realistically – not least due to the existence of specialist archive collections such as the Institut mémoires de l'édition contemporaine (IMEC) in Caen and the ready availability of Google Books during the Covid pandemic, when much of this research was being conducted – that is where the bulk of the sources was to be found. While the findings relating to the professionalisation of translators in the publishing sector cannot be unproblematically mapped onto the wider translation sector in the nineteenth century without further study, some broad trends can be hypothesised: it seems likely, for instance, that translator income depended on the supply and demand for specific language pairs, on gender, and on geographical location, whatever the market sector. Furthermore, in the nineteenth century, the various language industry sectors were by no means separate entities: the various language-related professions had not yet (and indeed have still not yet) fully coalesced into wholly discrete professional sectors. As Kleinman (2005: 76) points out, Masson does not differentiate between *traducteurs* and *interprètes*, while working in a ministry *bureau de traduction* also involved a range of language-related tasks such as press monitoring and language teaching.

8 *Professional Translators in Nineteenth-Century France*

Translators, then as now, often combined their translation practice with other remunerative activities, both within and outside translation and other language-related work. William Duckett translated for the *bureau de traduction* during the French Revolution, taught English at Masson's alma mater the Collège Sainte-Barbe, wrote a *Nouvelle grammaire anglaise*, and published French versions of Ludwig of Bavaria's German verse (Kleinman 2005: 34; Berthier 2012: 22). Louis-Mathieu Langlès (1763–1824) translated a number of travel narratives from English in the early decades of the century, mostly relating to his main profession as a librarian and teacher of Persian at the École Spéciale des Langues Orientales in Paris. Later in the century, Léopold Courrouve dit Pold (dates unknown) ran a translation agency, *L'Athénée polyglotte*, that also offered a range of business-to-business services such as copying, research support, copywriting, and accountancy. It would therefore be somewhat anachronistic to map today's distinction between translation for publishing and translation for other sectors – particularly marked in the modern French market (Pickford 2014) – onto the nineteenth-century context. Nineteenth-century translators worked in businesses and government ministries, for the church and for special interest groups, for the press, for the medical profession, for the telegraph service. They worked in a society in which translation was ever more visible in the public sphere, in broadly multilingual urban settings in which language contact was frequently a daily experience and where language and translation issues were an integral part of the processes of modernisation, industrialisation, and democratisation (D'hulst and Koskinen 2020: 1).

In historiographical terms, one of the ambitions of this book has been to adopt a range of approaches, using various historical lenses to build up a multifaceted picture of nineteenth-century translation practice and the extent to which it can be framed as professional. In the main, it understands "professionalism" in a broad sense, acknowledging its fuzzy boundaries and seeking to account largely for the experiences of people who earned money, mainly or exclusively, from their skill in languages, often coupled with other translation-adjacent forms of writing and business-to-business services. It begins with a broad-brush, bird's-eye view of the translation sector as a whole in Chapter 1, homing in in subsequent chapters on the literary translation sector, then on the experience of individual translators across their careers, and finishing by putting one well-known translator under the microscope for an in-depth study of his daily working practices. The methods of book history are a constant thread running throughout the book, while individual chapters draw in turn on the debate on professional identity, recent work on translation in archives, legal history, cultural economics, workplace studies, and the emerging trend for bio-bibliographical databases.

Introduction 9

* * *

Chapter 1, "The Emergence of a Mass Market for Translation", sets the framework for subsequent chapters by outlining the broad translation market in nineteenth-century France, drawing in part on material previously published in French in the *Histoire des traductions en langue française* volume IV (Chevrel and Masson 2012), covering the nineteenth century. It takes a top-down approach to the issue of how translation was organised into various sectors, beginning with the revolutionary drive to put translation on a solid administrative footing as a tool of the new republic and studying the practice as a form of soft power. It examines the factors that played into the growth of a modern marketplace for translation and the emergent possibilities for bilinguals to build a lifelong translation career in the service of the state or in the fast-growing business services sector.

Chapter 2, "Tracing an Emergent Discourse of Translatorial Labour", teases out the threads of the longstanding, and long-overlooked, strand of discourse on literary translation as a form of labour. Tracing this strand of discourse back as far as mid-eighteenth-century England and Germany, it focuses on translatorial identity in seeking to understand how everyday translators – arguably the most professionalised of all writers, in this paradoxical corner of authorship, with its inverse relationship between prestige and professionalism – thought and wrote about themselves and the bread-and-butter work they did. It examines the flurry of labour metaphors for translation in the early nineteenth century, comparing translators to stonebreakers and slaughterhouse workers, as long-atomised practitioners began the lengthy process of coalescing into a recognisable socio-professional category as the marketplace matured. It concludes with a close reading of the metaphor of translation as Jacquard-programmed loomwork in translations of Walter Scott and Willibald Alexis (W. H. Häring).

Chapter 3, "Tracing Translators in Publishers' Archives", draws partly on material previously published in French in a special issue of the journal *Meta* on translators' archives, edited by Anthony Cordingley and Patrick Hersant in 2021. It draws on the surviving set of translation contracts and correspondence from four nineteenth-century publishers' archives held at IMEC, Caen, to sketch out an array of positions in the field in Bourdieusian terms, taking into account factors such as the language and literary genre translated and the gender and social capital of individual translators.

Chapter 4, "Developing a Legal Framework for the Nineteenth-Century French Literary Translation Market", approaches translation history from the as yet under-exploited angle of legal history, seeking to account for the professionalisation of translation in the publishing sector via the development of a legal framework for the practice. It studies a number of nineteenth-century court cases involving translated books that, over the

10 *Professional Translators in Nineteenth-Century France*

decades, established a body of jurisprudence that anchored the authorial status of translators. It then focuses specifically on the issue of translatorial moral rights, drawing on further evidence from the set of sources used in Chapter 3 to establish a link between the social capital of individual translators and the extent to which they were able to assert their moral rights in dialogue with publishers. The evidence once more points to the unusual, if not unique, situation of translatorship as a form of authorship, in which a high level of ongoing professional practice correlates to a weak bargaining position in the assertion of moral rights.

Chapter 5, "The Economic Lives of Nineteenth-Century Women Translators", similarly seeks to introduce a new research paradigm into translation history by studying the careers of two nineteenth-century literary translators, Louise Swanton-Belloc and Emma Allouard, through the lens of cultural economics. It studies literary translation as part of the artistic labour market, taking a close look at the contrasting economic lives of two women in the translation field. It draws on theoretical work identifying the specific economic features of artistic careers to flesh out their career trajectories in two distinct marketplaces for labour, one granted significant state support, the other subject to market forces.

Chapter 6, "The Life and Career of Auguste-Jean-Baptiste Defauconprêt, Inventor of the 'Lingual Steam Engine'", the final chapter of the book, provides a detailed portrait of one translator's working practices. Defauconprêt was well known in his day as the hugely prolific translator of Walter Scott and James Fenimore Cooper, among others. The chapter outlines his life in Paris and London before taking a close look at his working practices in response to persistent rumours that circulated at the time that he was outsourcing much of his work. It weighs the evidence on both sides of the debate, using indicators such as dates of publication to calculate the output attributed to him and to his son, Charles-Auguste, said to be his principal helper. It concludes with a detailed look at the breakneck chronology of Defauconprêt's translation of Walter Scott's *Peveril of the Peak*, published in French within a couple of weeks of the English original, and assesses Defauconprêt's innovative role as a literary translation entrepreneur.

The book then concludes with a brief coda outlining some of the resonances between past, present, and future in terms of professional translation practice and a chapter-length appendix providing the details of the sources used in Chapters 3 and 4, including detailed accounts of their correspondence, contracts, and other publishing transactions. It is hoped that this will provide ample material for other scholars to take in new directions.

Acknowledgements

I would like to acknowledge a number of debts of gratitude. First of all, thanks to the series editors, Chris Rundle and Pekka Kujamäki, for

Introduction 11

accepting the initial proposal. This book has been two years in the writing and several more in the planning: my appreciative thanks to the editors, particularly Elysse Preposi, for their forbearance as deadlines moved and moved again as I changed jobs and countries halfway through the process. Thanks also to my colleagues at the Faculty of Translation and Interpreting, University of Geneva, for their warm welcome. I must single out Danielle Thien for special thanks in answering my many, many emails with constant patience and good humour. Back in Paris, thanks to the friends and colleagues who generously helped me access archival material at a distance, saving me days of travel, not to mention reducing the project's carbon footprint – Gábor Gelléri, Anne-Florence Quaireau, Klara Buda, Maren Baudet-Lackner, and Olivia Reneaud-Jensen. Similarly, thanks to professional genealogist Carolyn Alderson for accessing Louise Swanton-Belloc's papers at Girton College, Cambridge, on my behalf, and to editor Johnny McFadyen at the Virtual Scriptorium for his eagle eye in helping prepare the manuscript for submission. Thanks to Olivia Guillon for her willingness to share her expertise in cultural economics, and to two long-standing friends and colleagues, Leïla Pellissier and Alison E. Martin, for letting me bounce ideas off them for over 20 years. And above all, thanks to my marvellous family, Fred, Fergus, and Hazel, for everything, every day.

1 The Emergence of a Mass Market for Translation

In 1833, the *Revue Britannique* printed an anonymous article entitled "De l'art de traduire et des différens [sic] systèmes de traduction" [On the art of translating and the various systems of translation]. Nestled in a lengthy exploration of the "génie" [spirit] of translation from Homer to the (nineteenth-century) present day, it included a brief comment on the burgeoning demand for translation services as a result of an expanding economy across the continent and the internationalisation of economic exchanges, leading to growth conditions for the translation sector: "la traduction est devenue un métier : les rapports entre les différentes nations d'Europe s'étant multipliés, la connaissance des diverses langues est devenue familière à beaucoup de gens" [translation has become an occupation: since the various nations of Europe have multiplied their exchanges, knowledge of their languages has become familiar to many people] (Anonymous 1833: 44).

The phrase "est devenue un métier" implies a step change of some kind, a shift from uncoalesced, atomised translation practice of the sort conducted ever since humans began to trade across language barriers to a fully-fledged professional footing. As this book seeks to demonstrate, it would be a mistake to think of this as a tidy (or indeed completed) process. Translation has always been done for gain, for free, for fun, for love; it has always been done privately, collectively, amateurishly, officially, playfully, for leisure, and for learning, and no doubt always will. Yet to the anonymous author writing for the *Revue*, something had changed in recent years. The marketplace for translation had grown to such an extent that it could now support a significant body of translators who, crucially, were aware of themselves and each other as workers operating in the same space, thereby creating the conditions for a process that shared some – but by no means all – of the features of professionalisation. For the anonymous author, at least, translators were now an identifiable socio-professional category.

DOI: 10.4324/9781003173090-2

The Emergence of a Mass Market for Translation   13

* * *

Translators working within the publishing field are, like authors, often represented in research discourse as the sole agents behind their creative output (Stillinger 1991). However, this overlooks the fundamentally collaborative nature of their practice, long recognised in non-literary translation by scholars such as Holz-Mänttäri (1984), whose theory of translational action outlines the translator's place within a chain of command. Recent scholarship has begun to explore translation as a collaborative practice more thoroughly (Cordingley and Frigau Manning 2017; Monti and Schnyder 2018; Freeth 2022), in recognition of the fact that, by and large, translators work within networks, other members of which – authors, commissioners, copy-editors, for instance – also contribute to the translational project with greater or lesser degrees of agency. Similarly, genetic translation scholars (Cordingley and Montini 2015) have set out to uncover traces of collaborative practice in the genesis of translated works, while translation sociologists have applied Bruno Latour's Actor-Network Theory to the field, leading Hélène Buzelin (2011) to coin the term "translating agent" to encompass the complex hybridity of the roles involved in generating translated text.

In historical terms, groups of translators working in more or less formalised networks and collectives have attracted some attention. El Ghazi and Bnini (2020) outline the key players at the Bait al-Hikma in Abbassid Baghdad. Pym (2014) has explored the case for the so-called Toledo school, concluding that its cohesiveness has long been overstated. Guénette (2020) studies the network of translators working between French and English at the court of Queen Consort Henrietta Maria of England in the early to mid-seventeenth century. Such groups have been constant features of translation practice throughout history, crystallising the political, cultural, and ideological networks inherent in intercultural transfer. Importantly, the formalisation of such groups was one step on the path towards translation meeting the threshold for the sociologically defined profession outlined by Milan (2021: 51) as "the idea of service provision, remuneration, increased social and legal regulation, development of training, certification, whether academic- or non-academic based, institutionalization, and a sense of being a collective body, indeed a general sense of social recognition". It should be noted that this process is still ongoing.

Eighteenth-century France saw the institution of more or less formal translator collectives in a number of arenas. In the institutional arena, 1721 saw language service training institutionalised to a certain extent with the establishment of the *école de jeunes de langue* in Paris, building on *ad hoc* work in earlier centuries to train interpreters to negotiate French interests at the Sublime Porte. The pupils were taken into the Collège Louis

14 *Professional Translators in Nineteenth-Century France*

le Grand at the age of eight to study Latin, Turkish, and Arabic; they were often children of former French-born dragomen themselves, forming interpreting dynasties, but many students were eventually put off by the limited pay and career prospects and did not remain in service (Dehérain 1922 [1991]: 325–6). Masson (1877: 42) outlines the establishment of a ministerial *bureau de traduction* at mid-century, in 1762, under the auspices of Edmé-Jacques Genêt (1726–81), its role being to streamline the intelligence-gathering process by combing European newspapers for military intelligence, thereby reducing the costs of spies in the field in wartime while improving the reliability of the information collected (Kleinman 2005: 77). Patrice Bret (2016) studies the development of an informal translator collective which specialised in mineralogy around the Dijon-based encyclopedist Louis-Bernard Guyton de Morveau (1737–1816) in the decades leading up to the revolution, both building on and playing into the development of science as a social and professional activity by combining the dissemination of mineralogical knowledge, mainly from Germany, with experimental practice. The collective, referred to by contemporary Parisian scholars as "[le] bureau de traduction de Dijon", produced over 70 pieces for publication alongside others presented orally; its most productive member, Claudine Picardet (1735–1820), translated 30 percent of the collective's output of 474 pages between 1781 and 1787, working from four languages. The group's translations were checked and approved by Guyton de Morveau himself, who added comments and references, pointing to a concern for quality control (Bret 2016: 129–30).

As Masson (1877) demonstrates, the revolution and its need to disseminate information across France to speakers of all regional languages was a significant milestone in the bureaucratisation of translation practice. Early in 1790, Dugas (first name unknown), a parliamentarian from the Tarn département in the south of the country, contacted the authorities to offer his services translating decrees into the languages spoken across the south. He oversaw the translation of revolutionary decrees for 30 départements and contributed a number of translations himself. The process of bureaucratisation was clearly as yet incomplete, as the decree of 14 January 1790 governing the translation process failed to make it clear who was to pay for the work. While Dugas was eventually paid 6,000 livres for this work in October 1791, the next stage of the project – over 60 new manuscripts, completed in June 1792 – went unpaid (Simonin 2013). Interestingly, the "entreprise Dugas" [Dugas enterprise], as the undertaking was known, was characterised by a high degree of professionalisation: the translators were lawyers thrown out of work by recent events and keen to prove their revolutionary zeal (Pic 1989), while the project as a whole gave rise to a new category of public employee, the *vérificateur*, whose role was translation quality assessment (Simonin 2013). A March 1792 report on the chain of responsibility for the translations reflects a degree of awareness of the need for quality control and standardisation in the translation process:

> J'ai ensuite comparé beaucoup d'articles traduits en idiomes à ces mêmes articles en original. J'ai trouvé les traductions très littérales. Comme presque tous les mots qui y sont employés pour des mots français corrompus, on peut sans savoir les idiomes apprécier la fidélité de chaque traduction, sinon avec une entière certitude, du moins avec une grande vraisemblance ... L'approbation d'un seul député du département qui se trouve à la fin de chaque traduction ne me paraît pas offrir une garantie suffisante, surtout si ce député n'a pas été choisi par le ministre, mais par M. Dugas, et c'est ce que je crois. Il est à remarquer à ce sujet que l'approbation de la traduction faite en l'idiome du département de l'Aveyron et la signature Bourres qui la suit sont d'une écriture assez semblable à celle de la traduction même ... peut-être que cette approbation a été donnée par l'auteur même de la traduction ... Je crois qu'il serait important de faire vérifier chaque traduction au moins par un deuxième député du département, choisi par le ministre.

> [I then compared many articles translated into regional languages to the same articles in the original language. I found the translations very literal. Like almost all words used for corrupted French words, there is no need to know each language to judge the faithfulness of each translation, if not with complete certainty, at least with a high degree of confidence ... The approval by a single député from the département at the end of each translation does not seem to be to be a sufficient guarantee, especially if the deputé was not chosen by the minister, but by M. Dugas, which I think is the case. On this point, it should be noted that the approval of the translation into the language of the Aveyron and the Bourres signature beneath it are in a similar hand to the translation itself ... the translation may have been approved by its own author ... I think it would be important to have each translation checked by at least a second député for the département, chosen by the minister.]

> (Quoted in Simonin 2013)

While the translation programme eventually proved too costly for the revolutionary government to maintain, it nonetheless remains an interesting example of the drive to embed translation into the political framework of the nation, with some of the bureaucratic infrastructure to match.

* * *

By definition, translators are active within a supranational framework. As a result, they are figures of political, cultural, and economic significance.

16 *Professional Translators in Nineteenth-Century France*

Much research to date within the subfield of translator studies (Chesterman 2009) has focused on translators as political and cultural intermediaries. The role of translation and translators within the global economy has equally attracted some attention, both from within translation studies and business studies (Holden and Michailova 2014), though little research has been conducted from a diachronic perspective (one notable exception is Reinert 2011). In terms of translation history, the institutional role of translators has been a recent focal point (Wolf 2015; D'hulst and Koskinen 2020). However, little, if any, work appears to have been done within translation history from an economic or business perspective, other than a broad treatment of trust as a fundamental concept underpinning translation (Pym, Rizzi and Lang 2019). Exploring the history of translators as a workforce, as employees and entrepreneurs, is a blank spot on the research map that this chapter aims to fill in part, by exploring various figures of the translator as key stakeholders within the nineteenth-century French administration and economy. While the various language industry sectors largely overlapped then as now, with translators frequently earning an income from a range of language-related practices such as teaching and language manual authorship, the development of a highly centralised and structured bureaucracy on meritocratic principles did also lead to full-time, stable translation careers in various branches of the French administration. At the same time, the growth of an international industrial and knowledge economy opened up business opportunities for enterprising language specialists. Accordingly, this section focuses on the development of the translation market, broadly defined, before turning to two areas in which translators achieved a high degree of ongoing professional practice, as administrative employees and as freelance entrepreneurs, pointing to a slow process whereby language specialists gradually came to specialise in specific language industry sectors. It will become clear that what differentiates their status – and indeed differentiates them from literary translators in the same period – is not so much the content they translated, but the extent to which their legal and administrative status implied a full-time presence in the field of translation, considered either as a sub-field of the broader language-related professions or in contrast to other fields of intellectual endeavour and authorship.

The Rise of a Modern Translation Market

The economic significance of translation as a facilitator of international trade is apparent from a study of official business notices posted in the closing decades of the eighteenth and early decades of the nineteenth century. Looking across the Channel to the UK, for instance, the *London Gazette* regularly featured business announcements by translators practising in partnership with ship-brokers, insurance brokers, accountants,

The Emergence of a Mass Market for Translation 17

commercial agents, and notaries. Alongside the generally rising economic tide in France and Britain in particular (O'Brien and Keyder 2011), several factors played into the growth of the translation market and the increasing availability of potential recruits with the requisite language skills. While multilingualism had long been the norm in parts of Europe such as the Hapsburg Empire (Wolf 2015), and indeed in much of France, forms of bilingualism involving a centralised national language and a regional language were not necessarily of economic benefit to the speaker, since the latter tended to embody a low form of linguistic capital. Mastering another language with high market value was, however, now within reach of more people than ever before, for a number of reasons. Exposure to foreign languages via international travel was increasingly easy, comfortable, and affordable, with improvements to tourist infrastructure such as hotels, regularly scheduled transport services, travel guides, and middlemen offering services such as language brokering and currency exchange (François 2012). While would-be British tourists were unable to visit Napoleonic France, the years after 1815 saw a huge increase in cross-Channel travel. Regular passenger services began to run from Brighton to Le Havre in 1816; a steamship service between Dover and Calais was launched in 1821. By 1840, an estimated one hundred thousand people were crossing the Channel annually (Buzard 1993: 41). Improvements in transport systems also made print more widely available at affordable prices, while printed material itself fell in cost due to new technologies such as the steam-driven press and stereotyping. This in turn led to rising literacy rates (Chartier and Martin 1990a).

Foreign-language reading material was widely available in urban centres, in bookshops and circulating libraries. Giovanni Antonio Galignani and his English wife Anne Parsons founded the first English-language bookshop on the continent in Paris in 1800. Across the Channel in London, a large French community descended from the 12,500 émigrés who crossed the Channel annually during the revolutionary years (Carpenter 1999: 40; Reboul 2014; Kelly and Cornick 2013) formed a sizeable market for French books. Visitor guides to London in the early decades of the century record French coffee houses and several bookshops, including Dulau, Deboffe, and de Conchy (Feltham 1807: 319). The trade in French books was lucrative enough for an English-language trade publisher like Henry Colburn to work in the sector, bringing out around 50 books in French or on topics of interest to French readers (Saglia 2013: 56). A number of new bilingual dictionaries for modern European languages, especially French and English, came onto the market in the early nineteenth century, reflecting increased demand for up-to-date language, both standard and colloquial (Marello 2009: 89). Bilingual dictionaries were also available for specialist topics, such as maritime trade (Daniel

18 *Professional Translators in Nineteenth-Century France*

Lescallier, *Vocabulaire des termes de marine anglais et français, avec un dictionnaire de définitions et un calepin de termes de commerce maritime* [Lexicon of English and French Naval Terms, with a Dictionary of Definitions and a Section of Terms for Maritime Trade], 1777; Hendrik Willem Lantscheer, *Woordenboek der Fransche zee-termen, bijeen verzameld en in Hollandsche en gedeeltelijk in Engelsche kunstwoorden overgebragt* [Dictionary of French Maritime Vocabulary Compiled in Dutch with a Partial English Technical Translation], 1811), and mineralogy (Johann Heinrich Lorenz Pansner, *Französisch-deutsches mineralogisches Wörterbuch* [French and German Mineralogical Dictionary], 1802). Those who could not afford to purchase such books could consult them in circulating libraries or, if in Paris, at the Bibliothèque nationale, which opened to "le tout-venant" [the general public] in 1833 (Bruckmann 2018). For the self-motivated student, teach-yourself language manuals were readily available, by authors such as Lewis Chambaud, whose numerous publications included titles like *The Rudiments of the French Tongue: or, an Easy and Rational Introduction to French Grammar, Wherein the Principals of the Language Are Methodically Digested* (1802). Anyone preferring more guided study could call on one of the language teachers listed in commercial gazettes. As early as 1790, the *Almanach astronomique et historique de la ville de Lyon* listed 16 language teachers offering individual classes in Italian, Spanish, Dutch, Flemish, German, Latin, and English.

All of these developments meant that mastering a foreign language with high market value was now within grasp of a far wider swathe of the population than in the previous century. As the journal *L'Artiste* wrote in 1840,

> il n'y a plus au pays de France … que quelques laides populaces des faubourgs qui ne s'expriment point en [anglais]; encore n'est-il pas rare de voir des échopiers sur les boutiques desquels on lit: English spoken here. [in France there are now just a few unprepossessing hoi polloi in the faubourgs who do not speak English; and even there it is by no means rare to see shopkeepers with signs on their shops reading: English spoken here].
>
> (P. B. 1840: 284)

Latin and Greek lost ground as schools shifted to teaching modern languages, lower in symbolic capital but potentially higher in economic capital. The major lycées in Paris had their own English, German, and Italian teachers from the turn of the nineteenth century. An 1829 report by the very first *ministre de l'instruction publique*, Henri de Vatismenil, introduced modern language teaching in all secondary level schools, highlighting the economic importance of modern languages for "les besoins des professions commerciales, agricoles, industrielles et manufacturières" [the

The Emergence of a Mass Market for Translation 19

needs of professions in trade, farming, industry, and manufacturing] (Puren 1988: 47). Modern languages were largely taught by the grammar-translation method, using translation as a language acquisition tool (Laviosa 2014: 4), and the practice of *thème* and *version* (translation out of and into French), inherited from the study of classical languages, remained a fundamental teaching practice. A typical textbook on the English language would be the 1870 *Clef de la langue anglaise en vingt leçons, avec une règle de grammaire complète, un thème, une version et un vocabulaire pour chacune des leçons* [A Key to English in Twenty Lessons, with a Complete Set of Grammar Rules and a Prose and Version Translation for Each Lesson] by Louis Lauwereyns de Roosendaele, who taught English at a school in Béthune. *Thème* and *version* were two of the four papers comprising the *agrégation d'anglais* examination, established in 1849 to create a pool of qualified teachers. This helped enshrine their place in English teaching in France, where they remain part of the core modern language university curriculum to this day (Levick, Ní Ríordáin and Poncharal 2021). This early exposure to the practice of translation no doubt raised it as a potential career in the minds of many students seeking to make use of their skills in the burgeoning knowledge economy (Jacob 2014). Quality control remained problematic, however: the *Revue de Paris* warned in 1832 of "les écoliers qui vendent leurs versions à un libraire pour payer les cachets de leur maître d'anglais" [the schoolboys who sell their French translations to a bookseller to pay for their English lessons] (F. D. 1832: 295).

Economists of the period were well aware of the significance of translation as a growth lever for international trade. Baron Augustin-François de Silvestre (1762–1851) published an *Essai sur les moyens de perfectionner les arts économiques en France* [Essay on the Means of Perfecting the Economic Arts in France] in 1800–01, which demonstrated a thorough grasp of the issues raised by translation in the nascent knowledge economy. He recommended controlling the flow of knowledge into and out of France by establishing specialist translation services with institutional support. His essay is worth quoting at length on this point:

> Les étrangers recueillent avec avidité tous les ouvrages utiles qui paraissent en français, et les faisant bientôt passer dans leur langue, ils profitent des découvertes qui nous appartiennent. La supériorité de notre sol, la multitude des livres qui nous sont propres, et peut-être, notre paresse naturelle, nous empêchent de faire à leur égard ce qu'ils font au nôtre, et leurs découvertes ne nous sont connues que par d'heureux hasards; mais pour ne parler ici que des arts économiques, on sait qu'il paroît fréquemment d'excellens ouvrages allemands, suédois et anglois sur l'économie rurale. Ces ouvrages sont perdus pour nous; et le gouvernement qui sent les avantages que l'introduction de certaines pratiques utiles pourroit procurer à la France, devroit, ce me semble, suppléer à l'apathie

20 *Professional Translators in Nineteenth-Century France*

des particuliers pour ce genre d'occupation. Je pense qu'il seroit bon d'établir sous l'inspection du Ministre de l'Intérieur, un bureau de traductions, toujours en activité, dans lequel on s'occuperoit à faire passer dans notre langue les différents ouvrages étrangers qui traitent des Arts économiques. Ces ouvrages seroient publiés au nombre de cinq ou six chaque année, et ils nous mettroient au courant des progrès que ces Arts font chez les Nations étrangères, soit parce que des hommes de génie ont porté sur eux leurs regards, soit parce que l'esprit public plus perfectionné a recueilli et rendu vulgaires, des faits dont nous n'avons pas encore apprécié l'importance.

[Foreigners avidly welcome all the useful books published in French, quickly translating them into their own languages and taking advantage of the discoveries that belong to us. The superiority of our soil, the multitude of books proper to us, and perhaps our own natural laziness prevent us from doing to them what they do to us, and their discoveries are known to us only by fortunate happenstance; but, even just considering the economic arts, we know that excellent German, Swedish and English works are frequently published on the rural economy. These works are lost to us; and a government aware of the advantages that introducing certain useful practices could bring France should, it seems to me, make up for the apathy of individuals for this kind of occupation. I think it would be good to establish a translation bureau under the supervision of the Ministry of the Interior, that would be kept busy providing French translations of the various foreign works dealing with the economic arts. Five or six works would be published each year, bringing us up to date with the progress of such arts in foreign nations, either because men of genius have turned their gaze on them or because a higher level of public discourse has taken up and made common knowledge of facts whose importance we have yet to appreciate.]

(Silvestre 1802–03: 92)

The main thrust of Silvestre's argument was the risk to the French economy of losing out on knowledge transfer due to the haphazard nature of translation provision when left to the individual efforts of private citizens. Developing a centralised, systematic conduit for importing economic knowledge was, he recognised, crucial to the future of the new French republic. Translation was proving fundamental to bureaucratisation and the development of a service economy driven by intellectual labour; at the same time, the economic importance of proper language planning was an increasingly significant consideration. One fascinating example from mid-century survives in the French national archives in a report written on 12 October 1853 by the engineer and social reformer Frédéric Le Play (1806–82), a member of the planning committee for the inaugural

The Emergence of a Mass Market for Translation 21

universal exhibition in Paris in 1855. The report insists on the importance of hiring administrative staff with foreign language skills for the exhibition to maximise its economic benefit and French soft power. Again, it is worth quoting at length:

> La connaissance de la langue française est plus répandue en Europe que celle de la langue anglaise, sous ce rapport, les relations des jurés appartenant aux diverses nations seront plus faciles à Paris qu'elles ne l'ont été à Londres. Cependant j'ai entendu beaucoup d'industriels insister sur les obstacles qu'ils trouveraient, dans l'ignorance où ils sont de la langue française, à prendre part à la nouvelle Exposition. Je pense donc qu'il conviendrait d'indiquer, dans la publication qui doit émaner du Gouvernement français, que la Commission supérieure de l'Exposition aura mission de pourvoir à cette difficulté, qu'on introduira autant que possible dans chaque jury français des personnes ayant la connaissance des autres langues européennes, et que, dans tous les cas, on comprendra des agents ayant ce genre de connaissances parmi les personnels administratif de l'Exposition. Il importerait surtout que des agents parlant facilement les principales langues européennes se trouvassent dans un Bureau de renseignements qui serait attaché en permanence à l'Exposition de Paris, et dont le défaut s'est gravement fait sentir à Londres au début de l'Exposition de 1851. Il serait à désirer que le public européen sût le plus tôt possible que de telles précautions seront prises : des avis conçus dans ce sens contribueraient, j'en suis assuré, à augmenter le nombre d'exposants anglais.[1]

[Knowledge of French is more widespread in Europe than of English, so the discussions by panels from various nations will be easier in Paris than they were in London. However, I have heard many industrialists insisting that their lack of French would cause hindrances if they were to take part in the new exhibition. Therefore I think it would be useful to indicate in the publication that the French government is to put out that the exhibition's governing commission will be tasked with removing this difficulty by putting people on each panel with knowledge of other European languages as far as possible, and that the administrative staff will in all cases include people with language skills. Above all it is important to put staff fluent in the main European languages at a permanent information desk at the Paris exhibition, as its lack was sorely felt in London when the exhibition of 1851 opened. It would be

---

1 See the file shelfmarked F/12/3183 at the *Archives nationales*, Pierrefitte-sur-Seine. All subsequent references to documents from the *Archives nationales* will be footnoted with the relevant shelfmark number.

22 *Professional Translators in Nineteenth-Century France*

preferable to inform the European public as soon as possible of these precautions: notices to this effect would, I am sure, increase the number of English exhibitors.]

The lessons Le Play learned from the failure of language planning at the London exhibition of 1851 seem to have borne fruit, as over 50 per cent of exhibitors at the Paris event came from abroad, including thousands from Britain (Anonymous 1855).

Translators in the French Civil Service

The *exposition universelle* of 1855 foregrounded the importance of foreign language skills in international relations, making translation a key governmental tool and an element of soft power. From the very beginning of the century, the French authorities demonstrated their awareness of the crucial role of translation professionals by bringing them into the civil service.

While the roots of the French administrative state lay centuries back, the revolution and the Napoleonic era ushered in new egalitarian principles for the employment of civil servants:[2] they were now appointed by a centralised government, entering a career based on the principles of a transparent hierarchy, pay structure, and progression that was applied to a common standard across government departments. The creation of a stable body of employees at ministries, départements, and communes established *fonctionnaires* as a socio-professional category in their own right – a category that included many translators. Indeed, translation could be a useful stepping stone in a portfolio administrative career leading to positions of some power: to take one example, Maurice-Ernest Flesch (1842–1910) studied law and began as a translator at the Ministry of Foreign Affairs in 1859 before taking up consular posts in Damascus, Smyrna, Calcutta, and Shanghai. He was awarded the Légion d'Honneur in 1886 and finished his career as *ministre plénipotentiaire* in Port-au-Prince, Haiti. Furthermore, language services were given an increasing legislative framework. As early as 1804, the *Dictionnaire universel, géographique, statistique, historique et politique de la France* laid out a new legal status for interpreters: "Sous la monarchie il y avait des interprètes du roi pour les langues étrangères. Il y a maintenant un interprète assermenté de la préfecture de police" [Under the monarchy there were the royal interpreters for foreign languages. Now there is a sworn interpreter at the police prefecture] (Prudhomme 1804, quoted in Peñarroja 2013: 122). In 1811, an imperial decree stipulated the conditions for appointing *traducteurs jurés* [sworn translators] together

---

2 See https://www.napoleon.org/histoire-des-2-empires/articles/napoleon-et-la-naissance-de -ladministration-francaise/ (accessed 6 December 2021).

The Emergence of a Mass Market for Translation   23

with their duties and remuneration. Highlighting the gendered nature of language work in the public sphere, it added that "En cas de nécessité absolue, une femme peut être admise comme interprète, si d'ailleurs elle n'est récusée ni par le ministère public, ni par l'accusé" [In case of absolute necessity, a woman can be accepted as an interpreter, if she is not turned down by the public ministry or by the accused] (quoted in Peñarroja 2013: 125).

Institutionalising translation had been crucial for the fledgling republic as a means of controlling the import and export of information. The same was true of Napoleonic France: Napoleon wrote to the Duc de Cadore in 1810 to recommend requesting regular translations of every paper printed in regional or foreign languages in the kingdom as a means of uncovering potential dissent (*Correspondance* 1866: 267). Colonial expansion likewise called for new translation infrastructure as a matter of urgency. Shortly after the revolution, the *école des langues orientales* had been tasked with teaching its *jeunes de langue* students modern Oriental languages "pour la politique et le commerce" [for politics and trade]; Arabic was its most-studied language, and again translation was a fundamental teaching method (Messaoudi 2015). The war ministry hired 69 Arabic interpreters in the 1830s: the first "bureau arabe" was established in Algiers in 1833 (Messaoudi 2015; Monteil 1961). Messaoudi (2015) identifies three key interpreter profiles: *jeunes de langue* scholars who studied Arabic academically in Paris, Eastern Christians recruited during the Egypt expedition earlier in the century, and Maghrebi Christians and Jews recruited in Tunis. Their language skills often left much to be desired, according to one experienced interpreter who wrote a history of the service (Messaoudi 2015: 145). Being a colonial language broker could be a dangerous business: Louis Bracevich, a military interpreter who had worked for Napoleon in Egypt, died in 1830 aged 58 as a result of a nervous fever contracted after a stressful meeting with Hussein, Dey of Algiers, during which he had to inform him that the French were taking over the city (Féraud 1876: 177). Bracevich's son Auguste later applied for a job as a translator at the Ministry of Foreign Affairs, quoting his father's service to the nation (Pickford 2012a: 155–7).

An 1844 decree set up a "bureau arabe" with an interpreter in each Algerian subdivision. An imperial decree dated 13 November 1857 set the pay scale for military interpreters at "six francs par séance entière de jour, et neuf francs par séance entière de nuit" [six francs per full session by day, nine francs per full session by night] exclusive of "la traduction par écrit qu'ils peuvent être appelés à faire des pièces de conviction rédigées en langue étrangères" [written translations that they can be called on to provide for court exhibits in foreign languages]. This points to the increasing specialisation of labour between written and spoken language transfer.

24 *Professional Translators in Nineteenth-Century France*

Back in France, the career paths of translators in the French administration can be tracked in their personnel files in ministry archives and the *Archives nationales*. To take one example, Léopold Isoard (1822–87) began his career as an auxiliary translator at the Ministry of Trade in 1843, translating and analysing legal documents in German, English, Dutch, Spanish, and Portuguese.[3] There is little clue as to how the Paris-born 21-year-old had mastered such a range of languages. It was unlikely to have been in a formal educational setting, since Portuguese – for instance – was not taught as a modern language at French schools and universities until the twentieth century.[4] Two years later, he was moved to the *Bureau des législations étrangères* [foreign legislation office] to work on texts relating to England. He then moved in 1848 to the *Bureau des législations des douanes* [the customs legislation office], writing reports on economic issues such as the herring fishing industry. These were his first steps on the administrative ladder. He moved on to occupy various positions as sub-prefect in small towns across France – Saint-Affrique, Gray, Coutances – before promotion to prefect (i.e. head of the local authority) in the Aveyron and Deux-Sèvres. As late as 1865, when he was prefect for the Aveyron in southern France, he requested a transfer back to the Manche, where he had previously been sub-prefect: it was a much more convenient posting for his Scottish wife. He made the case to his hierarchical superior that he was eminently suited for a post near the Channel because "je connais cinq langues étrangères et particulièrement l'anglais, dont je fais l'usage comme du français" [I know five languages, particularly English, which I am as fluent in as French]. A confidential report in his personnel file details his political opinions, appearance, manners, and family income and background: "[il a] toujours appartenu aux partis de l'ordre" [he has always belonged to the parties of order]; his appearance and tenue were "très convenable" [very suitable]; his father had held a high-ranking position at the Ministry of Trade and was a chevalier de la légion d'honneur, while an earlier forebear had been archbishop of Lyon. The file consists of a series of pre-defined categories, one of which applies to Isoard's wife, Sophia Murray, requesting details of the "Noms et âge de Madame, caractère, valeur comme femme du monde, esprit, relations sociales" [names and age of wife, character, value as a woman of the world

---

3 Shelfmark AN F/iBI/163/1. All unreferenced quotations in this section are from the relevant files documenting each translator's career in the Ministère des Affaires Étrangères archives, La Courneuve.

4 https://capmagellan.com/les-100-ans-de-lenseignement-du-portugais-en-france/ (accessed 17 December 2021).

The Emergence of a Mass Market for Translation   25

(i.e., social asset), spirit, and social relations].[5] Madame Isoard, the report continues, was the daughter of Lord Cringletie, a leading Scottish judge; her older brother was married to the Duchess of Leeds's granddaughter. This surprisingly detailed family tree points to the crucial role of social capital in forging an administrative career in nineteenth-century France.

At a less granular level, translator careers can be tracked in the successive national, royal, and imperial almanacs that were an important record of administrative infrastructure. Translator posts were established, shifted, and abolished to meet the needs of various services, some in quite unexpected administrative outposts: in 1833, for instance, the *administration des lignes télégraphiques* [telegraph network administration] department at the *Département de l'intérieur et des cultes* [Department for Home Affairs and Religion] had not one, but two translators (M. Vergé[6] temporarily standing in as head translator, and M. Perrot d'Etivareilles, deputy head translator), in its nine-strong staff. Taking an example from mid-century, a study of the *Almanach royal et national* for 1844 shows the extent to which language services were threaded throughout the French administrative services. It lists translators and interpreters not only at the telegraph office (M. Vergé now confirmed as head, with M. Perrot d'Etivareilles still as deputy), but also at the *Département de la marine et des colonies* [Department for the Navy and the Colonies]; the *Section de la législation commerciale et de tarifs et douanes à l'étranger* (the division in charge of trade legislation and foreign tariffs and customs, where Léopold Isoard had worked briefly); the *Bureau des lois et archives* [Bureau for Laws and Archives]; the *secrétariat général* at the *Bureau de la prefecture* [general secretariat at the prefecture office]; three *secrétaires-interprètes* [secretary-interpreters] at the *Département des affaires étrangères* [Department of Foreign Affairs]; the *Cour de cassation* [Court of Cassation] library; and the *Direction des affaires de l'Algérie* [Office of Algerian Affairs]. The same names feature repeatedly across the years, pointing to a relatively small, stable pool of highly experienced language specialists.

While insights into the daily work of such translators are scarce, one rare archival document does shed some light on how one language service functioned. The French national archive holds a list of staff members at the *Direction de la Presse* for 1863, with details of employees at the various foreign-language press desks, their monthly wages, and, fascinatingly,

---

5 She is described as having "un peu de bizarrerie dans le caractère. Elle est grande et maigre et conserve un accent écossais très prononcé" [a slight oddness of character. She is tall and thin and has kept a strong Scottish accent].

6 Charles-Thomas Vergé, born in Lisieux on 28 July 1783, was granted a pension by Louis-Philippe on 11 December 1845, after 42 years, 2 months, and 15 days in service (*Bulletin* 1846: 733).

26 *Professional Translators in Nineteenth-Century France*

confidential notes on various translators working on English, German, Italian, and Spanish news sources. The translators listed include a number of names that suggest foreign roots: Hollander, Schwartz, Glück, Chelchowski, Birmingham senior and Birmingham junior, Vandenbrule, Galeazini, Sterbini, and Rempp. Wages ranged from 1,200 francs for the clearly rather junior Glück at the German desk to a generous 7,200 francs for the Chevalier de Saint-André at the English desk.[7] Most revealing of all are the notes penned in confidence by the head translator, Charles Le Comte. In the English service, Faillant was a "bon rédacteur" with "plus d'imagination que de jugement" [skilled writer with more imagination than judgement], who knew Spanish as well as English. The German specialist Barthe was "un homme très instruit (ancien précepteur du prince camerata) mais lent et maladif" [very learned man, former tutor to the prince camerata, but slow and sickly] with very poor eyesight: he was often absent for lengthy periods on health grounds. Montgomery had "bonnes manières" and "connaissance suffisante de l'anglais" but "rédaction malheureusement très faible" [good manners and enough knowledge of English but sadly very weak writing skills]: he could be trusted to read the papers and give an oral summary. He was also one of the longest-standing members of the team and was a useful institutional memory. Last but not least, Courtois at the English desk was an

> Excellent sujet – dans la force de l'âge. Coup d'oeil prompt – jugement solide – travailleur sérieux – employé hors ligne – bonne rédaction française – santé robuste – (a perdu, depuis la dernière organisation, 50 fr par mois, qui lui étaient attribués sur le fonds des correspondances du midi).

> [Excellent subject – in the prime of life – a quick eye – solid judgement – reliable worker – peerless employee – good French writing skills – robust health – (lost 50 fr per month in the last reorganisation, attributed to him from the Midi correspondences budget).][8]

This last comment points to a perennial problem for translators working as civil servants: while their working conditions were established by decree to a certain extent, they were by no means exempt from ministerial whims. On 16 March 1822, the député Pierre-François-Jean Bogne de Faye

---

7 According to https://www.historicalstatistics.org/Currencyconverter.html, these are equivalent to 5,606 euros and 33,638 euros in 2015, the most recent year available for comparison. The archival document does not make it clear if the sums are monthly or annual, presumably the latter.

8 Shelfmark AN F/18/310.

The Emergence of a Mass Market for Translation   27

(1778–1838) took part in a parliamentary debate calling for fixed working conditions:

> En 1816 on supprima par économie, dans un ministère, le bureau de traduction qui se composait de trois employés qui recevaient chacun 5,000 francs de traitement ... C'étaient des hommes très méritants qui avaient rendu beaucoup de services; on leur accorda à chacun 4,000 francs de pension, l'économie qui en résulta ne fut que de 3,000 fr. Peu de temps après on sentit la nécessité d'avoir un bureau de traducteurs. On le recomposa en renommant d'autres personnes bien dignes sans doute de cet emploi, et on leur donna 12,000 fr de traitement. On ajouta six employés; de sorte que le bureau des traducteurs coûte maintenant 50,000 fr, au lieu de 15,000 fr indépendamment des 12,000 fr de pension accordés aux employés réformés.
>
> [In 1816 a ministry made savings by closing the translation office with three employees, each earning salaries of 5,000 francs ... They were very worthy men who had served the country well; they were each given a pension of 4,000 fr, so the saving was just 3,000 fr. Soon after the need for a translation office was felt. It was reopened, appointing other people no doubt well suited to the position, and they were given salaries of 12,000 fr. Six employees were hired, so the translation office now costs 50,000 fr, rather than 15,000 fr, independent of the 12,000 fr of pension granted to the employees who lost their jobs.]
>
> (Mavidal and Laurent 1877: 545)

Recruitment was, in principle, meritocratic, but as the above examples show, not all those who ended up working for the ministries were entirely competent. Mastery of source and target languages was uneven; some workers were slow, or rarely at their desks. As the example of the Birminghams father and son and of Barthe, the former royal tutor, suggest, knowing the right people helped. Ministers were responsible for choosing suitable candidates: the Ministère de l'Intérieur published a decree on 16 May 1869 reserving the right to appoint applicants with useful language skills (*Annales de l'Assemblée nationale* vol. 14, Journal officiel, 1873).

As a result, this area of civil service employment may have been less open to cronyism and ministerial whim than other sectors, as translator recruitment did require some specialist skills above and beyond straightforward clerking duties. Translators were often foreign-born or from French border regions and were hired on the basis of their language experience. An undated letter in the personnel file of Maurice-Ernest Flesch's father Maurice (1798–?), himself an English, Spanish, and Arabic translator at the Ministry of Foreign Affairs, requests a post for his son and includes a specimen of his handwriting and a sample translation. Applications in

28 *Professional Translators in Nineteenth-Century France*

other files refer to previous experience in foreign language teaching or include foreign diplomas with sworn translations, reflecting a degree of awareness of the linguistic component of translatorial competence at least, if not the full range of skills required (Malmkjaer 2009). In some cases, however, there must be some doubt over the linguistic competence of some of these translators: as has been shown, knowledge of Arabic among trained military interpreters was sometimes insufficient, and one wonders how in-depth the skills of a translator like Barthélémy-Eugène Coquebert de Montbret (1785–1847) really were,[9] as he was recruited in November 1828 to translate at the Ministry of Foreign Affairs from "toutes les langues d'Europe et quelques unes de celles de l'Asie" [all European languages and some from Asia]. Either way, translators were keen to emphasise their specialist skills as a means of differentiating themselves from a purely secretarial function – not least because they felt that their additional skills required adequate compensation. Auguste Bracevich (1805–68), who worked at the Ministry of Foreign Affairs after his father's death in French service, wrote to his superior in 1846 that

> l'ordonnance Ministérielle, *qui établit plusieurs catégories*, dit que les expéditionnaires *seuls* commenceront à 1,500 fr, et dans aucune langue *du monde*, un traducteur ne peut être assimilé à un copiste. *Traducteur* de plusieurs ouvrages auxquels la presse a accordé de grands éloges ; traducteur comptant onze ans de services, je me borne à demander de n'être pas traité aussi mal que le dernier des copistes.
>
> [the ministerial decree, which establishes several categories, states that only copying clerks are to start at 1,500 fr, and that in no language in the world can a translator be equated with a copyist. As a translator of several works highly praised in the press, with eleven years in service, all I ask is not to be treated as badly as the lowliest copyist (emphasis in the original)].

For much of the nineteenth century, when entering the civil service and building a career was still arbitrary to some extent (Thuillier 1980), social capital was a clear advantage. In May 1855, Jean-Louis-Sébastien Duca began his application by foregrounding his family connections:

---

9 Coquebert de Montbret's sister Jeanne-Cécile was married to the eminent mineralogist Alexandre de Brongniart, further underscoring the value of social capital in building a civil service career. See the Coquebert de Montbret family tree on http://www.geneanet.org (accessed 11 January 2022).

The Emergence of a Mass Market for Translation   29

Seul petit-fils de Louis-Sébastien Mercier, auteur dramatique et du *Tableau de Paris*, membre de l'Institut et du Corps législatif, j'ai passé une partie de ma jeunesse en Allemagne et en Italie, où j'ai suivi des cours universitaires ; et je serais heureux maintenant, de retour en France, de pouvoir consacrer ma vie au service de mon pays ... Des études que je crois compléter, scientifiques et littéraires, et la connaissance de plusieurs langues étrangères, mon vif désir de me rendre digne de mon aïeul, mes efforts et mon zèle, pourront peut-être appeler plus tard votre attention sur moi, et vous prouver que je m'efforcerai de mériter une position que je ne puis solliciter aujourd'hui, que par votre bienveillance.

[The only grandson of Louis-Sébastien Mercier, playwright and author of the *Tableau de Paris*, member of the Institute and the legislative body, I spent part of my youth in Germany and Italy, where I took classes at university; and now, back in France, I would be happy to devote my life to the service of my country ... Studies in science and literature that I plan to complete, my knowledge of several foreign languages, my keen urge to prove myself worthy of my forefather, my efforts and zeal may later bring me to your attention and prove to you that I will strive to merit a position that I can only request today by your goodness.]

Along with his application, he sent a letter of recommendation from a family friend in parliament. Similarly, the British-born translator Henry Nicolas (1811–87) owed his recruitment to the support of his father-in-law, who held an important administrative position at the Assemblée Nationale.

Translators who found ministry employment were not immune from financial difficulties, however. The personnel file of the Italian interpreter and naturalised French citizen Antonio (Antoine) Buttura (1771–1832) records payments of between 1,000 and 1,500 francs annually from 1816 to 1821, which were then withdrawn. He wrote repeatedly to the ministry to request money or a position to support his wife and young children, pleading with the minister of foreign affairs in 1826,

Je ne viens pas réclamer contre la suppression de ma place ; Votre Excellence l'a voulu, je m'y soumets : mais je viens vous supplier, au nom de Dieu et de l'humanité de ne pas me retirer à la fois toute sorte d'appui, et d'empêcher la ruine totale d'un père de famille qui sert la France avec honneur depuis 29 ans.

[I am not writing to argue the suppression of my position; your Excellence wished it, I submit: but I write to beg you, in the name of God and humanity not to withdraw all sort of support at once, and to

30 *Professional Translators in Nineteenth-Century France*

prevent the total ruin of a father who has served France with honour for twenty-nine years.]

The response from the head accountant struck a note of regret:

> quelqu'effort que j'aie tenté pour obtenir un recours de M. de Damas, il s'y est refusé constamment et il m'a même défendu ... de faire à l'avenir aucune avance à M. Buttura.

> [whatever I try to obtain a review of his case from M. de Damas, he has always refused and he has even forbidden me ... from advancing M. Buttura any money in future.]

Buttura then tried his hand at writing and teaching but was thwarted at every turn: publishing was in crisis and his attempts at teaching were undercut by "un grand nombre de jeunes professeurs, et par les cours que fait donner au plus bas prix la soi-disant Société des Méthodes" [a large number of young teachers, and classes given by the so-called Society of Methods at the lowest cost]. The file contains one final, poignant letter to the ministry from his widow: "La malheureuse famille de cet homme estimable mort de chagrin, n'espère plus qu'en vain, et elle ose se flatter que vous ne l'abandonnerez pas dans sa détresse si peu méritée" [the unfortunate family of this estimable man who died of grief, now only hopes in vain, and dares flatter itself that you will not abandon it in a distress so little deserved].

The case of Julien Olszewiec (1822–?) demonstrates that even rare language skills came second to social status. Olszewiec was appointed to a position as a Polish translator in 1852, but then stripped of his position on the basis of a secret police investigation into his background:

> Plusieurs polonais, qui ont connu parfaitement sa famille, affirment que le sieur Julien Olszewiec est d'une origine très obscure ... il serait le fils de juifs très pauvres et aurait quitté fort jeune sa patrie, soit pour aller chercher fortune, soit pour se soustraire à la conscription russe.

> [Several Poles, who knew his family perfectly, state that Julien Olszewiec, Esq., comes from a very obscure background ... He is thought to be the son of very poor Jews, having left his home country at a very young age, either to seek his fortune or to avoid conscription by the Russians.][10]

---

10 Olszewiec seems to have indeed been quite an adventurer: he left Poland in 1840 aged 18, travelled to Rome via Geneva, and nearly married a Polish princess. In 1852, he applied to change his Polish surname to the French equivalent, Verne, giving rise to a long-lived

The Emergence of a Mass Market for Translation   31

Applicants with the requisite language skills but who were short on social capital or without ministerial backing could be hired on temporary contracts, sometimes for years on end. Auguste Bracevich was one such: his personnel file contains numerous letters complaining about the iniquities of his position as a temporary hire, seeing other, more recent recruits being given permanent contracts on higher pay. His file closes with a letter from his landlord informing Bracevich's employer that he had disappeared, leaving debts of nearly 300 francs. Such situations meant that potential translators from modest backgrounds, whatever their language skills, were liable to be dissuaded from applying for civil service positions, not least because their employment risked coming to a sudden end, making it difficult to maintain a stable family life. Furthermore, in the early decades of the nineteenth century at least, interpreters on overseas missions were expected to advance their own costs: Amédée Jaubert (1779–1847), posted to Constantinople, spent 12,000 piastres of his own money on expenses.[11]

The nature of the work carried out by civil service translators – largely legal and personal documents and foreign press clippings – brought them into competition with the burgeoning freelance translation market. In 1879, a group of sworn translators complained in writing to the Ministry of Foreign Affairs that one member of the translation department was unfairly undercutting them for his own personal enrichment:

> Le Chef de la traduction, M. Duca, s'est prévalu de sa situation pour accaparer, à son profit personnel, la généralité des pièces en langues étrangères qu'il y a lieu de traduire après législation, et, dans ce but, il a fait insérer, dans les Journaux ou Bulletins officiels, que le Ministère des Affaires étrangères se charge de faire opérer les légalisations et les traductions légales. À cet effet, un garçon de bureau nommé Lutz arrête au passage la plupart des documents que l'on porte au Ministère afin de les faire légaliser, et il se permet même de mettre à contribution les personnes qui sollicitent le visa de leurs passeports. Si Votre Excellence jugeait à propos de prescrire une enquête au sujet de ces agissements, qui lèsent les droits acquis d'un grand nombre d'honorables pères de famille, ce serait un acte de justice dont lui sauraient infiniment gré les

---

but mistaken rumour that Jules Verne was a Polish Jew. See http://www.societejulesverne.org/bulletin/195.php (accessed 11 February 2022).

11 It is hard to calculate exactly how much this amounts to, but as a point of comparison, in 1807, the French consul Joseph Rousseau paid an escort of 20 fusiliers 30 piastres each for the journey from Aleppo to Biregik (modern-day Birecik, Türkiye), a distance of some 150 kilometres. He calculated that his total expenditure of 20,765 piastres for May, June, and July 1807 when he travelled from Aleppo to Baghdad was the equivalent of 31,148 francs 10 sols. This included a gift for the pasha valued at 3,796 piastres (Deherain 1925: 179–80, 184).

32 *Professional Translators in Nineteenth-Century France*

confrères de M. Duca, ayant droit comme ce dernier à exercer envers le public leurs fonctions de traducteurs jurés et d'en retirer les ressources nécessaires pour les faire vivre.

[The head of translation, M. Duca, has taken advantage of his situation to enrich himself by taking over all the foreign-language items to be translated following legislation and, with this goal in mind, he has had notices printed in official gazettes and bulletins to the effect that the Ministry of Foreign Affairs will translate and notarize legal documents. An office boy by the name of Lutz stops most of the documents brought to the Ministry to be legalised and even takes it upon himself to take payment from people requesting stamps for their passports. If Your Excellency thought it appropriate to start an enquiry into this behaviour, which goes against the rights of a large number of honourable fathers, it would be an act of justice for which M. Duca's colleagues would be infinitely grateful, being entitled just as he is to offer their services to the public as sworn translators and make a living by it.]

This letter of complaint seems to have had an effect eventually, as Julien Pillaut's 1910 law manual states that "Pour obtenir la traduction légale d'un acte, les particuliers peuvent s'adresser aux traducteurs assermentés près les tribunaux (le ministère des Affaires Étrangères ne fait pas de traduction pour les particuliers)" [To obtain the legal translation of a certificate, private individuals can contact sworn court translators (the Ministry of Foreign Affairs does not provide translations for private individuals)] (quoted in Peñarroja 2013: 124). This clash between public service and the private sector opens the door to another little-researched dimension of translation history: early translation entrepreneurship. Freelance translators worked as sole traders, in partnership with other related businesses in the international trade sector, or even as agency managers, growing out of the informal translation groupings discussed earlier in this chapter. Freelance translators advertised their services as early as the first edition of the Bottin business directory, France's long-time equivalent to the *Yellow Pages*, in 1797.

Translation Entrepreneurs

As we have seen, it would be anachronistic to describe the role of translators in the nineteenth-century business sectors as wholly professional in modern sociological terms. Yet from the very beginning of the century, translators were working in business-to-business services, offering their language skills as part of the burgeoning knowledge economy and international trade.

The Emergence of a Mass Market for Translation 33

In the early nineteenth century, the need arose for a legal framework for handling translation issues arising from international trade disputes. The 1812 *Code de commerce* recognised the need for a legitimate authority in language disputes, stipulating that *courtiers-interprètes* (combining the function of brokers and interpreters) and *conducteurs de navire* (ship agents) alone could translate declarations relating to imports. In the 1840s, they were still being individually appointed by the king (*Bulletin* 1840: 184). In this highly under-researched area, the best sources are again collections of legislative texts which tell us that, for example, the Marseilles stock exchange had 50 such broker-interpreters appointed by a decree of 1813, increased to 54 in 1888 (*Annales* 1888: 386), and commercial gazettes listing the services of experts such as M. Pellecat of Rouen, who oversaw the arrival of the *Spéculateur* from Porto Maurizio, Italy, on 3 February 1823 with a cargo of 151 barrels of olive oil and 6 boxes of tiles (*Nacelle* 1823: 4). Interestingly, the 1813 code stipulated a series of set fees for broker-interpreters alongside emergent occupations that are now highly professionalised, such as surgeons and midwives – an implicit acknowledgement of the professional linguist's specific expertise. Similarly, the decree stipulated rates of payment per word, line, or even syllable, pointing to a rationalist quantification of translation services, taking account of regional variations in the cost of living:

> Les traductions par écrit seront payées, pour chaque rôle de trente lignes à la page, et de seize à dix-huit syllabes à la ligne, savoir : – À Paris, 1 f. 25 c. – dans les villes de quarante mille habitans et au-dessus, 1 f. – dans les autres villes et communes, 75 c.

> [Written translations will be paid, for each task of thirty lines per page, and sixteen to eighteen syllables per line: – In Paris, 1 f. 25 c., in towns with a population of over forty thousand, 1 f., in other towns and communes, 75 c.]

Evidence of this billing model survives in a rare 1810 invoice for clerking and translation services submitted to the *sénat conservateur de Nancy* for a series of land acquisitions. The invoice is dated 2 October in Aix-la-Chapelle (Aachen) and signed J. C. von Asten, translator for the Roer prefecture.[12] It lists the texts handled, such as a "contrat d'acquisition de la ferme de Clarenhoff à Frechen" and a "permission pour un conduit d'eau" [acquisition contract for the Clarenhoff farm in Frechen and permission for a water conduit]. Von Asten charged two francs per "feuille d'écriture", or

---

12 The Roer was a French département on the modern-day German and Dutch borders from 1798 to 1814.

34 *Professional Translators in Nineteenth-Century France*

sheet: the high cost may have been due to the archival nature of the documents in question, some of which dated back to the fourteenth century (Figure 1.1).

The status of such language experts was not legally defined or regulated in the nineteenth century: an 1848 edition of the *Journal du Palais* records

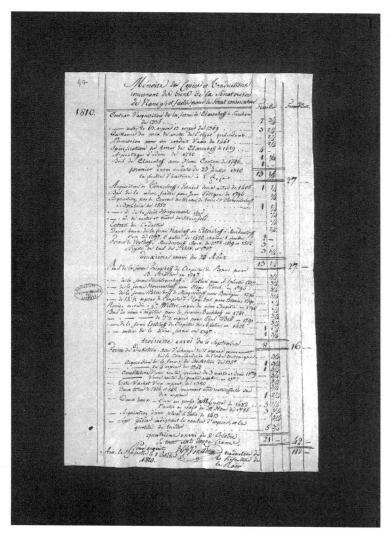

Figure 1.1 An invoice issued on 2 October 1810 by the translator J.C. von Asten in Aix-la-Chapelle. Image courtesy of the *Archives nationales*, Pierrefitte-sur-Seine.

The Emergence of a Mass Market for Translation 35

that magistrates could call on "toutes les personnes qu'ils jugent dignes de leur confiance" [anyone they deem trustworthy]. However, a de facto, if not de jure, form of accreditation existed, since, the *Journal* continued,

> il existe près d'un grand nombre de tribunaux des individus investis de leur confiance, et qui prennent le nom d'interprètes jurés; c'est parmi eux que les magistrats fixent ordinairement leur choix ... [Ils sont] reçus pour une ou plusieurs langues, après rapport de l'un des membres de la cour ou du tribunal, et le ministère public bien entendu; le titre qui leur est ainsi conféré est tout personnel et ne peut être transmis.

> [many courts have a pool of trustworthy individuals who call themselves sworn translators; magistrates generally choose from among them ... [They are] hired for one or several languages based on a report by a member of the court or tribunal, and the public ministry of course; the title conferred on them is wholly personal and cannot be passed on.]
> (*Journal du Palais* 1848: 612)

Accreditation was obligatory in Paris: "il n'y a que les experts qui ont été agréés par la cour royale qui soient admis à prêter serment devant elle, en audience publique" [Only experts approved by the royal court are allowed to swear an oath in public audiences at the court]. Interpreters also had legal liabilities: "L'interprète est responsable du dommage résultant pour les tiers d'une traduction infidèle, dans le cas de fraude ou de faute grave" [Interpreters are liable for damages caused to third parties by an unfaithful translation, fraud or gross misconduct] (*Dictionnaire du notariat* 1857: 106).

Translators also worked in other business arenas. While commercial gazettes from the very early years of the nineteenth century still listed translators under general headings such as "language teaching" and "interpreting", the roles were more clearly delineated by the 1820s, when translators were listed under their own heading, just after "tractomètres"[13] and before "traite des noirs (commission)" [the slave trade commission]. François-Marie Marchant de Beaumont (1769–1832), author of an 1818 tourist guide to Paris, assured readers that

> Celui qui est peu familiarisé avec la langue française, n'a pas à craindre de ne trouver à Paris personne capable d'entendre son langage. Il y existe des interprètes de toutes les langues de l'Europe et de l'Orient, et des bureaux de traducteurs assermentés.

---

13 A device for measuring pulling force, usually used to measure the strength of draught animals.

36 *Professional Translators in Nineteenth-Century France*

[Visitors unfamiliar with French need not fear finding no-one in Paris who speaks their language. There are interpreters for all the languages of Europe and the Orient, and bureaus of sworn translators.]

(Marchant de Beaumont 1818: 32)

Translators were indeed beginning to realise the benefits of formalising the loose groupings of the eighteenth century, pooling resources and effort, achieving economies of scale, and offering a wider range of languages. Commercial gazettes list men – and occasionally women – working as language brokers across the tertiary sector in interpreting, translating, teaching, and even accountancy. The translation sector was developing as a crucial tool of the emergent service sector: entrepreneurs established translation agencies as early as the 1810s. The *Almanach du commerce* for 1815 features an advertisement for a translation agency managed by a certain Nunez Taboada (who was probably Manuel Nuñez de Taboada, author of a number of Spanish-French dictionaries in the early nineteenth century) since its establishment in 1811. The advertisement made it clear that he ran his business on purely rationalist principles:

Cet établissement, également nécessaire à la politique, au commerce, aux transactions sociales, à l'ordre judiciaire et aux lettres ; cet établissement, dont le but est de centraliser et de régulariser en même temps des fonctions de la plus haute importance, présente toutes les garanties que le vœu du public et celui des particuliers peuvent s'en promettre. Des traducteurs, aussi recommandables par leur moralité que par leurs lumières, dont les travaux sont d'ailleurs soumis à une révision confiée à des littérateurs d'un mérite reconnu, et couverts par la responsabilité individuelle du directeur du département, M. E. Nunez Taboada, répondent par leur zèle, leur discrétion et leur intelligence, au choix et à la confiance dont on honore son établissement.

[This establishment, equally necessary to politics, trade, social transactions, the legal order, and literature, whose aim is to both centralise and regularise functions of the highest importance, presents every guarantee that the public and private individuals could wish. Translators, as recommendable for their morality as their intelligence, whose work is subjected to revision by men of letters of acknowledged merit, and under the individual responsibility of the department director M. E. Nunez Taboada, respond with zeal, discretion and judgement to the choice and confidence with which his establishment is honoured.]

(de la Tynna 1815: 22)

Such ventures were becoming important cogs in the increasingly modern business world. The legal scholar Jean-Marie Pardessus (1772–1853)

The Emergence of a Mass Market for Translation   37

defined these early translation agencies in an 1825 book on commercial law as follows:

> L'étendue des relations commerciales et les rapports qu'elles ont établis entre des individus de nations différentes, occasionnant l'emploi fréquent d'actes rédigés en langues étrangères, il s'est formé, dans différentes villes, des établissemens où l'on traduit tous les actes et documens, en quelque langue qu'ils soient rédigés, et où réciproquement on rédige des notes ou lettres en langues étrangères. En général, il n'y a pas acte de commerce à faire une traduction quelconque ; mais celui qui, par spéculation, réunit diverses personnes pour faire les traductions qu'on lui confie, forme en cela un établissement qu'il est naturel de ranger parmi les agences d'affaires, et de considérer comme une spéculation commerciale.

> [The extent of trading contacts and the relationships they have established between individuals of different nations, requiring the frequent use of documents in foreign languages, has led to the creation in several towns and cities of establishments where all sorts of acts and documents are translated, whatever language they are in, and where conversely notes and letters are written in foreign languages. In general, merely translating a document is not a commercial undertaking, but anyone who speculates by bringing together a number of people to translate documents entrusted to him thereby founds an establishment that can naturally be classed as a business agency and considered a commercial speculation.]

> (Pardessus 1825: 287)

A number of such agencies are recorded in advertisements across the century, often with names that made grand-sounding claims to universal expertise, such as Jacques Barzilay's *Bureau de traduction pour le commerce, les sciences et la littérature* [Translation bureau for trade, the sciences and literature]. Few records of the business practices of such agencies survive, but one brochure did somehow find its way into the collection of Louis-Lucien Bonaparte and from there to the Newberry Library, Chicago. The Athénée Polyglotte agency was founded at 28 rue Feydeau, Paris, in 1850 by Leopold Courrouve dit Pold, a sworn translator to the imperial court in Paris. The brochure starts with a grandiloquent declaration by the founder of his dream of

> Un vaste édifice, à l'aspect monumental et sévère, aux abords faciles, sorte d'Athénée universel, où le savant, l'homme du monde, le jurisconsulte, le voyageur, le commerçant, l'industriel, l'artisan, le prolétaire, l'étranger et mille autres auraient trouvé centralisées toutes les

38 *Professional Translators in Nineteenth-Century France*

ressources qu'offrent l'intelligence, la science et la civilisation de notre grande Capitale.

[a vast edifice, monumental and severe in appearance but easy to access, a sort of universal Atheneum where the scholar, the man of the world, the legal expert, the traveller, the trader, the industrialist, the craftsman, the proletarian, the foreigner and a thousand others would have found in one place all the resources offered by the intelligence, scholarship, and civilisation of our great capital.]

(Courrouve dit Pold 1861: unpaginated)

Political events had forced Courrouve dit Pold to scale back his ambitions, however – perhaps fortunately, since he begins presenting his services with the misspelled axiom "times is money", casting doubt on either his knowledge of English or his proofreading skills. As the ambitious opening description suggests, the agency offered a wide range of knowledge services including writing, fact-finding, accountancy, civil engineering, dispute resolution, patenting, market research – and translation. The presentation of the translation services on offer is worth quoting at length:

Aujourd'hui que la vapeur, l'électricité, la civilisation du monde ont pour ainsi dire supprimé les distances, renversé les frontières et rendu les communications internationales instantanées, de quel avantage n'est-il pas pour le commerçant, pour le savant même, d'être immédiatement au courant de ce qu'on lui écrit, informé de ce qui se fait et se publie à l'étranger ? Que d'honorables négociants, d'habiles industriels se trouvent dans l'embarras faute de pouvoir obtenir, à l'instant même et exactement, la traduction d'une dépêche télégraphique, d'une lettre commerciale, d'une commande faite en langue étrangère ? Quel ennui, quelle appréhension, quand il faut recourir à l'obligeance d'un ami, quelque fois même se mettre à la discrétion d'un étranger ou d'un concurrent pour avoir connaissance d'une missive renfermant des secrets de métier ou de famille que l'on ne voudrait confier qu'à soi-même!

[Today, now that steam, electricity, and a newly civilised world have, as it were, suppressed distances, overthrown borders and made international communication instantaneous, what an advantage is it not for the merchant, for the scholar himself, to know immediately what has been written to him, and to be informed of what is happening and being published abroad? How many honourable traders and skilled industrialists have found themselves in difficulties for the want of an immediate, accurate translation of a telegram, business letter, or order in a foreign language? How troublesome, how worrisome, when one must call on a friend, or even entrust oneself to a stranger or competitor to discover

The Emergence of a Mass Market for Translation   39

the contents of a missive containing trade or family secrets that one would wish known only to oneself!]

(Courrouve dit Pold 1861: 7–8)

Immediate, accurate access to commercially sensitive information was clearly a major selling point. The agency manager made a point of foregrounding the expertise of his team of freelancers, consisting of sworn court translators and language teachers. His own area of expertise was scientific translations and descriptions of machines: he boasted 20 years of experience had thoroughly familiarised him with their typical style (or, in today's parlance, their textual features) and personally guaranteed accuracy and discretion. The agency handled a wide range of languages including regional French patois and extra-European languages such as Hebrew, Turkish, Arabic, and Persian. The brochure concludes with the agency terms and conditions: payment upfront, no discounts, extra charges for delivery (Figure 1.2).

The *Athénée polyglotte* agency seems to have been active for a number of years, advertising its services in the daily press alongside hernia bandage manufacturers and odourless water closets (*Gazette des tribunaux* 1856: 860). The last trace of its activity is an approval for funding from the Ministry of Trade in 1869. Yet its two decades or so were no match for the longevity of another early French translation agency that eventually became one of the world's leading communications multinationals, the Havas Group.

Charles-Louis Havas (1783–1858) was born in Rouen. He moved to Portugal in his early 20s as a trading company representative, married the owner's daughter, and set up in international trade with his London-based brother-in-law. Ruined by the fall of Napoleon, he became the Paris correspondent for a wealthy financier, translating the latest financial news as soon as the European press came in (he spoke English and German, his wife Spanish and Portuguese). He quickly grasped that controlling the flow of information was one path to riches: just a few years earlier, it had been widely rumoured that Nathan Meyer Rothschild owed his successful speculation on the outcome of the Battle of Waterloo to advance information conveyed by homing pigeon. While the foreign press had long been translated piecemeal, Havas's great innovation was to streamline the process by centralising translatorial labour in an agency in close proximity to both the central post office where newspapers would arrive and to the dispatch centre where postal messengers would set out across France. This central location and the team of on-site translators gave him the edge in disseminating information in a timely manner. As the agency grew, he experimented with innovative solutions to speed up the process of information transfer, including lithography to avoid laborious hand-copying, telegraph

40 *Professional Translators in Nineteenth-Century France*

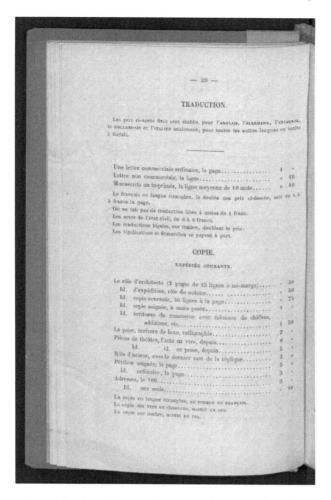

Figure 1.2 The price list from the advertising brochure for Léopold Courrouve dit Pold's *Athénée polyglotte* translation and business services agency. Image courtesy of the Newberry Library.

technology, and – perhaps inspired by the Rothschild example – sending information via homing pigeon: a dispatch sent by pigeon from the London stock exchange at eight in the morning would be at the Havas agency in Paris by two that afternoon, far faster than human travel and more practical for large quantities of information than the early forms of telegraphy then in operation. As a result, the Havas agency came to hold a quasimonopoly on news translation and onward dissemination. Balzac even critiqued the system in his *Monographie de la presse parisienne* in 1840:

The Emergence of a Mass Market for Translation   41

Le traducteur (genre disparu). Jadis, les journaux avaient un rédacteur spécial pour les nouvelles étrangères, qui les traduisait et les *premierparisait*,[14] ceci a duré jusqu'en 1830 ... Depuis, les journaux de Paris, ont eu tous le même traducteur, ils n'ont plus, ni agents, ni correspondants, ils envoient rue Jean-Jacques Rousseau, chez M. Havas, qui leur remet à tous les mêmes nouvelles étrangères, en en réservant la primeur à ceux dont l'abonnement est le plus fort.

[The translator (an extinct genus). Formerly, newspapers had a specialist writer for foreign news, who translated and headlined it, that lasted until 1830 ... Since then, the Paris papers have all had the same translator, they no longer have agents or correspondents, they send to M. Havas at rue Jean-Jacques Rousseau, who gives them all the same foreign news, handing it first to those who pay the highest subscription.]

(Balzac 2002 [1840]: 40)

This made Havas a pivotal figure in the control of information, criticised again by Balzac for his monopoly position: "Le public peut croire qu'il y a plusieurs journaux, mais il n'y en a en définitive qu'un seul journal, celui de M. Havas" [The public may believe there are several newspapers, but in fact there is just one, M. Havas's] (Balzac 1840: 245). Havas was also attacked for the quality of his output, since his translators were required to work to extremely strict deadlines – a complaint familiar to many freelancers today. *L'Ami de la religion* wrote in 1861 that another religious publication

se plaint, ce matin, de l'inexactitude et des erreurs de la traduction de l'allocution pontificale, faite par l'agence Havas et publiée par la plupart des journaux. On reçoit, dit-elle, cette traduction ; il est tard ; on ne veut pas être devancé, et on l'envoie à l'imprimerie sans la lire. Nous regrettons ... que la plupart des journaux aient publié cette ... version ; elle [est] remplie de contre-sens, de fautes grossières.

[complains this morning of the inaccuracy and errors in the pope's speech as translated by the Havas agency and published in most papers. We have received this translation, it says; it's late, we want to be first, and it is sent to the printers without being read. We regret ... that most newspapers printed this ... version; it is full of mistranslations and dreadful errors.]

(*L'Ami de la religion* 1861: 834)

---

14 A "premier-Paris" was the lead article in a newspaper: see https://www.cnrtl.fr/definition/premierpariser (accessed 12 June 2022).

42 *Professional Translators in Nineteenth-Century France*

Despite the criticisms, Havas's enterprise flourished. His death in 1858 was marked by the press in his hometown of Rouen: "Par ses traductions de tous les journaux importants de l'Europe, par le nombre de ses correspondants à l'extérieur, il a concouru puissamment à la transformation de la presse de notre pays qui, avant lui, n'était que médiocrement au courant des nouvelles des autres peuples" [By his translations of all major European newspapers and by the number of his foreign correspondents, he powerfully contributed to the transformation of our national press, which, before him, had only mediocre knowledge of news from other peoples] (*Nouvelliste de Rouen*, 25 May 1858, quoted in Dubuc 1959: 135).

By the late nineteenth century, translation remained an unlikely career choice. An 1887 careers guide for boys by Bernard-Henri Gausseron, himself a language teacher and translator of Swift, failed to mention it as a potential path for budding linguists (Derome 2021: 54). The number of people claiming professional translator status remained small. A March 1896 census of industries and professions included a category for translators, interpreters, and broker-interpreters, with 371 responses – 328 men, 40 women, and a tiny handful of unknowns – the majority declaring their status as "petits patrons travaillant seuls" (i.e. sole traders) (*Résultats statistiques* 1901: 381).[15] At the end of the century, there were roughly as many freelance translators as there were professional estate agents (341), twice the number of funeral parlours (191), and one-tenth the number of land surveyors (3,725). The figure does not include translators employed by the civil service or employed by publishers; nor does it include the large number of occasional translators with portfolio careers in and outside the languages sector. While translators may have lagged behind surgeons (15,790) and midwives (13,496) in number and in terms of the sociological threshold for professionalisation, forming a relatively small body of practitioners, they nonetheless remained a crucial cog in the machinery of international trade and communication, their role increasingly structured by early language business agencies and the legal framework of business and government.

---

15 For the sake of comparison, the two main professional bodies for translators in France today, the *Societé française des traducteurs* and the *Association des traducteurs littéraires de France*, have around 2,600 members between them.

2 Tracing an Emergent Discourse of Translatorial Labour

We begin this chapter not in nineteenth-century France, but in 1770s Germany via 1790s Britain. Following the Europe-wide success of Laurence Sterne's *Life and Opinions of Tristram Shandy*, rendered into German in 1774 in a classic translation by Johann Joachim Christoph Bode, Anglophile German authors were inspired to write their own eccentric novels incorporating Sterne's typical textual features such as discontinuity, digression, hypertrophy of the narrative discourse, and atrophy of the narrative itself (Sangsue 1987: 9), and – more importantly for this chapter – a studied awareness of the book's own materiality as a print artefact positioned within a particular communications circuit (Darnton 1982; Pickford 2018). One such author was Christoph Friedrich Nicolai (1733–1811), a writer and, significantly, bookseller, whose Sterne-inspired *Das Leben und die Meinungen des Herrn Magister Sebaldus Nothanker* (1773–6) contained a discussion over several pages between the eponymous hero and a doctor on the state of the modern German publishing industry, particularly the phenomenon of *Übersetzungsfabriken*, or translation factories. Translated into English by Thomas Dutton in 1798, *The Life and Opinions of Sebaldus Nothanker* compared the manufacture of translations to weaving linen and knitting stockings to fulfil orders for the military. Like many professional practices, translation for the publishing trade gave rise to a hierarchy of various classes and ranks:

> [A] translator from the English, for example, ranks higher than a translator from the French, as being scarcer. A translator from the Italian expects to be solicited before he begins to work, and will not always be content to be tied down to any particular day for the delivery of his work. As for a translator from the Spanish, there is scarce a single one to be had. And this is the very reason why people frequently undertake to translate from this language without understanding a syllable of it. On the other hand, translators from the Greek and Latin are so numerous, that they are never sought after, but come for the most part

DOI: 10.4324/9781003173090-3

44 *Professional Translators in Nineteenth-Century France*

to offer their services. In addition to all these, there are translators, who do nothing their whole life but translate; – translators, who make their translations at their leisure hours by way of amusement, in the same manner as our young ladies employ themselves with ornamental needlework, knotting and filligree [sic]; fashionable translators who accompany their translations with a preface, in which they assure the public, that the original is excellent; – learned translators, who improve upon their work, accompany it with remarks, and assure us that the original is very bad, but that they have made it tolerable; translators, who translate themselves into originals; these worthy gentry get hold of a French or English book, leave out the beginning and end, alter and improve the remainder at leisure, put their name boldly in the title page, and publish the book as their own production. Lastly, there are translators who make their translations themselves, and some, who get them made by others.

(Nicolai, tr. Dutton 1798: 1.153–5)

This fascinating insight into late eighteenth-century editorial translation practice is worthy of note in several ways. Firstly, it sketches out a hierarchy of literary and linguistic capital in the international marketplace for cultural goods, theorised in recent years by scholars such as Pascale Casanova (1999), Louis-Jean Calvet (2007), and Johann Heilbron and Gisèle Sapiro (2002), anticipating a Bourdieusian field of literary translation that we will return to in greater detail in later chapters. Secondly, it offers a precious glimpse of the range of translatorial self-identities (Sela-Sheffy and Schlesinger 2011) at play at a time when the modern publishing market was coming into being. Thirdly, it points at various models of translatorial practice approaching the sociological threshold for professionalism, foreshadowing the categories defined by modern sociological studies of the translation profession such as Kalinowski's sense of vocation (2002) and full-time vs. part-time practice (Heinich 1984; Vitrac 2000; Guillon 2020). Strikingly, at a distance of nearly 250 years, it will read to any working translator as an instantly recognisable description of current literary translation: the respective literary capital of individual languages may have changed, Latin and Spanish may have swapped places, but the overall pattern still fundamentally holds true.

Above all, it makes it clear that even in the eighteenth century, literary translation was a *business*. It had its purchasers and suppliers, skills gluts and shortages that dictated remuneration, deadlines and the availability of work, information asymmetries that impacted recruitment and pricing (Chan 2008), and dubious practices such as intellectual property piracy and unacknowledged subcontracting. Then as now, translators seeking to enter the field and maintain an active presence within it faced

Emergent Discourse of Translatorial Labour   45

issues of fungibility, status quo bias, and opportunity cost. They had to be in the right place at the right time, to network, and to market themselves.[1] They had to work fast to turn a profit. In short, in the words of Sebaldus Nothanker, it is wise to consider "the translating business in the wholesale, (after the same manner as an Irish contractor engages to furnish the grand fleet with salt-beef)" (Nicolai, tr. Dutton 1798: 1.158). Interestingly, this aspect of translation as a business practice is reflected in a little-known alternative meaning of the term "translator", now obsolete though recorded in the *Oxford English Dictionary* as late as the 1920s, as a person who mends old clothes and shoes, and by extension second-hand boots and clothes and the trade in them.

While the previous chapter focused broadly on a macro-description of translation as a sector of the economy and government, this chapter – and the rest of the book – zooms in on the sector of the nineteenth-century translation industry that is most clearly evidenced in the archival and historical record. Translation for publication was a significant market in its own right and one that has left an abundance of sources for the translation historian to explore. This is not to claim that the findings of this and subsequent chapters can be unproblematically expanded to other sectors – far more research is needed on professional translation practices in sectors other than the publishing trade – but as Sebaldus Nothanker makes clear, there was at the very least a perceived degree of continuity between book translation and modes of production in other sectors, from cottage-industry weaving, abattoirs, and military supply chain management to proto-Taylorist factory production lines; there is no reason to think that these modes of translational production do not also apply to non-literary translation in sectors other than the publishing trade, as indeed Havas's experiences in news translation outlined in Chapter 1 suggest.

Sebaldus Nothanker was not alone in envisioning translation as a form of authorial labour within a competitive literary marketplace. Comparisons with the labour-for-hire model and accusations of hackery are found as early as the early eighteenth century. "Iscariot Hackney"'s (i.e. Richard Savage's) 1732 satire on contemporary authorship, *An Author to Be Let*, outlines the sort of dubious literary practices associated with publishers such as the notorious Edmund Curll:

---

1 See, for example, Christian Garve's attempts to break into translation, hampered by his geographical location in Breslau where the latest French and English books were hard to come by. Many of his letters to Christian Felix Weisse complain about losing translation commissions to rivals closer to the heart of the publishing trade in Leipzig (quoted in Zille 2021: 128).

46 *Professional Translators in Nineteenth-Century France*

> 'Twas in his Service that I wrote Obscenity and Profaneness, under the names of *Pope* and *Swift* ... I abridg'd Histories and Travels, translated from the French what they never wrote, and was expert at finding out new Titles for old Books.
>
> (Hackney 1732: 4)[2]

While Rogers and Hopkins (2005: 81) caution against taking such satires too literally, they do seem to have reflected contemporary practice to a certain extent; these sharp business practices, including hack (pseudo-) translation, brought authorship perilously close to then-emergent common law torts such as passing off, associated with the intangible assets of intellectual property (Pickford 2011).

Such comparisons track with a broad trend across the eighteenth century away from translation from the classical languages, whose high literary and educational capital brought a concomitantly high degree of prestige to translation practice, to modern European languages, whose lesser degree of social exclusivity brought about a corresponding decline in the prestige of translation as a form of authorship. This shift went hand in hand with a significant rise in the sheer number of books being translated (Wilfert 2012). The work of the hack translators satirised by "Iscariot Hackney" did indeed neatly map onto the core characteristics of the emergent factory system, including the use of unskilled labour in downplaying linguistic competence in hiring decisions;[3] the putting out system in carving the text up into separate signatures; economies of scale in the manufacture of texts; location near key industry resources, particularly spatialised in

---

2 On Edmund Curll's notorious career, see Rogers (2021).

3 See, for example, Fielding's satirical commentary on translation practice in the 1730s in *The Author's Farce*: "Bookweight: a translator too is what I want at present, my last being in Newgate for shop-lifting. The rogue had a trick of translating out of the shops as well as the languages.

Scarecrow. But I am afraid I am not qualified for a translator, for I understand no language but my own.

Book. What, and translate Virgil?

Scare. Alas! I translated him out of Dryden.

Book. Lay by your hat, sir, lay by your hat, and take your seat immediately. Not qualified! Thou art as well versed in thy trade as if thou hadst laboured in my garret these ten years. Let me tell you, friend, you will have more occasion for invention than learning here. You will be obliged to translate books out of all languages, especially French, that were never printed in any language whatsoever" (Fielding 1730: 26). A similar mock conversation features in the *Mercure de France* in 1829, in which "Mercure" advises "M. De Chompré" to translate from fashionable English, which he does not speak; this is no obstacle for Mercure, who suggests "pour traduire vite et bien, il faut traduire une traduction toute faite" [to translate fast and well, translate a translation that's already been done] (Anonymous 1829: 507).

Emergent Discourse of Translatorial Labour   47

English in the expression "Grub Street" (Cross 1985); centralisation in collective workshops; and standardisation and uniformisation of output.

As a result, framing translation as a form of proto-industrial practice became a relatively common trope from mid-century on. In 1774, Elie Fréron gave an account in the *Année littéraire* of the practice of enterprising authors seizing the business opportunities afforded by the expanding print market, taking on translation work which they then farmed out to low-paid – though not necessarily incompetent – hirelings:

> Vous ne sçavez peut-être pas, Monsieur, qu'il y a dans Paris des Manufactures de ces sortes de Traductions. L'Entrepreneur fait d'avance son marché avec des libraires qui lui paient tant la Feuille in-4° ou in-12°; supposons trois ou quatre louis, & cette supposition n'est pas gratuite. L'Entrepreneur intelligent fait venir des ouvriers qui lui taillent de la besogne, moyennant 24, 18, 15 & quelquefois 12 livres par Feuille. Vous voyez le profit immense qu'il retire, sans qu'il se donne la moindre peine.

> [You may not know, sir, that there are factories for these sorts of translations in Paris. The entrepreneur agrees on terms in advance with booksellers who pay a given amount for a quarto or duodecimo sheet; say three or four louis, and this supposition is founded. The smart entrepreneur brings in workers who do the hard work for 24, 18, 15, sometimes 12 livres a sheet. You see the vast profit he makes without the least effort.]

> (Fréron 1774a: 298)

FréronIn another issue of *L'Année littéraire* the same year, Fréron alluded to a "Bureau général des traductions d'ouvrages anglais, Bureau qui commence à être fort connu" [general translation bureau for English works, which is beginning to become very well-known] (1774b: 76), specialising in travel narratives. Van Tieghem (1914) suggests this is a jocular reference, though Fréron's tone is hardly humorous at this point. I have been unable to locate any trace of any such institution. Yet the expression itself shows that as early as the mid- to late eighteenth century, translational labour was organised enough to draw (satirical) attention.[4] In particular,

---

4 See also Louis-Simon Anger, writing in 1828: "Environ vingt-cinq ans avant la révolution, au plus fort de notre anglomanie politique et littéraire, Le Tourneur, écrivain passable, mais spéculateur plus habile encore, éleva dans Paris une manufacture de traductions qu'on pouvait comparer à ces ateliers d'horlogerie, où de simples ouvriers fabriquent des pièces grossières, qu'ensuite les maîtres repassent et signent de leur nom pour les mettre dans le commerce. De cette manufacture de Le Tourneur sont sortis un grand nombre d'ouvrages dégrossis d'abord par ses garçons traducteurs, puis repassés, signés et publiés par lui" [Some 25 years before the revolution, when our political and literary Anglomania was at

48 *Professional Translators in Nineteenth-Century France*

translation practice became far more open to women, whose role in the so-called translation factories of mid to late eighteenth-century Germany is explored in Willenberg (2008).

Such comparisons continued well into the nineteenth century. The next section will study one particular strand of the discourse surrounding translatorial (self-)identity for evidence of how low-status translators thought about their own professional practice. At this early stage in the crystallisation of a professional field for translation for publishing, the practice stood at a crossroads. Two distinct economic models lay ahead. For some elite practitioners, particularly working from classical languages and with authorial status in their own right, translation seemed a perfect fit for the economic model of authorship, involving an individualistic "star system" approach to status improvement (Sela-Sheffy 2006: 246). For hack translators churning out translations by the hundredweight for their publishing taskmasters, the practice likely seemed more akin to a straightforward collective form of waged labour. These two potential directions of travel hint at the complex status of literary translation as a creative, economic, and professional practice, at the crossroads between creative writing and the language industry sector, leading to equally complex expressions of professional translatorial identity.

Studying Translatorial Identity

Issues of translatorial identity began to be studied in earnest following the sociological turn in translation studies in the early years of the twenty-first century. Sela-Sheffy (2011: 1) sees the question as a natural trajectory of translation studies, building on earlier work on norms and the invisibility topos. The earlier assumption of a monolithically submissive habitus (Simeoni 1998) has become increasingly nuanced in studies that "zoom in on translators' and interpreters' own understanding of their role and status [to build a picture of] a dynamic and multi-layered cultural construct, collectively produced and re-produced through social struggles" (Sela-Sheffy 2011: 2). Yet as Sela-Sheffy makes clear, in 2011, little such work had at that point focused on professional translatorial identity: exceptions include Choi and Lim (2002) on professional translators in Korea and Van Dam and Zethsen (2008) on the status of translators employed in the Danish industry.

---

its height, Le Tourneur, a decent enough writer and even smarter speculator, established in Paris a translation factory that could be compared to the clock-making workshops where ordinary labourers manufacture rough pieces for the masters to polish, sign and sell. From Le Tourneur's factory poured numerous works in rough drafts by his apprentice translators and polished, signed and published by him] (Anger 1828: 316).

Since Sela-Sheffy wrote her introduction to Sela-Sheffy and Schlesinger (2011), research on translatorial identity has expanded rapidly. Innovative recent studies have begun to investigate marginal forms of translatorial identity such as that of translation students (Singer Contreras 2022). Some such work has focused on literary translators, beginning perhaps with Reine Meylaerts's study of author-translators in diglossic societies (Meylaerts in Sela-Sheffy and Schlesinger 2011): the issue has been explored in depth in PhD dissertations on translators of Modern Greek poetry into English (Georgiou 2020) and translated urban vernacular in Sweden and the UK (Smalley 2014: Chapter 7), and in discussions of competition and cooperation among literary translators (Tekgül 2016; Misiou 2023). A sign of the increasing importance of research on literary translator identity is the omnipresence of the term in Kaindl, Kolb, and Schlager (2021), with over 50 occurrences. This specific focus on identity stands on the shoulders of more impressionistic collections of translator biographies and portraits such as Jean Delisle's *Portraits de traducteurs* (1999), *Portraits de traductrices* (2002), and *Traducteurs par eux-mêmes* (2021); Agnes Whitfield's *Métier du double: Portraits de traductrices et traducteurs littéraires* (2005); and Esther Allen and Susan Bernofsky's *In Translation: Translators on Their Work and What It Means* (2013). These collections are not explicitly framed in terms of identity but can usefully serve the translator studies scholar as *a posteriori* evidence (Eberharter 2021). Again, it is worth noting that such collections tend to focus on literary translators to the detriment of other sectors of the translation industry; Delisle (2021) is an exception, offering autobiographical vignettes of government translators in Canada.

A glance at the list of contributors to Allen and Bernofsky (2013) hints at a potential stumbling block in research into translatorial identity in the literary translation sector. The book, published by Columbia University Press, is a beautiful object with high production values, reflecting the symbolic capital afforded to literary translation as a creative practice by the authors. The 16 translators invited to reflect on their translatorial practice and identity for the volume – including such luminaries as David Bellos, Haruki Murakami, Alice Kaplan, and Lawrence Venuti – all have multiple, overlapping professional identities as academics, literary critics, and creative writers. It would prove impossible in practice to unpick the threads of their various professional habitus to isolate a specific translatorial identity. All 16 bring significant intellectual and/or literary capital to their translation practice from the adjacent fields of literature and literary scholarship, rendering them visible in a field in which, as Venuti (1995) makes clear, invisibility is the norm. Indeed, high literary and/or intellectual capital correlates in these cases with amateur translator status, not in the sense of the *quality* of their translational output, but in the sense that their presence in

50 *Professional Translators in Nineteenth-Century France*

the field is sporadic rather than ongoing, corresponding to the "dilettante" end of the professional spectrum (Heinich 1984: 266), or what Lahire (2006) describes as occasional players of the game. This foregrounds the fundamental paradox at the heart of literary translation as a form of authorial practice: translation is typically valued for the invisibility of the translator-as-writer's voice, placing the typical means of accruing symbolic capital through authorial practice out of reach. As a result, uniquely in authorship (with perhaps ghost-writing), the most visible translators tend to import literary capital from outside the field, such that literary translators with high literary capital gleaned from their multiple professional identities that necessarily limit their presence in the field are more prominent than literary translation practitioners with a sole professional identity present in the field full-time, who tend to work with authors and genres that are lower in literary capital to ensure a steady flow of work.[5]

First-person accounts of translatorial identity by translators with a sustained, or even full-time, presence in the field have historically been scarce, almost by definition: such practitioners have typically had little motivation to expend time and effort on non-remunerative, self-reflexive forms of writing.[6] Genetic approaches to translation criticism (Cordingley and Montini 2015) are valuable but rely on the survival of material that again tends to correlate with high literary capital. Translator studies scholars have displayed initiative in making excellent use of alternative resources such as translator-publisher correspondence (Paloposki 2021), bibliographic catalogues (Santana López and Travieso Rodríguez 2021), and translatorial paratext (Vanacker 2021). Scholars have particularly recognised the value of translatorial paratext as a tool for research, compiling anthologies such as Cointre and Rivara (2006), Hayes (undated), and the rich collection of

---

5 Such professional literary translators will in some cases translate multiple novels per year: for instance, Swedish translators working for the Harlequin romance brand will regularly translate 12 full-length books a year on a freelance basis (Hemmungs Wirtén 1998: 115). In rare cases, literary translation is even conducted on an employment basis, distancing the practice from the exceptional economy of the arts and placing it squarely in the standard labour market: Harlequin Japan employed 400 English-to-Japanese translators in 1998, for example (Shibamoto Smith 2005).

6 As Kaindl (2021: 11) points out, full-time translators are today increasingly able to achieve visibility by maintaining an active online presence, for instance contributing to the TOLEDO translation diaries website or writing blogs. One high-profile example is full-time translator Daniel Hahn's translation diary blog series recording the process of translating Diamela Eltit's *Jamás el fuego nunca* for Charco Press, which ran from January to November 2021, subsequently published by Charco Press as *Catching Fire: A Translation Diary* (2022).

translator prefaces held at the Centre d'études du 19e siècle Joseph Sablé at the University of Toronto.[7]

The next section uses such sources, direct and indirect, to shed light on one underexplored aspect of the (self-)identity of translators working at the professional end of the spectrum, who had a sustained presence in the field and for whom translation was – as far as can be established at this historical remove – a significant source of income. It deliberately turns the focus away from the historically visible practitioners who entered the field by leveraging literary and/or intellectual capital garnered in other fields of intellectual practice, such as Charles Baudelaire, whose much-researched translations of Edgar Allen Poe (Salines 2004: 12) have – despite his flawed English – historically overshadowed earlier versions by Isabelle Meunier, Alphonse Borghers, and Léon de Wailly, among others (Lemonnier 1928).[8] Léon de Wailly (1804–64) was a highly experienced translator by the time he came to translate Poe in 1856, having translated Sterne, Swift, and Fielding, among others; nonetheless, his versions of Poe were – and still are – displaced by Baudelaire's, though the latter had very little translation experience prior to his work on Poe (Salines 2004: 255). The marginalisation of other Poe translators is such that the editor of Poe's works in the prestigious Pléiade collection, Yves-Gérard Le Dantec, chose to exclude stories by Poe not translated by Baudelaire (Salines 2004: 21). Baudelaire's extra-translational literary capital has therefore entirely displaced de Wailly's professional standing as a translator.

A second category of amateur translators that this chapter will not explore in depth are those who worked occasionally on non-fiction titles relating to their own areas of expertise. Such translators again typically had a sporadic presence in the field of translation for publication. A study of nineteenth-century mathematics translators, for instance, shows that in this specialist field, translators into French were frequently students, engineers, and educators, often co-opted by senior figures in the network behind the publication of mathematics journals (Chatzis et al. 2017). In contemporary terms, the participation of such practitioners in

---

7 For Hayes's online anthology, see https://scholarworks.umass.edu/french_translators/ (accessed 25 May 2022). For the Centre d'études du 19e siècle Joseph Sablé collection, see http://sites.utoronto.ca/sable/recherche/banques/prefaces/traducteurs.htm (accessed 25 May 2022).

8 See examples from Baudelaire's translation practice: "I am an Epicure. I am delicate in my tastes, choice in my acquaintance, careful in my loves and fastidious in my country-houses. / Je suis un véritable Épicure; délicat dans mes goûts, réservé dans mes accointances, tendre dans mes amitiés et mes amours, je ne suis cruel et dédaigneux que pour mes pauvres maisons de campagne" and "Then she made the shepherd call All the heav'ns to witness truth. Never lov'd a truer youth. / Puis elle contraignit le berger à appeler Tous les cieux en témoignage Qu'il n'avait jamais aimé une fille plus candide" (quoted in Salines 2004: 26).

52 *Professional Translators in Nineteenth-Century France*

translation was rooted in their communicative and above all their extra-linguistic competence (knowledge of languages and of mathematics); at the professional end of the spectrum, translators display the full range of translational skills, including instrumental-professional, psycho-physiological, transfer, and strategic competence (Malmkjaer 2009). Translators working within the publishing trade on a regular basis typically also took on a range of related roles as part of a sustained network rooted in the publication communication circuit. To take one example, the well-known eighteenth-century German translator Christian Felix Weisse, whose translation bibliography runs to 90 titles, regularly acted as a publishing go-between, putting publishers in touch with translators; he also took on a range of ancillary publishing roles as copy-editor, author, and even proto-literary agent. His central role in the communication circuit enabled him to envision his translated texts as raw materials that he could "syndicate" and recycle across a range of media (Zille 2021: 125, 167, 169).

Translation as Industrial Labour in the Nineteenth Century

The emergence of quasi-professional translation for publishing went hand in hand with the growth of a modern publishing market, driven by a number of forces, including improvements to printing technology such as the steam-driven press, the development of modern advertising techniques, and improved transport links enabling better distribution to a wider readership, all of which in turn fed into rising literacy rates that generated a virtuous circle for print consumption. Modern management techniques began to emerge on the back of the Industrial Revolution (Pollard 1965) and, like many other business sectors, printing and publishing embraced Adam Smith's principles of the division of labour. Instead of producing pins, they produced books. Various functions became increasingly specialised. Publishing became increasingly separated from bookselling (Haynes 2010). Print workshops broke tasks down into separate functions; apprentices specialised in specific skills such as composition or bookbinding, which was in turn subdivided into forwarding, or sewing and putting on the cover, and finishing, or tooling the cover (Kinane 1993: 11). And, in France, Britain, Germany, and doubtless other European countries, beginning in around the 1730s, texts were carved up among translation service providers on a division of labour basis for just-in-time delivery, sometimes with quality control procedures built into the process.[9]

---

9 See, for example, the *Anti-Jacobin Review*'s passing reference to a copy-editing process: "The doctor [Henry Hunter] was a professional translator from the French. His chief work in that way was his translation of Lavater [1789–98]; this, luckily for him, passed through

Emergent Discourse of Translatorial Labour   53

This section will focus particularly on one specific translator profile which emerged at this point as the communication circuit increasingly came under the sway of a modern capitalist market structure: the translator as industrial labourer. The vast majority of translation for the publishing trade was not the work of leading literary lights such as Chateaubriand, Baudelaire, and Mallarmé, whose translational output has attracted disproportionate scholarly attention; nor was it high in the symbolic capital required to enter the literary canon. The mass of translations forming part of what came by the mid-nineteenth century to be termed "la littérature industrielle" [industrial literature] (Sainte-Beuve 1839) was churned out by nameless, unsung translators who laid little claim to any form of symbolic or intellectual capital and who instead sought to make use of their linguistic capital in a marketplace that, for major European languages, was crowded indeed – giving their language skills weak exchange value, as Sebaldus Nothanker reminds us. Such translators may well have identified with the eighteenth-century strand of discourse on hack translatorial practice outlined above. Their own paratextual commentaries, as well as third-party epitextual comments, regularly continued to frame translation as an industrial process and translators themselves as manual labourers, child workers, women carrying out piecework, slaves, and even steampowered machinery.

* * *

In 1822, a certain Mrs. Mainwaring published the "historical tale" *Moscow; or, the Grandsire*, set during Napoleon's invasion of Russia a decade previously. Now forgotten, the novel was fairly standard publishing fare for the day, featuring in the same list as titles such as Maria Edgeworth's *The Wife* and Alicia McGennis's intriguingly titled five-volume Scottish adventure *Strathbogie, or the Recluse of Glenmorris*. Mrs. Mainwaring's novel seems to have sunk without trace: it was included in lists of recent publications in various journals, but it does not appear to have been reviewed or reprinted. A glance at the first sentence suggests its fate might not have been wholly undeserved:

In allowing imagination to personify such causes as might have given effect to those dreadful occurrences, which surprised and paralysed the human mind, during a period comprising all the horrors of romance, exemplified in the terrible light of truth, it is by no means the intention, accurately to detail the whole of the French campaign against Moscow, or, in other words, the campaign of death; but to follow the

---

other hands before it went to press, it would otherwise have made as pitiful an appearance as his translation of Sonnini" (Anonymous 1805: 256).

54 *Professional Translators in Nineteenth-Century France*

individuals whose fate interests the writer it is to be feared, much more than the reader; and to endeavour to prove how much is left to our own direction in the good or evil fortune that befals [sic] us mortals; intending thereby ever to keep in view our dependence on that gracious Providence, who often snatches from portending evil the good who may have strayed into mischief, while the wicked are suffered to proceed in the path marked out by their passions, and left to the punishment brought on themselves by the pursuit; without presuming to call in question the attribute of universal benevolence attributable to an All-merciful creator, who delighteth not in evil, but rejoiceth in good.

(Mainwaring 1822: 1.1–2)

Whatever the novel's intrinsic qualities, as a historical romance in the vein of Walter Scott, it was undeniably part of a fashionable literary trend. As such, it seemed a viable commercial prospect to one French publisher, eager to tap into the reading craze prompted by Scott's enviable success. The subject matter showcasing a recent French military humiliation does not seem to have been a stumbling block for the Paris-based publisher Masson. The translation came out just a year later, in 1823, the work of a certain Pierre Dubergier (1756–1828).[10] Little is known about the translator: the Bibliothèque nationale de France catalogue records him as a Bordeaux-based lawyer, novelist, and translator and ascribes a number of otherwise anonymous translations dating from the 1820s to him, some on the basis of Barbier's *Dictionnaire des ouvrages anonymes*.[11] Other titles attributed to Dubergier include translations of Regina Maria Roche's *The Maid of the Hamlet* and Alexander Sutherland's *St. Kathleen; or, The Rock of Dunnismoyle*. If we take his attributed output in the first half of the 1820s at face value, he seems to have been relatively prolific for a handful of years: Quérard (1853: 126) ascribes 26 multi-volume translations to him between 1820 and his death in September 1828. It therefore seems fair to describe him as a jobbing translator for the publishing trade for most of the decade, specialising in precisely this sort of fashionable sub-Scottian output.

10 Cointre and Rivara (2006: 289) identify the translator as a woman, Mme Dubergier. They also misspell the title, which retains the English spelling for Moscow. The frontispiece identifies the translator only as "M******, auteur de Jeunesse et folie, traducteur des Ruines du Château de Damismoyle [=Dunnismoyle], de la Femme criminelle, etc, etc."

11 See https://data.bnf.fr/fr/12998347/dubergier/. There was a lawyer named Dubergier active in Bordeaux in the 1790s: as president of the counter-revolutionary *Club Monarchique*, described at the time as an "orateur fallacieux et impératif" (Challamel 1895, 150), he presumably turned to translation later in his career after the turmoil of the revolutionary years.

The dearth of detail about Dubergier's later career in translation is in itself revealing about the minor social status of such jobbing translators in the nineteenth-century French publishing market. The low status of such figures clearly correlates with low visibility and agency. Outside the texts they translated, the loci in which their voices can be heard tend to be rooted in the private sphere, in letters and archival material, where recovering them is a painstaking, time-consuming, often haphazard process. Translation history has done good work to uncover the lives of individual translators (Brown 2005; Zille 2021), though much remains to be done. As explored in Chapter 3, it is largely in such archival sources, rarely afforded the dignity of publication, that we catch glimpses of the practicalities and constraints of professional translation careers and the human-interest stories that lie therein. Yet when we do, they can be revealing indeed, opening windows onto little-explored issues such as translation workload, expectations of productivity, and cash flow difficulties – the crunch point where the accelerating "labor time of translating" (McMurran 2009: 23) ran into the financial demands of family life.[12] One example is a letter from Christian Felix Weisse recounting how illness severely impacted his workflow in early 1778, threatening his income, the stability of his family unit, and potentially the reputation and future of a daughter described in another letter as "leichtfertig" [flighty]:

> Ich hatte diesen Winter so viel zu übersetzen angenommen z.B. <u>Courtney Melmoths freymüthige Gedanken in 3 Th. Miss Moore Abhandlungen für junge Frauenzimmer</u>, andere kleinere Arbeiten ungerechnet, dass ich, da mich meine Krankheit beÿnahe [sic] 6. Wochen gekostet, kaum fertig werden konnte. Sie werden sagen, liebster Freund, dass ich als Übersetzer wenig Lorbeern einärndten werde, Sie haben Recht: wäre ich ledig, so hätte ich gewiss ein besserer Dichter u. grösserer Gelehrter werden wollen: aber wo der Kreis der Familie sich sich [sic] so erweitert

---

12 My analysis in this chapter runs largely counter to McMurran (2009), who makes the case that fiction translation in particular was "not industrialized hackwork" and that attitudes about translating "were often noncommercial" (2009: 56–7). My analysis covers the full range of translation for publication, where evidence of translation experienced as labour is plentiful: see for instance Willenberg (2008) for abundant quotes from translators' correspondence and contracts making clear the financial constraints and time pressure many faced. Serial publication and the twice-yearly book fairs in Leipzig and Frankfurt, for instance, acted as powerful forces driving the synchronisation of labour. I also focus on a slightly later period, when "market demands" had firmly "collapsed the distinctions between task-oriented work and timed labor" (McMurran 2009: 65). I share the point of view of Leah Orr (2017: 144) that the working conditions of individual translators were shaped by their own social capital and the literary capital of the text they were working on.

56 *Professional Translators in Nineteenth-Century France*

hat, dass die Ausgabe die Einnahme übersteigt, muss man bisweilen mehr auf Gewinnst als auf Ehre sehen.

[This winter I took on so many translations, e.g. Courtney Melmoth's Liberal Opinions in three parts, Miss Moore's Essays on various subjects, not counting other, smaller projects, that I could scarcely finish everything after my illness cost me nearly six weeks. You will say, my dear friend, that I shall harvest few laurels as a translator and you are right: if I were single, I would surely have become a better poet and a greater scholar: yet when the family circle has grown so much that outgoings exceed income, profit must sometimes come before honour.]
(quoted in Zille 2021: 69: emphasis in the original)

Such financial woes did occasionally make it into print, albeit in jocular fashion. The nameless English translator's 1756 preface to Félicité de Biron's *The Adventures and Amours of the Marquis de Noailles and Mademoiselle Tencin* points to the very real cash flow problems faced by workers in an age when friendly societies and other mutual insurance schemes were in their infancy:

Besides, as Delays and Revisals are terrible Things to Translators, who seldom happen to be over-loaded with Cash, the pretty Manner of delivering a few Sheets of Copy into the Printer's Hand on a Saturday Night, for which he's down with the Dust, is a most convenient Way of Dealing and makes us Drudges go thro' our Work with cheerful Hearts.
(quoted in Hughes 1919: 55)

Paratextual spaces also allowed translators to develop and present their public-facing translatorial identity in a range of ways. Some, such as Anne Plumptre, used footnotes to exhibit their erudition and challenge sexed norms around scholarship (Pickford 2012b). Dubergier, granted space to express himself in a preface to his translation of Mrs. Mainwaring's novel – perhaps to justify the decision to publish the novel, given its unpromising subject matter for French readers, a question he also touches on – took a different, and perhaps rather surprising, tack. He chose to frame his working practice in somewhat dehumanising and derogatory terms, critiquing his fellow translators as "paresseux ou peu spirituels ... n'ayant point d'idées à eux" [lazy or lacking in wit ... with no ideas of their own]; he continued, "ce sont des machines à traduction, trop heureux lorsqu'ils ne méritent point de la part de leurs lecteurs le nom de machines à vapeurs" [they are translation machines, all too fortunate when they do not deserve to be called steam engines by their readers] (Dubergier in Mainwaring 1822: 1.ii). In so doing, he joined a lengthy list of commentators on translation who, like Sebaldus Nothanker, developed the metaphor of literary translation as (industrial) labour. This strand of discourse has been largely overlooked in literary translation research, though it was surprisingly prevalent well into the early decades of the nineteenth century. As such, it inevitably shaped attitudes towards and expectations of literary translation, particularly in terms of the debate around the translator's duty of faithfulness. After all, industrialisation meant foregrounding the values of faithful reproduction by definition.

The metaphor of translatorial labour tracks closely to industrial practices, even in spatial terms. Georg Forster's "Studierstübchen" [little study], where he functioned as a self-described "Uebersetzermaschine" [translating machine], was described in terms akin to an artisan's workshop: "In jeder Ecke ... steht ein Tisch, darauf ein Band von Cook; Papier und ein Dintenfass; völlig nach Fabrikenart" [in every corner ... stands a table, on it a volume by [James] Cook, paper and an inkwell, just like a factory] (quoted in Willenberg 2008: 230). Other commentators took the metaphor in different directions, highlighting the potential capacity for alienation of translational labour. The literary journal *Le Corsaire* combined several such images in one in 1838, commenting on another Walter Scott production from the indefatigable Defauconprêt (see Chapter 6) in terms of the (gendered) unpaid work of spousal amanuenses, child labour,[13] and most strikingly of all to the modern eye, slavery:

> six tombereaux de traductions par le Fauconpret à vapeur, trois brouettées par des épouses laborieuses, deux boisseaux par les enfants en dessous de sept ans, et une truellée par les gens de peine ; les titres, notes et préfaces traduits par un nègre[14] descendant du Domingo de Paul et Virginie.
>
> [six dust carts of translations by the steam-powered Fauconpret, three wheelbarrows full from hard-working wives, two bushels by children under the age of seven, and a trowel's worth by hard labourers; the titles, notes and prefaces translated by a Negro descended from Paul and Virginie's Domingo.]
>
> (Quoted in Hermetet et al. 2012: 550)

13 The review was printed three years prior to France's first child labour law of 1841, which set the minimum working age at eight. Child labour was the object of a campaign and two government inquiries in the 1830s: when the law came into force, 150,000 children worked in French factories, representing around 12 per cent of the workforce (Weissbach 1977: 268–9).

14 The alternative meaning of 'ghostwriter' is certainly an underlying presence, having been in use since the 1750s, and would certainly be thematically appropriate given Defauconprêt's literary reputation. See https://www.cnrtl.fr/etymologie/n%C3%A8gre (accessed 30 May 2022). However, the isotopy of labour and the reference to Paul and Virginie's Domingo suggest that the primary reference here is indeed to enslaved labourers.

58   *Professional Translators in Nineteenth-Century France*

By the 1830s, the image of the translator as labourer had become a recognisable social type in the Paris publishing ecosystem, portrayed as such
by Édouard de la Grange – himself a translator from the German of works
by Heine and Jean Paul, among others – in the compendious overview of
contemporary Paris society, *Paris ou le Livre des Cent-et-Un* (1831–4):

> Parmi toutes les espèces d'industries qui font gémir la presse à Paris et
> qui se partagent les vastes champs de la littérature, il en est une plus
> pénible que celle du manœuvre qui broie le sable et la chaux ; il en
> est une dont le salaire est quelquefois inférieur à celui du paveur ou
> du tailleur de pierres ; je veux parler des traductions ... Courbé sur
> la pensée d'autrui, et semblable à une presse mécanique, le traducteur
> est forcé de reproduire, dans un temps donné et dans un français trop
> souvent barbare, les inspirations des auteurs exotiques ; labeur ingrat
> d'ouvriers faméliques, sorte de grosse littéraire transcrite à tant le rôle ;
> et les hommes qui vivent de cet ignoble métier, on les compte par mil-
> liers dans la capitale du monde civilisé ; essaim bourdonnant, troupe
> sans nom comme sans gloire, depuis celui qui traduit à la ligne sous
> l'échoppe de l'écrivain public, jusqu'à celui qui travaille à la feuille dans
> son galetas solitaire.

> [Of all the types of industry that makes the presses of Paris groan and
> share the vast fields of literature, one is more back-breaking than the
> labourer who crushes sand and lime; one whose salary is sometimes
> lower than that of a paver or stonemason; I mean translations ... Bent
> over someone else's thought, like a mechanical press, the translator is
> forced to reproduce, in a given time and all too often barbarous French,
> the inspirations of exotic authors; thankless labour of starving workers,
> a sort of literary rough draft transcribed at so much per role; and the
> men who live by this ignoble trade count in their thousands in the capi-
> tal of the civilised world; a buzzing swarm, a troupe without name or
> glory, from the one who translates by the line in the public writer's stall
> to the one who works by the page in his lonely garret.]
>
> (de la Grange 1833: 240)

De la Grange continues with a description of the various stages such
"productions à la vapeur" [steam-powered productions] pass through on
the way to publication, in terms reminiscent of Adam Smith's division of
labour or even a proto-Taylorist production line:

> Dès l'aube du jour, on voit [les traducteurs de pacotille] accourir la
> plume sur l'oreille dans les ateliers du traducteur entrepreneur; ils se
> pressent sur les bancs noircis par l'encre ... Puis viennent les correcteurs
> chargés de biffer les contre-sens grossiers ; puis les puristes qui effacent

impitoyablement la foule innombrable des car, des si et des mais, repoussent avec énergie la cohorte pesamment armée des que et des comme, et font disparaître les délits grammaticaux ; puis enfin les _polisseurs_ et les _vernisseurs_ qui retouchent le style, sèment les points d'exclamation et d'interrogation, et, réunissant tous ces lambeaux épars, en forment un ensemble à peu près homogène.

[From dawn, hack translators are seen running, quills behind their ears, to the workshops of the entrepreneurial translator; they throng together on ink-blackened benches ... Then come the correctors in charge of crossing out the grossest errors of meaning, then the purists who pitilessly erase the countless host of sinces, ifs and buts, energetically repelling the powerfully armed cohort of thats and ases, and get rid of offenses against grammar; then come the polishers and varnishers who touch up the style, sow exclamation and question marks around, and gather up all the scattered shreds to form a more or less homogeneous whole.]

(de la Grange 1833: 242–3, emphasis in the original)

Though Frederick Winslow Taylor's principles of scientific management still lay some decades in the future, economists were indeed beginning to apply operational research to book production. It is perhaps no coincidence that Edouard de la Grange's analysis of the hack translator as a production line worker came out the year after Charles Babbage's widely read 1832 study _On the Economy of Machinery and Manufactures_, with its detailed analysis of printing processes and the costs of book production.[15] Babbage's book came out in a French translation by Edouard Biot in 1833 as _Traité sur l'économie des machines et des manufactures_. Underscoring both the competitive nature of the translation business and its relatively tight-knit communities, the work was retranslated the following year by J. E. Isoard, a former head of division at the Ministry of Trade – and doubtless a close relative of Léopold Isoard, whose career was detailed in Chapter 1.[16]

15 Babbage's book was itself a cutting-edge technological artefact, machine-printed and with a gold-stamped title on cloth binding, which was brand new technology at the time. See https://historyofinformation.com/detail.php?entryid=537 (accessed 30 May 2022).
16 A search on genealogy websites throws up a Joseph-Eugène Isoard related to Léopold, but though he has the right initials, his date of birth is given as 1822, making him too young for the project in question. It is not beyond the realm of possibility that the date of birth on the website is incorrect.

60 *Professional Translators in Nineteenth-Century France*

Translation as Loomwork: *Walladmor Shuttles between Languages*

This chapter closes with a brief study of how one particular work shuttled between three languages – English, German, and French – weaving a series of intricately patterned literary artefacts that comment ironically on their own translated nature.[17] We begin with Sir Walter Scott. The introduction to his 1825 novel *The Betrothed* opens with an amusing vignette in which a group of gentlemen gather to form a joint-stock company to write and publish the Waverley novels. The chairman (or "preses" in Scott's Hibernian English) takes the floor to present the venture, framing writing careers as inherently Smithian:

> It is indeed to me a mystery how the sharp-sighted could suppose ... scores of volumes could be the work of one hand, when we know the doctrine so well laid down by the immortal Adam Smith, concerning the division of labour.
>
> (Scott 1825: iv)

The gentlemen then debate the pros and cons of a recent invention that takes much of the effort out of writing by mechanising the process on the lines of a patent loom that turns raw hemp into a ruffled shirt. Applied to the writing process, the steam-powered book loom can handle set pieces from narratives "which are at present composed out of commonplaces, such as the love-speeches of the hero, the description of the heroine's person, the moral observations of all sorts, and the distribution of happiness at the end of the piece". The process of composing novels is explicitly compared to damask weaving, revolutionised in 1805 by Joseph-Marie Jacquard's new programmable loom using punched cards – an important precursor to modern computing technology and the artificial intelligence that is now once again on the verge of revolutionising translatorial labour. Relying on technology enabled the author, "tired of pumping his own brains, [to] have an agreeable relaxation in the use of his fingers" (Scott 1825: v). Some stockholders react with Luddite objections at bread being stolen from their mouths. One then opines that Mr. Dousterswivel's recent novel, *Walladmor*, was most probably written "by the help of the steam-engine" (Scott 1825: v). *Walladmor: Frei nach dem Englischen des Walter Scott, von W*****s* [Walladmor: Freely translated from Walter Scott's English by W*****s] was a German pseudotranslation in three volumes published in 1823–4, not by a Mr. Dousterswivel but by Willibald Alexis,

---

17 This section is particularly indebted to de Groote and Toremans (2014). My thanks to Brecht de Groote at the University of Ghent for drawing Scott's reference to Adam Smith to my attention.

the pseudonym of Wilhelm Heinrich Häring (1797–1871), who had previously translated Scott's poetry (Thomas 1951: 219). Häring later included Dousterswivel as a character in the preface to a further Scottian pastiche, *Schloss Avalon* (1827).

The *Westminster Review* attributed *Walladmor*'s composition to the lack of a genuine Walter Scott novel at the Leipzig book fair: German readers were instead presented with "the commodity manufactured and called Walladmor" (quoted in de Groote and Toremans 2014: 112). As we have seen, Scott himself compared *Walladmor* to a mechanically produced, steam-powered, derivative, mass market commodity; Häring wrote in volume three of the just-in-time translation process driven by the speed of the printing and distribution process and its negative impact on quality control.

Ach, Sir – wüßten Sie, welcher Noth ein armer Uebersetzer Walter Scottscher Romane in Deutschland ausgesetzt ist, würden Sie auch noch größere Freiheiten verzeihen. Der Buchhändler feilscht umher nach dem wohlfeilsten, der die Uebersetzung dann auch zugleich am besten liefern soll. Demnächst müssen die naß aus der Edinburger Presse Post um Post kommenden Bogen ohne Sinn und Zusammenhang übersetzt werden; ja, es trifft sich oft, daß wir, wenn der Originalbogen mit zwei Sylben schließt, ein unvollendetes Wort übersetzen müssen.

[Oh sir, if only you knew how hard-pressed a poor translator of Walter Scott's novels is in Germany, you would forgive even greater freedoms. The book dealer casts around for the cheapest translator, who has to deliver the translation immediately as best they can. The proofs that come from the Edinburgh presses, passed from staging post to staging post, still wet when they arrive, must be translated without sense or coherence; when the signature ends with two syllables, we even often have to translate an incomplete word.]

(Alexis [Häring] 1824: unpaginated preface)

Germany's ersatz Scott was translated into English in turn in 1824 by Thomas de Quincey, weaving the second weft in a complex translational pattern. De Quincey's English translation adopted a new set of punched translational cards, correcting Häring's eccentric Welsh geography and leaving out some key characters altogether (de Groote and Toremans 2014: 119).[18] He then offered to pass the shuttle back to Häring, inviting him to translate his own English version back into German, which he

---

18 "But still, my dear sir, it *did* strike me, that the case of a man's swimming on his back from Bristol to the Isle of Anglesea [sic], was a little beyond the privilege granted by the most *maternal* public" (de Quincey 1851: 144).

62 Professional Translators in Nineteenth-Century France

would then bring back into English. In an unconscious echo of Sebaldus Nothanker, he compared this to-and-fro translation to darning stockings until all the original silk has been replaced with worsted (de Groote and Toremans 2014: 120).

Walladmor likewise came out in Dutch, Swedish, Polish, and French translations, adding further intricate detail to the book's transnational, translational weave (Thomas 1951: 231). The French version came out in 1825, based not on the original German, but on de Quincey's English; it was attributed to Walter Scott in the French national library catalogue for some time (Thomas 1951: 231). The title page attributed the translation to Auguste-Jean-Baptiste Defauconprêt, "traducteur de la collection complète des romans historiques de Sir Walter Scott" [translator of the complete collection of Sir Walter Scott's historical novels], whose career is explored in depth in Chapter 6. The novel opened with a prospectus touting for subscribers for a new *Bibliothèque des romans anglais et américains*, translated by Defauconprêt and, in an (ironic?) echo of Scott's gathering of Waverley novel stockholders, a "société de gens de lettres français et anglais". The idea behind the new collection was to organise literary imports along rational lines to guide French readers through the mass of contemporary English-language literature, casting aside the dross. Defauconprêt, who had been established in London for the best part of a decade, positioned himself as a key figure in cross-Channel cultural transfer, "capable de distinguer les bons ouvrages des médiocres" (capable of telling good works from mediocre ones) (Häring tr. de Quincey tr. Defauconprêt 1825: 3). As a translation entrepreneur, he set up a team of "collaborateurs français et anglais capables de le seconder" (French and English collaborators able to back him up), who worked on the translations, copy-edited translation proofs, and provided suitable paratext in the form of notes (Figure 2.1).

This systematic approach to cultural transfer, he argued, would be a boon to publishers who, as Häring was pointing out in volume 3 of the German original, struggled to balance speed of output – crucial in beating the competition to market in an age before copyright – and quality control. His stable of translation professionals, he argued, afforded publishers "l'espoir d'être garantis des inconvéniens [sic] d'une concurrence dont le moindre n'est pas celui qui force les traducteurs de rivaliser de vitesse plutôt que d'application" [the hope of protection against the downsides of competition, not the least of which is forcing translators to compete in terms of speed rather than care and attention] (Häring tr. de Quincey tr. Defauconprêt 1825: 3). *Walladmor* was to be the first title in the new collection, presumably translated by the same team: yet only Defauconprêt's name appears on the title page as translator. It is intriguing to wonder exactly what Defauconprêt's nameless subcontractors thought

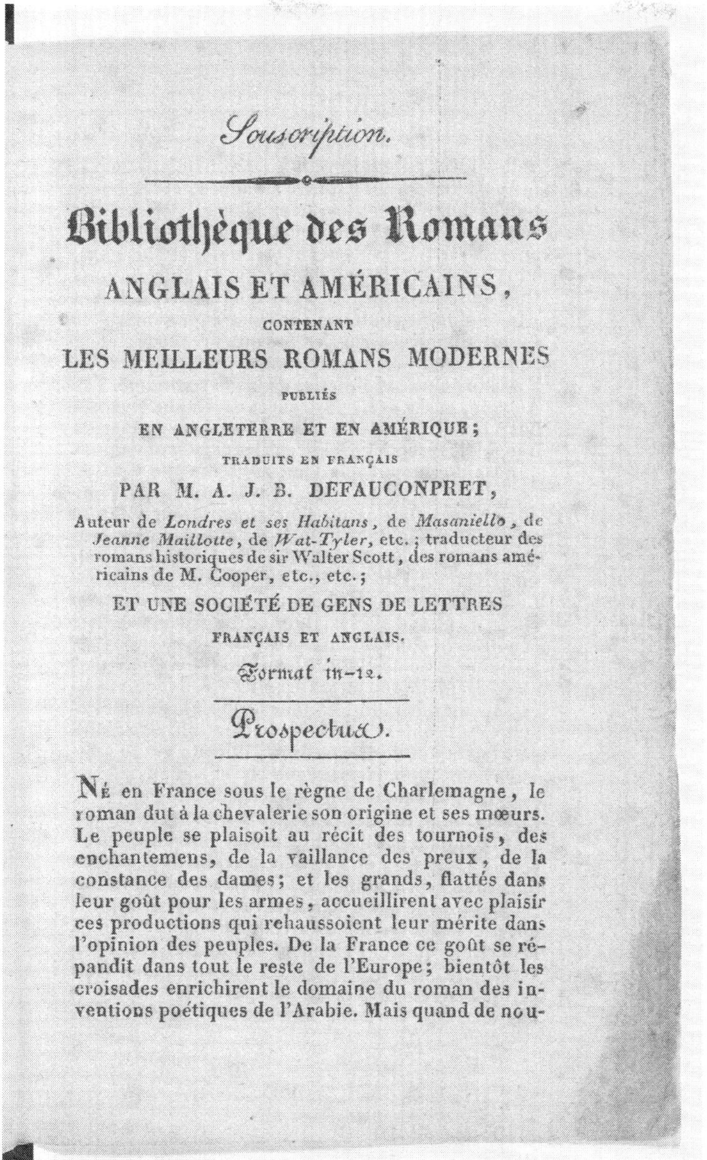

Souscription.

Bibliothèque des Romans

ANGLAIS ET AMÉRICAINS,

CONTENANT

LES MEILLEURS ROMANS MODERNES

PUBLIÉS

EN ANGLETERRE ET EN AMÉRIQUE;

TRADUITS EN FRANÇAIS

PAR M. A. J. B. DEFAUCONPRET,

Auteur de *Londres et ses Habitans*, de *Masaniello*, de *Jeanne Maillotte*, de *Wat-Tyler*, etc.; traducteur des romans historiques de sir Walter Scott, des romans américains de M. Cooper, etc., etc.;

ET UNE SOCIÉTÉ DE GENS DE LETTRES

FRANÇAIS ET ANGLAIS.

Format in–12.

Prospectus.

Né en France sous le règne de Charlemagne, le roman dut à la chevalerie son origine et ses mœurs. Le peuple se plaisoit au récit des tournois, des enchantemens, de la vaillance des preux, de la constance des dames; et les grands, flattés dans leur goût pour les armes, accueillirent avec plaisir ces productions qui rehaussoient leur mérite dans l'opinion des peuples. De la France ce goût se répandit dans tout le reste de l'Europe; bientôt les croisades enrichirent le domaine du roman des inventions poétiques de l'Arabie. Mais quand de nou-

Figure 2.1 Auguste-Jean-Baptiste Defauconprêt's call for subscribers opening the French translation of *Walladmor*, 1825. Image courtesy of the Bibliothèque nationale de France.

64   *Professional Translators in Nineteenth-Century France*

as they toiled away, their labour unacknowledged, to supply just-in-time translations of Scott's ironic musings on the mechanisation of literary composition and "la doctrine si bien établie par l'immortel Adam Smith relativement à la division du travail" (Scott 1825b: 3). One wonders if some were tempted to mimic the Luddites, smashing their literary looms to demand authorial recognition.

Conclusion

Did the general prevalence of a metaphor of standardised translatorial labour lead to a decline in the *belles infidèles* model and a concomitant rise in the fidelity paradigm? It seems impossible to measure a single metaphor's impact in shaping expectations of translational fidelity. Edouard de la Grange's pessimistic assessment of the literary translation industry in the early 1830s suggests the contrary was in fact true: every time a text went through another step in the translation process, "elle perd quelque chose de sa ressemblance avec l'original" [it loses some of its resemblance to the original] (de la Grange 1833: 134). A more optimistic assessment, such as that in Defauconprêt's *Walladmor* prospectus, might conclude that by rationalising and streamlining the translation management process, translation collectives with a high level of professionalisation could offer improved quality control and reduce errors by working on the principle of the aggregation of marginal gains (Walker 2023: 85).

Either way, the question soon became moot. Having arisen around the 1730s, the metaphor of translatorial labour was a constant, if minor, strand of translational discourse and identity for around a century in several national literary traditions, in both paratextual discourse by translators themselves and epitextual discourse by other commentators. Paradoxically, just as the metaphor of industrial literature was beginning to gather strength on the back of technological developments such as Friedrich Koenig's steam-powered press, patented in 1810 and in widespread use by the 1820s, metaphors of translatorial labour became less prevalent in the latter half of the century. By the time Sainte-Beuve published his famous essay on industrial literature in 1838, the metaphor was on its way out. This change can be attributed to a shift in the literary field, studied in Chapter 4, as a series of legal decisions in the French courts definitively established the basis for translation as a form of authorship – thereby ushering in an individualistic, rather than collective, understanding of translatorial labour. Translators may have remained, and indeed remain to this day, the "literary proletariat" (Apter 2006: xi), but their claim to authorship was now enshrined in French law.

3 Tracing Translators in Publishers' Archives

Translation studies has recently embraced an archival turn, offering scholars "an invaluable trove of primary sources ... [and] presenting a new vector through which to measure, critique, and conceptualize translation practice, its function and status in societies past and present" (Cordingley and Hersant 2021: 9). Though this development is to be welcomed for shining a light on the concrete realities and contingencies of historical translatorial practice, it must be acknowledged that without questioning the nature of the archival material used by translation scholars, we run the risk of creating new blind spots in translatorship research. Of particular concern is the fact that perhaps the most obvious and widely exploited source, author and translator archives, entails a degree of cultural gatekeeping by definition: their holdings therefore tend to reflect an atypically high degree of literary capital on the translator's part.[1] Seeking to account for the more typical experience of translators with low agency and low literary capital, this chapter follows Michelle Milan's lead in adopting an agent-centred approach within a socio-historical framework (Milan 2021: 50). It adopts a collective approach to translator history by drawing on research in archival holdings devoted principally to other actors in the

---

1 This has been apparent in the genetic approach to translation archives (Cordingley and Montini 2015; Agostini-Ouafi and Lavieri 2015; Nunes, Moura and Pacheco Pinto 2020; Cordingley and Hersant 2021). The conferences devoted to translator archives have tended to focus on "les grands traducteurs" [great translators], as the title of the 2015 conference *Les grands traducteurs dans les archives de l'IMEC* [great translators in the IMEC archive] explicitly stated: the author-translators featured at the event included Samuel Beckett, Maurice-Edgar Coindreau, Vladimir Nabokov, Henri Michaux, Adonis, Kateb Yacine, Abdellatif Laâbi, and Rainer Maria Rilke. The male-gendered nature of the term "grands traducteurs" proved apt in terms of the event's focus, if not exactly representative of a sphere of activity that is heavily feminised as a whole. The 2019 Marbach conference *Übersetzernachlässe in globalen Archiven* [translator records in global archives] followed suit, with papers on Brecht, Paul Celan, Hans Magnus Enzensberger, and Peter Handke, all far better known as authors than translators.

DOI: 10.4324/9781003173090-4

66 *Professional Translators in Nineteenth-Century France*

communications circuit, in which translators are a tangential presence. Reading such archives for the experiences and careers of unsung translators of forgotten books uncovers often moving, sometimes surprising stories about the men and women who translated for a living. Take the doctor and English teacher Jules Baytun Gébelin, for instance, whose Italian translation of the nautical signalling code mysteriously went missing in the post in May 1856 – reading between the lines, a convenient excuse for a project he was unable to complete – or the minor poet and journalist Jules Kergomard, paid to translate *Wuthering Heights* a good two decades prior to the first known French translation, by Théodore de Wyzewa, published in the early 1890s (see appendix). Kergomard's version was apparently never published, but its fleeting mention in a single payment record raises the tantalising spectre of an entirely new early French history of Emily Brontë's masterpiece, should the manuscript ever resurface.

Strikingly, these archives hold next to no translatorial output *per se*. They have next to nothing to offer translation geneticists aiming to retrace the genesis of translator manuscripts. They situate translators first and foremost not as producers of texts, but as workers within the publishing marketplace, as explored in Chapter 2. The holdings are dominated by contracts, payment records, and documentation relating to translation rights – explored in more depth in Chapter 4 – shedding light on the economic lives of literary translators, the topic of Chapter 5. This approach, reading translators as members of a socio-professional grouping through their tangential presence in publisher archives, lays bare a number of mechanisms operating within the nineteenth-century literary translation marketplace, many of which will resonate with modern-day practitioners. While much research in translator history has taken a microhistorical frame (Munday 2014) and focuses on individuals (Paloposki 2017; Kaindl, Schlager and Kolb 2021), studying a translator cohort (Ghadie 2013; van Bolderen 2021) offers the advantage of foregrounding patterns (or, just as importantly, *lack* of patterns) of practice across the wider field, particularly important in such a weakly structured field where the experiences of individual translators varied wildly depending on their position within it.[2]

Taking this collective approach and approaching nineteenth-century translators not as individuals, but as a socio-professional cohort extending

---

2 In a weakly structured professional field like literary translation, the microhistorical approach has one significant downside: its findings cannot be readily extrapolated to other practitioners. For instance, Chesterman's analysis of Douglas Hofstadter's manuscripts for his work on Françoise Sagan – copying the entire French book out by hand – reveals a working practice largely incompatible with the tight deadlines of modern mainstream trade press translation, pointing to an atypical relationship with the synchronisation of labour within the publishing cycle that is indicative of high agency on the translator's part (2021: 287). Full-time translators with an incentive to maximise their income display an entirely different relationship to translational labour time, working faster and on much shorter cycles.

across three-quarters of a century (no archival material survives for the first 25 years), offers a means of identifying the opposing poles that structured the broad field of nineteenth-century translation for publication in France. The sources in question were gleaned from the archives of four major nineteenth-century French publishers, Larousse, Flammarion, Hetzel, and Hachette, held at the Institut mémoires de l'édition contemporaine (IMEC) in Caen, France. IMEC, established in 1988 and based in Caen since 2004, now holds over 700 sets of archives in four categories – authors and artists, publishers and the book trade, journals and the press, and associations and organisations.[3] Tellingly, translators are not categorised as such in the archive metadata (Santana López and Travieso Rodríguez 2021). This chapter now turns to an exploration of IMEC's nineteenth-century publisher holdings in depth, drawing out the variables that emerge from the sources to sketch out a field of (more or less) professional translating for publishing in nineteenth-century France.

Structuring the Field of Translation for Publishing in Nineteenth-Century France

The bulk of the IMEC holdings stem from twentieth-century publishers; only four nineteenth-century publishers are represented, all with mainstream trade press profiles. Small specialist presses may well have had different practices. The possibility that the results below are unrepresentative is regrettable but unconfirmable and unavoidable. The information is at least reflective of practices within the mainstream publishing market. The lives of the translators in the set are written up in the appendix for ease of consultation.

The four publishers in question are Hachette, founded in 1826 by Louis Hachette (1800–64), best known for its schoolbooks and pioneering cheap railway editions; Hetzel, founded in 1843 by Pierre-Jules Hetzel (1814–86), best remembered for his collaboration with Jules Verne; Larousse, founded in 1852 by Pierre Larousse (1817–75), best known for his work in lexicography; and, more marginally, Flammarion, founded in 1875 by Ernest Flammarion (1846–1936) to publish works by his well-known astronomer brother Camille before moving on to mainstream literary output.[4] Hachette, Larousse, and Flammarion are still significant players in French publishing to this day. The earliest contract dates from 1825. The holdings for earlier decades are somewhat thin on the ground; the bulk of the sources is from the latter half of the century, reflecting not only

---

3 See https://www.imec-archives.com/archives/collection (accessed 17 June 2024).

4 For ease of reference, archival references will be included in short form in this and subsequent chapters as follows: HAC (Hachette), HTZ (Hetzel), LRS (Larousse), FLM (Flammarion), followed by the relevant IMEC file number.

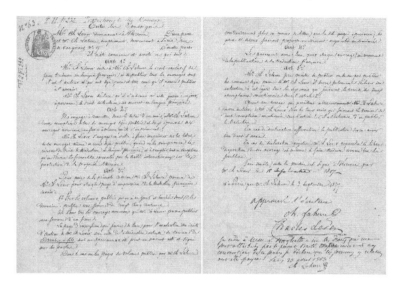

Figures 3.1a and 3.1b Translation contract between Charles Lever and Charles Lahure, September 1857. Images courtesy of Archives Hachette/IMEC.

improved record-keeping as publishing developed into a fully-fledged capitalist enterprise run according to modern management principles (Mollier 1988), but also the increasingly complex legal framework within which the sector operated, explored in the next chapter. Many of the documents from the 1850s on, for instance, concern the acquisition of translation rights which came into being as a result of bi- and later multi-lateral copyright treaties (Figure 3.1a, Figure 3.1b).

The archive holds a range of document types, from the aforementioned acquisition rights to translation contracts, sales and translator payment data, and general correspondence, including translator-led pitches and letters of complaint. Some contributors remain well-known to this day for their work in other spheres of intellectual and cultural endeavour – the geographer and anarchist Peter Kropotkin (FLM 8.5)[5] and the composer

---

5 Kropotkin to Flammarion, 18 December 1888: "Ma femme a traduit une nouvelle de Korolenko, un jeune auteur russe, tout à fait remarquable, qui s'annonce comme un continuateur de Tourguéneff ... J'ai revu la traduction con amore, puisque la chose me plaît. L'épreuve serait relue par un ami français ... Vous savez certainement que le droit de traduction du russe en toute autre langue et du français en russe est libre" [My wife has translated a short story by Korolenko, a perfectly remarkable young Russian author who promises to be an heir to Turgenev ... I have revised the translation *con amore* because I enjoy it. The proofs would be checked by a French friend ... As you must be aware, translations from Russian into other languages and from French into Russian are free (i.e. no acquisition rights to be paid)].

Camille Saint-Saëns (FLM 8.14)[6] both dabbled in translation and submitted proposals to Flammarion, highlighting the importance of broad networks of intellectual sociability and diluting literary translation's claim to be a wholly autonomous field of practice (Speller 2011; Lahire 2006). The majority, however, are lost to history. The nature of the archive means that some sources typically exploited in sociological research are entirely absent, such as parents' professions. Other categories, such as sex, are relatively complete. Others still, such as social status and geographical location, are partially present; some, such as the genre of book being translated, fall into more or less fuzzy categories. Some, such as payment data, are tricky to compare across a timespan of seven decades. However, the researcher has little choice but to work within the parameters of the sources that have survived, and despite the manifold hurdles, some variables and trends can be discerned across the aggregate sources to locate individual actors within the broader field.

This section proposes to sketch out the various positions aspiring translators could typically achieve within the field of translation for publication in nineteenth-century France depending on their own sociological characteristics – most notably their gender, social status, and place of residence – and on the characteristics of the books they worked on, particularly the original language and textual genre. It does so by drawing on the set of sources described above to outline a series of opposing characteristics that typically helped translators achieve a strong negotiating position with publishers, leading to favourable contractual conditions in terms of income and deadlines – or, conversely, weakened their position, thereby restricting them to less favourable financial and reputational outcomes.

Close reading of the surviving contracts and correspondence provides ample sources to justify differences in the professional experiences and career trajectories of nineteenth-century translators, shaped by a series of opposing poles that directly shaped the translation rates they were able to negotiate and, consequently, their income. The translation pricing model seems from the sources to have been based on a series of more or less binary criteria. As will be seen, perhaps unsurprisingly, men tended to outearn women; Parisians tended to outearn provincials; languages of lesser diffusion tended to outearn widely spoken ones; languages that embodied a translator's high social and educational capital tended to outearn languages that did not; and text types high in literary capital tended to

---

6 Saint-Saëns to Flammarion, 11 May 1910, on the short story *Cristoforo Molinos*: "Le temps m'a manqué pour traduire d'autres nouvelles des mêmes auteurs et je le regrette, car maintenant le temps me manque plus que jamais et dix ans de non-pratique m'ont fait oublier ce que je savais d'espagnol" [I have been short of time to translate other short stories by the same authors and I regret it, for now I am shorter of time than ever and ten years without using my Spanish have made me forget what I once knew].

70 *Professional Translators in Nineteenth-Century France*

outearn texts that did not. In concrete terms, a man occupying a position of some social importance in Paris and translating a Greek classic was in a much stronger negotiating position than a woman living in provincial France translating children's books from English. Between these two poles – dominant and dominated – lay a host of intermediary positions, depending on each individual translator's situation.

Language Flows

Taking all the contracts into account across the century, in terms of language flows, English unsurprisingly dominates the field, followed at some distance by German and the classical languages of Europe, then a relatively short tail of other (mainly) European modern languages (Table 3.1).

Table 3.1 Distribution of Translated Languages in the IMEC Archives

Language	Number of Translation Projects in the IMEC Archives
English	60
German	10
Latin	9
Ancient Greek	8
Russian	4 (including 1 FR>RUS)
Italian	4 (including 2 FR>IT)
Spanish	3
Arabic	2 (1 *Arabian Nights*, 1 FR>AR)[7]
Hungarian	2 (both FR>HUN)[8]
Danish	1[9]

7 HAC 18.11: Adrien Paulmier, formerly of the court of appeal in Algiers, self-published a translation of *Gil Blas* with the printers Jacques Arbieu in Poissy, west of Paris. He transferred the rights to the books to Arbieu to repay a debt of 4,000 francs. Arbieu sold them to Hachette in 1850.

8 Both come at the very tail end of the century. HAC 154.6: Victor Cherbuliez wrote to Hachette on 18 February 1899 that a Budapest publisher was hoping to buy the translation rights to his novel *Jacquine Vanesse*, adding, "Il est certain qu'une traduction en magyar ne peut être payée comme une traduction en allemand, et je suis d'avis que nous acceptions la proposition qui nous est faite" [A translation into Hungarian certainly cannot fetch the same price as a translation into German, and I am minded to accept the offer we have been made]. HAC 21.2: Charles Bernard Derosne wrote to Hachette on 27 April 1898 to claim payment for a Hungarian relay translation of Marion Crawford's *Three Fates*, produced via his own French version as was apparent from the numerous identical cuts.

9 HAC 65.9: On 15 November 1855, David Soldin signed a contract for 1 franc/page in-16° to translate Hans Christian Andersen's fairy tales. Hachette retained full rights to the translation and was still earning rights from Soldin's translation as late as 1976, when SAGEM paid 120 francs for the right to reproduce it.

These translation flows track closely with D'Hulst (2014: 129), who records English as taking over from Latin within the French translation market in 1819. The tail of languages he records from a wider sample is somewhat longer, with a further 13 languages, but the overall patterns are the same: from 1825 to the end of the century, the most translated languages after English and Latin are German, Italian, Ancient Greek, and Spanish, followed at a considerable distance by so-called "minor" European and extra-European languages: Russian, Portuguese, Polish, Dutch, Hebrew, Arabic, Chinese, Sanskrit, and Turkish. Similar trends are clear in the fine-grained analysis in Wilfert (2012), reflecting the mass marketisation of translation in an increasingly mature capitalist publishing sector.

Logically, translation flows were shaped by market demand and the supply of translators working in various language pairs. As a result, translator remuneration across the nineteenth century reflected a degree of hierarchy between modern European languages, with the exact position of a given language in the remuneration hierarchy depending on the supply of translators and the economic and literary capital associated with the language (Casanova 2002). As the Swiss novelist Victor Cherbuliez wrote in 1899, commenting on a proposed foreign rights sale, "il est certain qu'une traduction en magyar ne peut être payée comme une traduction en allemand" [A Hungarian translation clearly cannot fetch the same price the same as a German one] (HAC 154.6). Translators of languages of lesser diffusion tended to receive higher remuneration: translators from Danish, Bulgarian, and German all received slightly higher rates than the one franc per page for English that features in many contracts.[10] Classical languages obeyed their own logic with two separate economic strands, as will be seen below. In all cases, the centrality and literary capital of a language was just one of several factors shaping the relative negotiating positions of translator and publisher, and, consequently, the contractual conditions and remuneration a translator could hope to achieve.

Translator Gender

The cohort of nineteenth-century translators represented in the IMEC archives runs to some 80 individuals in all: 55 men (68.75 per cent), 24 women (30 per cent), and 1 or 2 who cannot be identified from their initials.[11] Some types of project are clearly distributed by gender, with women unsurprisingly absent from classical language translation and dominant in translating children's fiction. However, there is a fair chance that women

---

10 See, for example, HAC 65.9, HAC 33.40, and HAC 34.7.
11 This gender balance runs counter to the modern field, in which women represent some 70 per cent of practitioners (Pym et al. 2014).

72 *Professional Translators in Nineteenth-Century France*

are under-represented among the named translators. A number of contracts refer to unnamed subcontractors,[12] while a number of the named women are recorded in correspondence as having acted as translation subcontractors. Archival research into women translators is further hampered by changes of name on marriage, not even necessarily their own: Thérèse Bentzon, for instance, was known at birth as Marie-Thérèse de Solms, then on her mother's second marriage became Marie-Thérèse Cartier d'Aure, then on her own marriage Marie-Thérèse Blanc. She took her pen name from her mother's maiden name. Similarly, Amélie Chevalier de la Petite Rivière became Mme Paul Fliche. Pseudonyms (often masculine or neutral-sounding) are also an issue: Amélie Fliche wrote as Antoine Alhix, Emma Allouard wrote as Emile Jouan and Jouan-Rolland, while Mlle H. Gréard wrote as both Henri de Colosses and H. de l'Espine, a fact revealed only by a close-grained cross-comparison of archival sources, reading the relevant IMEC files against listings in the French national library catalogue. Much of this information is, of course, unrecoverable by its very nature. As Elisabeth Gibbels writes of a project to recover 250 historical women translators working in Germany,

> What was striking then and now is how little these women are known and how little information can be gained from online resources like the German National Biography database ... information is often gleaned from hard to access sources, such as journals, correspondence and publishing houses' archives. Even this information doesn't seem to impact on their inclusion in cultural memory.
>
> (Gibbels 2022: 13, 17)

As a result, it can only be hypothesised that female translators were disproportionately excluded from contractual protection for their labour, which left few traces in the archive outside of their correspondence with editors. However, the *fact* of subcontracting to (inexperienced young) women aligns with the experience of one fictional translator, Sophie Ulliac-Trémadeure's eponymous *Emilie, ou la jeune fille autrice* (1837), who sets out to alleviate her family's poverty by translating a philosophy book from German, only

---

12 See, for instance, the contract signed by Paul Lorain on 9 April 1856 (HAC 41.15): "M. Lorain se charge de traduire ou de faire traduire les romans & nouvelles indiqués ci-dessus ... Il se charge de revoir & corriger lesdites traductions tant celles qu'il fera faire par des collaborateurs de son choix que celles déjà imprimées dont. M. M. L. Hachette pourront faire l'acquisition" [M. Lorain agrees to translate, or have translated, the above novels and short stories ... He undertakes to read through and edit the translations, both the ones done by other people of his choosing and the ones previously printed that Messrs. L. Hachette may acquire in future].

to discover that her translatorial labour was to be elided in favour of an author with greater symbolic capital:

> Emilie, en écoutant son éditeur, rêvait déjà de gloire; elle comprenait la valeur que lui donnerait, dans le public et dans le monde littéraire, un travail de cette importance; M. Muller souriait à la pensée de voir le nom de sa petite-fille attaché à un ouvrage de ce genre; mais ils demeurèrent stupéfaits d'un même étonnement lorsque le libraire leur annonça, d'un air triomphant, qu'il avait la presque certitude qu'un auteur en réputation daignerait revoir la traduction et y mettre son nom.

> [Listening to her publisher, Emilie already dreamed of glory; she grasped the value a work of this importance would bring her in society and the literary world; Mr Muller smiled at the thought of his granddaughter's name on a book of this sort; but they were both struck dumb with astonishment when the bookseller triumphantly announced he was almost sure a reputed author would deign to revise her translation and put his name on it.]

(Ulliac-Trémadeure 1899 [1837]: 98)[13]

Sophie Ulliac-Trémadeure having herself had some experience in translating the novels of August Lafontaine from German under a variety of pseudonyms, Emilie's experiences no doubt mirror her own to some extent.

While none of the women in the cohort are now widely remembered – they obviously had less scope to make names for themselves in other fields of endeavour than the men did – some of them did achieve high levels of ongoing professional practice, as will be seen below. However, broadly speaking, their opportunities were limited by the languages they had access to. The majority of the women translated contemporary literature from English, many of them children's books and popular literature, placing them in the mass market where competition was fiercest and, consequently, contractual conditions least favourable. Some nineteenth-century female translators were able to leverage their social capital to make a name for themselves, such as Théophile Gautier's daughter Judith, wife of the poet Catulle Mendès, whose relay translations from the Chinese in *Le Livre de Jade* have attracted scholarly attention (Yu 2007) and are still in print. Such instances were rare, however, as most female translators simply did not have access to the classical languages and elite networks that afforded the most social and literary capital, and were thus in a relatively weak position when it came to negotiating with publishers.

---

13 My thanks to Anthony Glinoer at the University of Sherbrooke, Canada, for bringing this example to my attention.

74 *Professional Translators in Nineteenth-Century France*

Translator Income

In terms of income, while figures are hard to compare across the century, there is some indication that translators working in the editorial sector, then as now, were generally under-remunerated compared to other sectors. Evidence from works of fiction featuring translator characters points to incomes barely above the poverty level: where ministry translators were earning up to 5,000 francs a month as early as 1814, and Léopold Courrouve dit Pold was charging 8 francs per official document at mid-century (see Chapter 1), a fictional literary translator at mid-century such as M. de Charleval was able to earn just "de 8 à 10 francs par jour" (Muller 1858: 132). Though M. de Charleval was able to keep costs down by working from home, he ran into an unexpected productivity issue that reduced his income below the daily rate he had anticipated:

> L'antiquaire, en évaluant ainsi son salaire quotidien, avait compté sur sa rare connaissance des langues savantes, connaissance qui devait lui rendre le travail facile; mais il lui arriva une chose qu'il n'avait pas prévue. Il rencontra dans les ouvrages qu'il s'était chargé de traduire des assertions qui lui parurent douteuses, sinon tout à fait erronées. Il se livra, pour sa propre satisfaction, à des recherches qui lui firent perdre un temps considérable et rognèrent d'autant le prix de son labeur.

> [The antiques dealer, in estimating his daily income, had counted on his expert knowledge of scholarly languages to make the work easy; but something unforeseen happened. In the works he had undertaken to translate he found assertions that seemed to him dubious, if not outright incorrect. For his own satisfaction, he carried out research that took up a lot of time and reduced the cost of his labour by the same amount.]
>
> (Muller 1858: 132–3)

Mastery of labour time was indeed a key factor in determining a translator's autonomy and economic independence. Some elite translators working on classical texts were unencumbered by deadlines (or simply ignored them), such as the statesman and later president of the Senate Paul Challemel-Lacour (1827–96):

> Vous voudrez bien, j'espère, m'excuser de n'avoir pas répondu plus tôt à votre obligeante lettre au sujet de la traduction de Valère Maxime. Vous ne devez pas, je pense, attacher beaucoup d'intérêt à la publication immédiate de ce manuscrit. Peut-être, après avoir dormi si longtemps, peut-il dormir quelque temps encore sans inconvénient.

> [You will, I hope, forgive me for not replying earlier to your obliging letter on the translation of Valerius Maximus. You must not, I think, place much importance on the immediate publication of this manuscript.

Perhaps after sleeping for so long, it may slumber a little longer without inconvenience.]

(HAC 12.3, letter dated 29 May 1865)

The data on remuneration is not standardised across the board, making it challenging to analyse. Rates are given as lump sums or per page, often with various additional costs. Furthermore, the interplay of remuneration and labour time is a thorny issue: it has always been challenging for translators to measure the comparative difficulty of a text and judge ahead of time how long it will take to translate. Nor was the page a standardised unit of measurement, though occasionally contracts included specimen pages as a point of comparison for editor and translator: one such was included in the contract in Figure 3.1a. At mid-century, where per-page rates are indicated, they tend to hover around one franc a page: this was the rate in the Dickens contract signed by Paul Lorain in 1857. Miss H. Gréard received the same rate the same year for translating F. J. Smith's novel *Woman and Her Master*,[14] to be published under either her own name or her mother's: she was still translating in the mid-1870s, under her own name. It is to be hoped her per-page rate had increased in the meantime. The same offer was made in 1856 to Jules Baytun Gébelin for a French to Italian translation (HAC 7.39); a year later, Louis-Joseph Brossollet obtained a rate of 1 fr 20 cts for *The Wreckers* (HAC 8.3). Confirming the relative scarcity of German, Justin Charles Corrard was paid 1 fr 50 per page for Schiller's *Opuscules esthétiques*, also in 1857 (HAC 10.20).

Payment Based on Literary Genre

Perhaps unsurprisingly, the contracts point to a hierarchy of remuneration based on genre, which often mapped onto readerships with varying levels of spending power that also shaped the material appearance of the book itself (Pickford 2007). An 1860 Plutarch translation by Victor Bétolaud intended for "[les] gens du monde" [society people] (HAC 1.40) cost the publisher 3,500 francs,[15] over ten times higher than a typical translation payment for works for a popular readership or for children. Similarly, Jean-Louis Burnouf, professor of Latin eloquence at the Collège de France,

---

14 Given the date of publication and the fact that the work is described in the contract as a novel, I have identified it as the undated *Woman and Her Master: A Romance* by J. F. Smith (1804–90) rather than the better-known history with the same title by Lady Sydney Morgan. *La femme et son maître* was published in three volumes in 1859. The translator's name was given as Mme H. de l'Espine.

15 According to https://www.historicalstatistics.org/Currencyconverter.html, this is equivalent to 15,956 euros in 2015, the most recent year for which conversion is available (accessed 12 June 2024).

76   *Professional Translators in Nineteenth-Century France*

was paid 1,000 francs in 1825 for a translation of Cicero's *Catilinarian Orations* and *Brutus* "sur beau papier et en beaux caractères" [on fine paper and with fine type], intended for a wealthy readership prepared to expend economic capital to acquire its literary equivalent.

Translations of classical, canonical, and cutting-edge contemporary literature all commanded a premium, with higher-than-average rates paid for books by Clemens Brentano, Friedrich Schiller, Ivan Turgenev, and George Eliot.[16] Popular literature and children's books did not attract high rates, and their lack of literary capital was sometimes considered an embarrassment if at odds with the social capital of the translator. The Comtesse de Ségur's daughter Henriette Fresneau translated Agnes Harder's *Familienroman* [family saga] *Doktor Eisenbart* shortly after the turn of the twentieth century but preferred to keep her name off the finished product: "je désirerais ne pas faire connaître mon nom comme traducteur; si on peut mettre simplement mes initiales H. F. je le préférerais" [I'd rather not let it be known I translated it; I'd prefer it if it just bore my initials H. F.] (HAC 23.11). The image of translation as labour, the focus of Chapter 2, continued epitextually well into the twentieth century in the case of genres low in literary capital. Though it lies outside the chronology of this book, one revealing letter archived by the Hachette complaints department in 1924 sheds light on the longevity of the image, framing literary translations as an unwanted deluge of mass-produced commodities:

> À cette époque éloignée Vannes était un centre de traductions anglaises et les dames qui les composaient travaillaient en commun ou en concurrence pour ces traductions ou des ouvrages originaux sous des pseudonymes ou non suivant l'occurrence. Bien que ces personnes m'aient procuré parfois des ouvrages très intéressants ... j'ai fini par ne plus vouloir faire quoi que ce soit avec elles parce que je ne savais plus avec qui je traitais devant l'avalanche de leurs productions.
>
> [In those distant days Vannes was a centre for English translation and the ladies who wrote them worked together or in competition on translations or original work, at times with pen names, at times without. Though they sometimes procured me very interesting works ... I ended up not wanting to work with them at all because I no longer knew who I was dealing with given the deluge of projects.]
>
> (HTZ 4.1)

Far from holding the original sacrosanct, such books were often heavily formatted to fit a certain market niche. Novels translated for the periodical

---

16 See HTZ 9.40, HAC 10.20, HTZ 3.16, and HAC 4.2 respectively.

press, for instance, were cut to fit the cloth of the target publication, as revealed in an 1876 contract for the *Journal des villes et campagnes*: "M. Berlay aura le droit de réduire ce roman à quarante feuilletons simples et d'y faire tous les changements qu'il jugera convenables; il aura aussi le droit d'en changer le titre" [Mr. Berlay is entitled to reduce the novel to forty simple instalments and change anything he sees fit; he is also entitled to change the title] (HAC 21.2).

Translatorial Reputation and Social and Literary Capital

Overall, remuneration was dependent on a number of factors, including the translator's reputation; in 1855, Amédée Pichot, by then well known as a cultural intermediary between France and Britain, was offered the atypically high rate of two francs a page to translate Thackeray (HAC 43.37).[17] Most interesting from this point of view is the unusual economy of classical translation. Translators of classical texts were either paid significantly more than translators of modern European languages, or significantly less. Paul Challemel-Lacour was offered two francs per page for his Valerius Maximus, a project he seems never to have completed. Where contemporary novels from English of standard length generally earned their translators around 200 to 300 francs, the sums paid for classical translations were often considerably higher. In May 1865, Adolphe Bouillet, a history teacher in Paris, was paid 2 fr 80 a page for his translation of Aeschylus with a guaranteed minimum earning of 1,000 francs (HAC 3.2). Such high rates can be attributed to the considerable overlap between linguistic and social capital where classical scholarship is concerned. A number of the translators in fact include their social status in the contract: "Frédéric Bellaguet, chef d'institution", "Victor Bétolaud, professeur au Lycée Charlemagne", "Pierre-François Delestre, principal du collège de Tonnerre".[18] Such books were also liable to sell well within the school market. At the other end of the remuneration scale, some translators of the

---

17 Pichot writes on 18 May 1855 that he was offered two francs a page verbally but was paid one, which he accepted, preferring not to squabble with the publisher.

18 See HAC 1.4, HAC 1.40, and HAC 21.11 respectively. One particularly flagrant case of the importance of social status is a contract signed in 1879 by two teachers who were unable to fulfil a translation commission for a book on American contemporary history in a timely manner. They agreed to work with an unnamed third party on the condition that "Il est entendu que le tiers intervenant dans votre travail ne sera pas nommé, et que la traduction ne sera signée que de vos deux noms, Gustave Ovrée et A. Varembey, Chefs d'institution à Paris et anciens professeurs d'histoire au lycée Charlemagne" [It is agreed that the third party intervening in your work will not be named and that the translation will only be signed with your two names, Gustave Ovrée and A. Varembey, headmasters in Paris and former history teachers at the Lycée Charlemagne] (HTZ 9.28).

78 *Professional Translators in Nineteenth-Century France*

classics or of authors particularly rich in literary capital worked for free, speculatively, or with profit-sharing agreements that saw them potentially facing significant losses, situating themselves firmly within the realm of symbolic rather than economic capital. In 1870, Ernest Lavigne had 1,000 copies of his translation of Lucretius's *De Natura Rerum* printed by Hachette on a half-share of profits basis, with an agreement that he was to cover the cost of printing if the costs were not covered by sales by April 1871. The ledger records that Lavigne eventually had to pick up 840 unsold copies: his brief flirtation with publishing must have cost him a small fortune (HAC 33.8).[19] Another interesting example is the novelist and playwright Louis Judicis de Mirandol, who asked a friend to write to Hachette on his behalf in 1860 offering his translation of Boethius's *Consolation of Philosophy*:

> L'année dernière, l'Académie Française a proposé un prix de 4000 francs pour la traduction d'un ouvrage de morale, soit de l'antiquité grecque, soit de l'antiquité latine; M. Judicis … travaillait depuis plusieurs années à sa traduction; … sur mon conseil, il se décide à entrer en lice. Il faut pour cela que son livre soit imprimé et remis à l'Institut le 1er janvier 1861 au plus tard. Pouvez-vous vous en charger? … Quant à M. Judicis, il ne se fait aucune illusion sur le débit possible d'un semblable ouvrage, même rare comme il est, et couronné par l'Académie, comme j'espère qu'il le sera. Aussi s'en remet-il aux conditions que vous jugerez convenables.

> [Last year, the Académie Française put up a 4,000 franc prize for the translation of a work of morality, either from Ancient Greece or Ancient Rome. Mr Judicis … had been working on his translation for several years … on my advice he decided to enter. He needs his book to be printed and handed in to the Institute by 1 January 1861 at the latest. Can you take this on? … Mr. Judicis is under no illusion as to the potential sales of such a book, rare though it may be, and hopefully crowned by the Académie. He therefore agrees to whatever conditions you see fit.]

> (HAC 24.23)

Perhaps surprisingly, a translator's social and literary capital could outweigh their competence in the decision to publish. Any lack of translatorial

---

19 The 1870s were a difficult decade for Ernest Lavigne: in 1877 he sued the management of the Ecole Monge in Paris for unfair dismissal from his post as a Latin teacher "alors qu'il lui avait promis une carrière stable et durable" [after promising him a stable and lasting career]. See http://ark.bnf.fr/ark:/12148/cb36806777j (accessed 7 July 2022). He went on to publish *Le roman d'un nihiliste* in 1879 and a history of Russian nihilism in 1880.

Tracing Translators in Publishers' Archives   79

skill could be compensated by a judicious editing process, but the visibility afforded to a project by a well-placed, high-profile translator was worth its weight in gold. The most striking example of this comes in a rough draft of a letter from Louis Hachette to Jules Janin, the well-known "prince des critiques", dating from 1859. The letter, couched in highly diplomatic language, delicately critiques Janin's translation of Horace, which clearly left something to be desired though Janin was paid handsomely for his work:

> J'ai lu attentivement et comparé avec le texte pour plusieurs parties de votre travail et il ne m'a pas fallu beaucoup de temps pour reconnaître que votre système de traduction [crossed out: n'avait rien de commun avec le] est diamétralement opposé au mien. Je ne parle pas de l'intelligence du texte latin [crossed out: pour laquelle vous pêchez de temps en temps] qui doit rester au-dessus de toute atteinte et qui exigera quelques redressements sur votre manuscrit, mais de la liberté avec laquelle vous rejetez les formes et les expressions originales de votre auteur pour substituer des tours et des mots [crossed out: tournures toutes différentes]; je considère surtout vos additions et vos suppressions, le mélange de phrases et enfin l'à-peuprès et les libres imitations.

> [I carefully read and compared several passages from your work and it did not take me long to realise that your system of translation [crossed out: has nothing in common with] is diametrically opposed to mine. I do not mean understanding the Latin text [crossed out: which you get wrong from time to time] which must be beyond reproach and which will require some emendations to your manuscript, but the freedom with which you reject your author's original forms and expressions to substitute [crossed out: very different] turns of phrase and words; I mean above all your additions and suppressions, blending sentences, approximations and free imitations.]

The same file contains an exchange of letters with a copy-editor by the name of Sommer, who promises "une révision scrupuleusement consciencieuse sous le rapport de tout point où la traduction me semble s'éloigner du sens littéral ou du fond de la pensée d'Horace" [a scrupulously conscientious revision at all points where the translation seems to me to diverge from Horace's literal meaning or thought] (HAC 29.18). Janin earned a little over 1,800 francs from his translation by 1862, in an unusual one-third profit-sharing agreement – Hachette demanded two-thirds of the profits given the extra work involved in revising the translation – while Sommer was paid 400 francs for his detailed revision (HAC 29.18).

Generally speaking, then as now, networking was key to building a successful ongoing presence in the literary translation field (Risku and Dickinson 2017). A translator backed by an author was in a stronger

80 *Professional Translators in Nineteenth-Century France*

negotiating position, as shown by the career of Louise Swanton-Belloc, who attended the same intellectual salons in Paris as Prosper Mérimée and Victor Cousin. Among her close friends was Elizabeth Gaskell, who wrote to Louis Hachette in 1855,

> I do not know if *Cranford* will be one of my works which you will select for translation but if it were, I should be very glad as far as I am concerned, if you and Mme Belloc could come to any agreement, as I fancy she is well acquainted with the delicacies of the English language.
>
> (HAC 29.3)

As a result, unusually for a woman, Swanton-Belloc was in a position to dictate her terms to Hachette:

> Je suis toujours disposée à me charger de la traduction de Cranford, afin de répondre à l'aimable désir que m'a exprimé Mme Gaskell, mais il m'est impossible d'apprécier l'étendue du travail sur les fragments disséminés dans les gros volumes de *Household Words*. Il faudrait donc que vous eussiez l'obligeance de mettre à ma disposition le volume anglais de la dernière édition. Vous m'avez parlé aussi d'un mode de paiement à tant la page, dont vous devriez m'envoyer un spécimen. Ainsi que j'ai eu l'honneur de vous le dire, je n'ai jamais traduit au dessous de mille et douze cents francs le volume. Dans cette circonstance exceptionnelle, je réduirai à moitié, c'est à dire à 600 fr au volume. Quant au temps, je ne voudrais m'engager à livrer ma traduction que dans trois mois, quatre au plus, avec l'intention néanmoins de m'occuper exclusivement de ce travail et d'arriver plus tôt si cela m'est possible. Toutes les personnes auxquelles j'ai eu à faire savent avec quelle rigueur je tiens mes engagements et souvent j'ai devancé les époques fixées mais je veux me laisser un peu de latitude.
>
> [I am still prepared to translate Cranford in accordance with Mrs Gaskell's amiable wishes, but I cannot estimate the volume of work from fragments scattered in large volumes of *Household Words*. You must therefore be so kind as to send me the latest English edition. You also mentioned a mode of payment at so much per page and should send me a specimen. As I had the honour of informing you, I have never translated for under 1,000 or 1,200 francs a volume. In these exceptional circumstances, I will lower that by half, i.e. to 600 francs a volume. As for the deadline, I would like to undertake to hand in my translation in three months, four at most, with the intention of focusing exclusively on this project and completing it sooner if possible. Everyone I have had

dealings with knows how strictly I keep to my undertakings and I often hand projects in early but I wish to keep myself a degree of latitude.]

(HAC 29.3)

Her statements on translation reflect her disinterested approach to the practice, typical of translators keen to appear more invested in their own literary capital than in its economic potential as a form of labour: "En me chargeant de traduire en français *Highways and Byways*, je n'ai point cédé aux sollicitations des amis de l'auteur, mais bien à mon propre désir" [In agreeing to translate *Highways and Byways* into French, I gave in not to the entreaties of the author's friends, but to my own desire] (Pickford 2012a: 180). It was a luxury only some of her fellow translators could afford.

Translators in the Publishing Chain

Comparing sources on translator remuneration to other costs in the publishing archives makes it clear what a relatively minor cog in the publishing chain (Thompson 2010) translators were, at least in cost terms. Like other aspects of publishing, translation became an increasingly streamlined and integrated part of the book production process over the course of the century. Late in the period, translators began to be offered standard pre-prepared forms, such as one signed by Charles Berthoud in 1892 acknowledging payment for his translation of Ouida's *Guilderoi*, in which the author's name and book title were added later in a different hand (HAC 44.41) (Figure 3.2).

After mid-century, translator remuneration was commonly outstripped by the sums publishers paid to acquire the rights to desirable literary properties. Berthoud was paid 750 francs to translate *Guilderoi*; Ouida herself received an average of 800 francs per novel from Hachette for her translation rights. Between 1878 and 1888, she received a total of 9,000 francs for various novels (HAC 44.41).

It was clear that though the translator was an integral and indispensable part of the publishing chain, the oversupply of translators on the market worked to keep translation costs down. As one publisher told *Emilie la jeune fille auteur*, "Nous ne manquons pas de *manœuvres* pour la traduction des langues étrangères ... Nous payons fort mal, et fort peu" [We have no shortage of labourers to translate foreign languages ... We pay very badly, and very little] (Ulliac-Trémadeure 1899 [1837]: 44, emphasis in the original). As a result, publishers could out-earn translators by vast amounts if a book sold particularly well. The Parisian bookseller and publisher Gustave Barba (1805?–67) recorded in 1846 that Charles Gosselin (1795–1859) paid Auguste-Jean-Baptiste Defauconprêt 500 francs each for his Walter

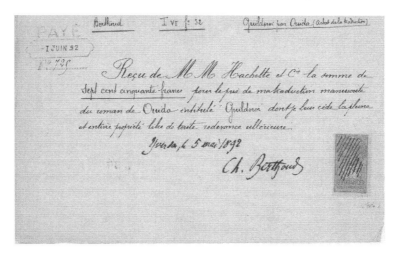

Figure 3.2 Pre-prepared form signed by Charles Berthoud to acknowledge payment for translating Ouida's *Guilderoi*, 5 May 1892. Image courtesy of Archives Hachette/IMEC.

Scott translations. He then sold Barba the right to reprint ten of the novels for a total of 65,000 francs. Another bookseller, M. Dauthereau, noted Gosselin's profits from his Walter Scott publications reached 45,604 fr 91 "dans une entreprise dont la dépense ne s'est élevée qu'à 85,682 fr 09 c ! J'en appelle à tous les négocians, quelle est la spéculation commerciale qui puisse présenter de pareils résultats?" [for a project whose outlay was just 85,682 fr 09 c! I call on all merchants, what commercial speculation can present such results?] (quoted in Pickford 2012a: 173).[20]

Two final documents from the IMEC archive shed interesting light on broader developments affecting the place of translation in the publishing sector within France and internationally, reflecting the increasingly defined and streamlined legal framework within which translators worked, explored in the next chapter. The first of these is a rare overt reference to collective organisation within the translation field, hinting at a nascent translator code of ethics – one of the key signs of professionalisation. French writers had been represented by a quasi-professional body, the Société des Gens de Lettres (SGDL), since 1838. In 1881, a now forgotten translator from Italian, Léon Dieu from Montbéliard in eastern France, wrote to Hachette to inform them that as an SGDL member, he was unable to cede his reproduction rights (HAC 19.20); this bears witness to early

20 See *Observations pour M. Dauthereau, contre M. Gosselin* (1830). Paris: Casimir.

Tracing Translators in Publishers' Archives 83

moves towards a collective defence of the economic rights of translators, continued in the twentieth century by bodies such as the *Société Française des Traducteurs* (founded in 1947) and the *Association des Traducteurs Littéraires de France* (founded in 1973). The latter decades of the nineteenth century also witnessed new business services springing up as the international circulation of books became increasingly subject to legal codification. These included literary agencies who handled translation rights, literary scouts who sought out interesting projects in other languages, and book packagers who handled part of the editorial process externally. Literary agencies arose in the British literary sphere in the latter half of the nineteenth century to handle the increasingly complex business of author copyright (Gillies 2007); French publishers then had no choice in many cases but to deal with them to acquire translation rights. Hachette negotiated with the famous A. P. Watt agency to acquire the translation rights for Wilkie Collins's novel *Blind Love* in the 1890s, for instance (HAC 63.2). A detailed contract between Hachette and an Italian translator, Mrs. Jean Darcy, from just after the close of the century formalises much of the hitherto unstructured work underpinning the international circulation of literature within a detailed legal framework. It is worth quoting at length:

> Art. 1. Mme Jean Darcy se charge de rechercher pour MM. Hachette et Cie et de leur signaler les romans les plus remarquables publiés à l'étranger. Elle leur en donnera une analyse aussi détaillée que possible, permettant de se faire une idée suffisante de la donnée générale de l'oeuvre. C'est d'après ce résumé que MM. Hachette et Cie détermineront leur choix, accepteront le roman ou le refuseront. Mme Jean Darcy fera toute la correspondance et toutes les démarches nécessaires pour assurer à MM. Hachette et Cie le droit exclusif de traduction en langue française ... Art. 2. Mme Jean Darcy fera exécuter la traduction par des collaborateurs de son choix. Les frais de travail seront rémunérés par MM. Hachette et Cie qui en fixeront le chiffre. Mme Jean Darcy sera tenue de revoir la traduction et de lui donner la forme littéraire la plus soignée ... Art. 3. Pour rémunérer Mme Jean Darcy tant de ses soins et démarches que de son travail personnel, MM. Hachette et Cie paieront à la remise du manuscrit, lorsqu'ils le jugeront définitivement au point et prêt à être envoyé à l'impression, un droit d'auteur de cinq pour cent du prix du catalogue sur les mille premiers exemplaires tirés ou à tirer.
>
> [Article 1. Mme Jean Darcy takes it upon herself to find the most remarkable novels published abroad and bring them to the attention of MM. Hachette et Cie. She will give them as detailed an analysis as possible, giving an adequate idea of the work's general interest. MM. Hachette et Cie will make their choice and accept or refuse the novel based on

84 *Professional Translators in Nineteenth-Century France*

this summary. Mme Jean Darcy will handle all the correspondence and administration needed to guarantee MM. Hachette et Cie exclusive French translation rights ... Article 2. Mme Jean Darcy will have the translation done by a team of her choosing. MM. Hachette et Cie will choose the rate and remunerate their work. Mme Jean Darcy will be responsible for revising the translation and putting it into excellent literary shape ... Article 3. To remunerate Mme Jean Darcy for her care and efforts and for her personal labour, Mme Hachette et Cie will pay a droit d'auteur of five per cent of the catalogue price for the first thousand copies printed or forthcoming upon completion of the manuscript when they deem it wholly ready for print.]

(HAC 21.21)

The process clearly ran into teething problems – the agreement quickly foundered when Hachette disputed whether Darcy was authorised to translate Gerolamo Rovetta's *Mater Dolorosa* – and within a few years the contract was null and void. Though short-lived, the agreement does bear witness to an increasing awareness by both publishers and translators that there was much to be gained if the processes whereby books were brought into French were streamlined. In a professionally structured field of translation, there was money to be made on both sides.

* * *

Translators are not equal before history. Paradoxically, those best remembered today – Chateaubriand for his Milton, Baudelaire for his Poe, Nerval for his *Faust* – were those whose presence in the field was amateur and sporadic, an occasional source of additional income rather than the economic mainstay of their lives. By combing the archives for evidence of the working conditions afforded to translators unknown precisely *because* translation was their main activity, this chapter has sought to recover the experiences of the men and women whose translation activity offered no power of consecration, no historical visibility. Jeanne Bignon, a translator of English-language children's literature from Autun (some 200 miles south-east of Paris) who worked in the 1870s and 1880s, may be forgotten, her name recorded in a single contract that stripped her of her moral rights (HTZ 1.41); but as a figure of the nineteenth-century translator, she is surely more representative than any of the great male writers we now associate with nineteenth-century literary translation practice.

4 Developing a Legal Framework for the Nineteenth-Century French Literary Translation Market

On 29 June 2021, the Paris court of appeal heard a case between a translator, anonymised in court proceedings as Monsieur E. X., and Paris-based publishers Editions de l'éclat.[1] The cause of the dispute was an academic translation for which both parties had signed a contract in July 2009. Following standard practice, the contract stipulated that the publishers were to judge the quality of the translation; if they deemed edits necessary, the translator had to be given the opportunity of making the changes himself. If he refused, the publishers had the right to bring a third party on board to edit the translation for a share of the original translator's remuneration.[2]

E. X. completed the translation ten months overdue, in August 2010. The publishers considered the original contract void as a result and entrusted the edits to a second translator, F. A. The book was published in April 2012 under F. A.'s name. In 2017, E. X. successfully sued the publishers for breach of contract and had the book – legally considered a counterfeit product – withdrawn from sale.

The case went to appeal. At the 2021 hearing, the publishers asked the court to recognise that E. X.'s work did not meet the standard required for protection under French intellectual property legislation. It was handed in far past the deadline, they argued: in failing to uphold his side of the contract, E. X. had neglected to fulfil his professional obligations, entitling the publisher to break off the contract. They claimed 18,000 euros from E. X. This claim was not upheld, and the publishers were sentenced on appeal to pay E. X. 5,000 euros.

More unexpected in legal terms was the outcome of E. X.'s second claim against the publishers. He had brought the counterfeit case on

---

1 See https://www.doctrine.fr/ for the full legal judgment. All quotes in this section, including in the footnotes, are from this document (accessed 3 October 2022).

2 For a brief overview of standard practice in French literary translation contracts, see https://atlf.org/wp-content/uploads/2021/10/CODE-DES-USAGES.pdf (accessed 11 May 2023).

DOI: 10.4324/9781003173090-5

86 *Professional Translators in Nineteenth-Century France*

classic grounds, arguing that translation was a creative act worthy of legal protection under French intellectual property law.[3] He bolstered his case with some 30 pages recording his translation choices, such as the use of the somewhat unusual *infinitif de narration* ("et Gonzalo de continuer" for "Gonzalo continues") and the high-register relative pronoun "lequel" rather than the more common "qui" to introduce relative clauses. The cumulative effect of such choices, he argued, was to create a distinctive translatorial voice that made his translation an *oeuvre de l'esprit* – a work of art that reflected the unique cast of the creator's mind. His argument was in line with over 200 years of French thinking on intellectual property, rooted in a framework dating back to the Revolution and beyond (Boncompain 2001). Yet in a radical break from previous legal decisions, the court ruled against E. X. on this point and dismissed his claim to be the author of a piece of original, creative writing.[4]

3 "Il expose que ce sont les choix d'un traducteur qui confèrent à sa traduction son caractère original et personnel et que l'objectif de fidélité qui s'impose au traducteur n'interdit pas de faire des choix, par exemple en modifiant la ponctuation, le nombre de phrases, les temps de conjugaison, une traduction simplement littérale n'étant pas possible. Il fait valoir qu'en l'espèce, il a pris le parti d'améliorer, autant que faire se pouvait, la lisibilité du texte de I J tout en respectant au maximum l'esprit de l'entreprise intellectuelle de l'auteur, retenant comme principes directeurs, d'une part, la fidélité au sens plus qu'à la lettre du texte dans la "langue source", même si sa traduction a été le plus souvent très fidèle à cette dernière, d'autre part, la lisibilité du texte dans la "langue cible", ce parti pris lui ayant permis de s'accorder une très raisonnable liberté d'interprétation et de composition quand elle était nécessaire."

[He made the case that a translator's choices are what give a translation its original and personal character and the translator's duty to be faithful is not incompatible with choices, for instance alterations to punctuation, the number of sentences, or tense, a straightforward literal translation not being possible. He brought it to the court's attention that in this case, he took it on himself to improve the legibility of IJ [i.e. the anonymised author] as best he could, while still respecting the spirit of the author's intellectual undertaking as much as possible, his guiding principles being both faithfulness to the meaning rather than the letter of the original, even if his translation was in most places very faithful to the letter, and the legibility of the target, this stance allowing him to take very reasonable freedoms in interpreting and rewriting where necessary.]

4 The grounds for the judgment were laid out in detail: "Enfin, la comparaison à laquelle se livre M. X de sa traduction des deux premiers chapitres de l'ouvrage de L.J avec celle des EDITIONS I.A.V. [i.e. the anonymised publisher] montre certes des différences ... mais ne permet pas de conclure pour autant que ces différences feraient de la traduction de M. X une oeuvre originale, éligible à la protection du droit d'auteur. Ainsi, et alors que la traduction proposée par M. X a été critiquée à plusieurs égards par l'éditeur qui a finalement choisi ... de recourir à un autre traducteur, l'appelant échoue à démontrer que sa traduction révèle l'empreinte de sa personnalité et peut bénéficier de la protection au titre du droit d'auteur.

Pour ces motifs, le jugement sera en conséquence confirmé en ce qu'il a débouté M. X de l'ensemble de ses demandes en contrefaçon dirigées contre la société EDITIONS DE L'ECLAT et M. A."

The judgment came as something of a shock to the French literary translation community, causing alarm in professional circles, for instance on the *Association des Traducteurs Littéraires de France* message board. While the jurisprudence on this point seemed to have been settled for decades, if not centuries, it came as a perhaps unwelcome reminder that the law develops over time – sometimes in unexpected directions.

Laws are not handed down from on high on tablets of stone: they have a history and a social context. Yet the development of a body of translation-related legislation is a relatively under-studied area of translation history, particularly as regards the literary sphere. Salah Basalamah's seminal monograph *Le droit de traduire: Une politique culturelle pour la mondialisation* (2009) lays much of the fundamental groundwork for this important field of enquiry. As its subtitle suggests, it offers a broad sweep – an "archaeology", to use its own term – of translation-related laws and rights from the eighteenth to the twentieth century, focusing in the first half on France and Britain and in the second on the major landmark statements on translation law, from the nineteenth-century congresses of the *Association Littéraire et Artistique Internationale* (ALAI) and the Bern convention to the Nairobi recommendation of 1976. A number of scholars have also written on translation and copyright with a more contemporary focus (Park 2019; Lee 2020) or a philosophical bent (Venuti 1995; Basalamah 2001), while others have focused on translation legislation in institutional settings (Wolf 2015; Merkle 2015; D'hulst and Koskinen 2020). However, detailed studies of the legislative backdrop to past translators' professional lives are still thin on the ground. This chapter returns to the primary sources of the nineteenth century – works of legal theory, accounts of court cases involving literary translators, and material from the IMEC archive studied in Chapter 3 – to flesh out some of the legal framework for translation that emerged over the course of the period. It will begin by outlining some of the significant court cases involving translation for publication in early- to mid-nineteenth-century France, before focusing particularly on the issue of moral rights. These are a useful proxy in assessing an individual

---

[In conclusion, M. X.'s comparison of his translation of the first two chapters of L. J.'s book with that published by the Editions I. A. V. [i.e. the anonymised publisher] does indeed reveal differences ... but does not allow the conclusion to be drawn that the differences are such as to make M. X.'s translation an original work eligible for *droit d'auteur* [i.e. author rights] protection.

Therefore, whereas M. X.'s translation was criticised on several grounds by the publisher who eventually chose ... to call on the services of a second translator, the appellant has failed to demonstrate that his translation bears the stamp of his personality and can be protected under *droit d'auteur* legislation. On these grounds, the judgment is confirmed in that all M. X.'s accusations of counterfeiting against Editions de l'éclat and M. A. are dismissed.]

88 *Professional Translators in Nineteenth-Century France*

translator's agency – their "willingness and ability to act" (Kinnunen and Koskinen 2010: 6) – and degree of investment in professional translation practice. The final part of this chapter seeks to demonstrate that a translator's agency and investment are reflected in, and determined by, their position in the translational field outlined in Chapter 3.

Translations and Translators in Court in the 1820s and 1830s

The history of French *droit d'auteur*[5] [i.e. author rights] legislation has been studied at length, most notably in Boncompain (2001), an impressively thorough study of the revolutionary period. The decades-long debate over author's rights, led by such literary luminaries as Voltaire, eventually led to the abolition of the *privilège* system (by which printers held exclusive permission to print a given title) in August 1789. Permission to print no longer stemmed from royal authority but from the natural rights of citizens to ownership of their own intellectual property. The National Convention's decree on author's rights of 1793 stipulated crucially that "Les auteurs d'écrits en tous genres ... jouiront durant leur vie entière du droit exclusif de vendre, faire vendre, distribuer leurs ouvrages dans le territoire de la République et d'en céder la propriété en tout ou en partie" [authors of writings of all sorts ... will hold the lifelong exclusive right to sell, have sold, or distribute their books in the territory of the Republic and cede ownership of them in whole or in part].

For translators working in the French market, of course, the devil was in the detail. Did they count as authors in the spirit of the decree? Did a published translation count as a legally protected unique expression of authorial personality, of the sort intended by the legislators? Or was translation, as an inherently derivative practice, unavoidably a form of intellectual piracy that deprived authors of their natural rights? The 1793 decree did not explicitly mention translators, though it did extend protection to composers and visual artists working in paint and drawing.

The derivative nature of translation naturally complicated translators' claims to authorial status, which was rooted in Enlightenment ideas of originality and inimitability (Mortier 1982; Woodmansee 1984). Various other European nations had already laid down their own laws on this point: writing in the 1830s, the legal commentator Augustin-Charles Renouard (1792–1878) gives the legal position in Belgium, the Netherlands, Russia, Prussia, and so on. However, France had pointedly decided *not* to make its position clear at this point. The topic of translators' rights was debated by legislators in the run-up to Napoleon's significant decree on printing and

---

5 I retain this term in French as it does not neatly map onto copyright; see Strowel (1993).

Developing a Legal Framework 89

bookselling of 5 February 1810, but the published decree made no mention of translators or translation (Locré 1819).[6] This left a clear gap in the French legislation: "est-ce contrefaire un ouvrage du domaine privé que de le traduire? ... Le silence de nos lois sur ce point est une lacune véritable" [Is translating a work in the private domain counterfeiting? ... The silence of our laws on this point is a real omission] (Renouard 1839: 38).

French legal opinion on the issue was divided. Jean-Marie Pardessus (1772–1853), a specialist in commercial and contract law, argued in his four-volume *Cours de droit commercial* that translations of French books published in France were by their very nature counterfeits: "Ce serait ... contrefaire un ouvrage publié en France, que de l'y traduire en latin, ou en langue étrangère" [Translating a book published in France into Latin or a foreign language in France would be counterfeiting] (Pardessus 1825: 35). In the absence of an international rights agreement, on the other hand, he considered French translations of foreign books to be perfectly licit:

> Les traductions d'ouvrages composés en langues étrangères par des auteurs qui n'auroient pas, en France, un droit d'édition exclusif, étant permises, l'intérêt des traducteurs les fait considérer, relativement au droit d'empêcher la contrefaçon, comme des ouvrages nouveaux, en ce sens que nul ne peut imprimer une traduction sans le consentement du traducteur, ou celui de ses ayants-droits.

> [Translations of books written in foreign languages without an exclusive right to publish in France are authorised; the interest of translators means they are considered in terms of the law against counterfeiting as new works, in the sense that no-one can print a translation without the authorisation of the translator or his beneficiaries.]
>
> (Pardessus 1825: 37)

What mattered for Pardessus, then, was the direction of the translation, into or out of French. Pardessus's expert opinion was shared by Etienne Blanc (1805–74), author of a legal treatise on counterfeiting. Renouard, on the other hand, pointed out that no cases had come before court related to out-of-French translations published in France, though it was a relatively common practice, and it was unclear what harm could come to the original

---

6 See, for example, the draft version of the legislation presented by M. le comte Regnaud on 25 November 1809: "L'individu qui aura fait le premier sa déclaration pour la traduction ou publication d'un ouvrage imprimé ou publié à l'étranger, jouira, en France, des droits d'auteur pour sa traduction ou sa publication en langue originale" [The first individual to declare a translation or publication of a book printed or published abroad will have authors' rights in France to their translation or publication in the original language] (Locré 1819: 83).

90 *Professional Translators in Nineteenth-Century France*

by such a publication: the difference in language was enough to avoid confusion and the readerships were unlikely to be the same (Renouard 1839: 38). He held that the principle of the circulation of ideas was of such importance that it was crucial to "laisser toujours ouverte à la civilisation française une communication directe et facile, dans sa langue, avec toutes les idées des autres peuples" [always give French civilisation direct, easy communication in its own language with all the ideas of other peoples] (Renouard 1839: 39). Consequently, the direction of translation, into or out of French, should not matter. Books should only be protected as intellectual property in their original language, and translators should be able to practice their art freely without fear of being accused of counterfeiting.

This gap in the legislation became increasingly problematic in the 1820s as the publishing trade modernised and expanded (Chartier and Martin 1990a; Rebolledo-Dhuin 2017; Wilfert 2012), leading to greater competition in the sale of books, with higher financial stakes at play. If it could be shown that translations were *not* afforded *droit d'auteur* protection in the terms of the law, then literary piracy would clearly become a lucrative business opportunity as the initial publisher of a translation would be taking all the financial risk by remunerating the translator and demonstrating the presence of a market for the book. As a result, a small cluster of court cases arose as printers, publishers, and translators tussled over legal ownership of the intellectual labour of translation, seeking to establish its boundaries. The primary sources for the details of these squabbles are the legal gazettes, dictionaries, and treatises recording details of the successive cases that shaped literary property law (e.g. Gastambide 1837; Renouard 1838–39; Dalloz 1857; Pouillet 1879). As is the nature of such compilations, the content varies little from one source to another. The accounts in the following paragraphs draw largely on the most readily available and compendious of these sources, Dalloz (1857).[7]

The first step in determining the legal ownership of literary translations was acknowledging that translation was an *oeuvre de l'esprit* rather than a purely mechanical operation. This meant demonstrating that the translator was an author in the terms of the National Convention decree – a claim that seemed (and still seems) counter-intuitive to many. Accordingly, it did not take long for a case to come up in court testing the claim that

---

7 A thorough study of court archives would doubtless reveal other cases, such as Laroche vs. Charpentier in the 1840s, briefly outlined in Laroche's biography in the annex, and Lindau vs. (Richard) Wagner, 6 March 1861: "celui qui a coopéré à la traduction d'un livret d'opéra n'avait pas nécessairement droit à figurer sur les affiches, surtout quand son travail avait été presque refait après la livraison au compositeur" [an individual cooperating with the translation of an opera libretto does not necessarily have the right to appear on the posters, especially when his work is almost completely rewritten after delivery to the composer] (quoted in Strömholm 1966: 149).

translators were – or, as one publisher argued, were *not* – authors under the terms of the decree.

The first such case involved not a translator, but two publishers. In 1821, the Parisian printer Auguste Bobée (1788–1849) brought out a set of plays by Goethe, including a new translation of *Götz von Berlichingen* by Albert Stapfer (1802–92). Two years later, in September 1823, Pierre-François Ladvocat – a thrusting, ambitious young commercial publisher described by one contemporary commentator as a "hardi spéculateur, esprit aventureux" [bold speculator and adventurous spirit] (Regnault 1833: 393) – took up Stapfer's translation in his own new collection of *Chefs d'oeuvre des théâtres étrangers traduits en français* [Masterpieces of Foreign Theatre in French Translation]. Bobée had the entire print run seized and sued Ladvocat for what he claimed was a counterfeit edition. The court heard that a careful comparison of the two texts revealed that Ladvocat's version was, "à la seule exception de mots changés et de quelques membres de phrases omis ou transportés" [with the sole exception of words changed and a few clauses left out or moved around], identical to Bobée's, especially in the first three acts, right down to the same typographical errors (Dalloz 1857: 457). However, a comparison of Stapfer's translation with the previous French translation by Friedel and de Bonneville, dating from 1784, contained only "des rapports et des ressemblances inévitables" [inevitable links and resemblances]. It seemed a cut-and-dried instance of counterfeiting and Ladvocat was accordingly found guilty on 28 January 1824. He was fined 100 francs.

But Ladvocat had not said his last word. His appeal was heard within a few months, in April 1824. He argued that the law on authorship of 1793 had been incorrectly applied by the court, since the National Convention decree

> n'a eu en vue que ceux qui composent un livre, qui font quelque ouvrage d'esprit, ... étendre ces dispositions aux traducteurs quand leur traduction d'un ouvrage, composé dans une langue vivante et très-répandue, ne suppose ni études spéciales, ni efforts de génie, c'est évidemment donner à la loi de 1793 une interprétation qu'elle n'avait pas dans l'esprit du législateur.

> [was solely aimed at those who write a book, whose work reflects their unique cast of mind ... extending the application of the decree to translators, when their translation of a book written in a widely spoken modern language requires neither special study nor the effort of genius, clearly interprets the law of 1793 in terms the legislator did not intend.]
> (Dalloz 1857: 457)

His appeal was rejected and his fine raised to 3,000 francs. M. Ollivier, *président*, M. Fréteau de Pény, *avocat général*, and M. Cardonnel,

92 *Professional Translators in Nineteenth-Century France*

rapporteur, decided that translation "était au nombre des propriétés lit-téraires auxquelles le fait et le délit de contrefaçon pouvaient être applicables" [was included in the literary properties to which the fact and offence of counterfeiting could be applied] (Dalloz 1857: 457). The *cour de cassation* recognised the principle that translation was a creative act.[8]

A similar case came before the court in 1830, when another ambitious young bookseller, Charles Gosselin, sued the translator Albert de Montémont (1788–1861) along with Montémont's publisher Armand Aubrée and printer François Rignoux, for counterfeiting Gosselin's edition of Walter Scott's *Ivanhoe*. Montémont and his team stood accused of substantial plagiarism in their 1829 edition of *Ivanhoe*, the first 11 chapters of which Gosselin claimed were a "copie servile, presque complète" [servile, almost complete copy] of his own 1818 edition of Defauconprêt's translation. The three accused mounted a spirited defence: they argued that the syntactic similarities between French and English meant translations were bound to hit upon the same phrasing, especially – one English paper reported – "in rendering an author like Sir Walter ... who [was] so precise, so technical, and so little under the influence of the imagination" (Anonymous 1830: 4). Rignoux also printed an 18-page pamphlet listing all of Defauconprêt's omissions and errors corrected in the new version as well as all the material added by Montémont (Figure 4.1).[9]

Yet it was to no avail. The court – including Augustin-Charles Renouard – sided with Gosselin, considering that Montémont's relatively minor cosmetic changes did not make up for the extensive swathes of plagiarised prose comprising around a quarter of the total text that reproduced a number of the Defauconprêt edition's typographical errors and mistakes in meaning. The principle was enshrined in the *Code pénal* article 425 that while minor plagiarism was an issue for literary criticism rather than the courts, major instances of plagiarism – described as "nombreux, consécutifs et serviles" [numerous, consecutive and slavish] – did indeed amount to counterfeiting an extant edition, even in the case of translations (Dalloz 1833: 135). Interestingly, the case does not seem to have harmed Montémont's career unduly, as he carried on writing and translating regularly until his death in 1861, including several more titles by Walter Scott.

Since the French legal system does not operate under the doctrine of *stare decisis* [i.e. the legal principle of determining points of litigation based on precedent], it took several more cases for various aspects of translatorial creativity to be recognised by the courts. Two additional cases from the early 1830s indicate further recognition of the translator's authorial

---

8 For a provocative reading of translators as *non*-authors, see Pym (2011).

9 My thanks to Gábor Gelléri of the University of Aberystwyth for generously taking the time to supply me with a copy of the pamphlet.

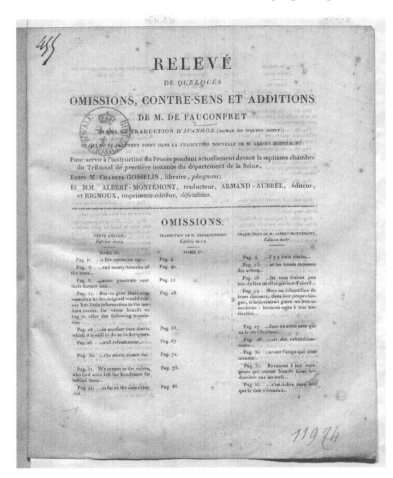

Figure 4.1 François Rignoux's list of errors and omissions in Defauconprêt's translation of *Ivanhoe*, presented to the court to counter accusations of plagiarism. Image courtesy of the Bibliothèque nationale de France.

rights, with the cases being brought this time not by publishers concerned first and foremost with potential financial losses, but by translators on their own behalf, keen to defend their own authorial status.

In 1829, Louise Swanton-Belloc (1796–1881), a leading English to French translator since 1818, began work on a 12-volume "série de lectures pour enfants" [series of readings for children] entitled *Éducation familière*. The series was based on the tales of Maria Edgeworth, to which Swanton-Belloc brought "une nouvelle classification et des rectifications scientifiques" [a new classification and scholarly corrections] (Renouard

94 *Professional Translators in Nineteenth-Century France*

1838: 120). For reasons unknown – perhaps because Louise Swanton-Belloc had too much on her plate[10] – her publishers, Alexandre Mesnier and H. Fournier jeune, entrusted the final four volumes in the series to a second, and vastly less experienced, translator. For her debut translation, Adélaïde de Montgolfier (1789–1880) – a close lifelong friend of Swanton-Belloc's – retained the original title and arrangement of the material, while the publishers continued to advertise the edition under Swanton-Belloc's name, suggesting she was the sole translator for the entire project (*Annuaire* 1872: 62).

The discrepancy in experience between the two translators may explain what came next. Perhaps motivated to some extent by an urge to protect her translatorial reputation, Swanton-Belloc sued for infringement of her intellectual property. The court decided on 27 December 1831 that the title, format, and classification of the volumes were the property of the translator on the grounds that "cette dame pouvait soit achever son ouvrage, soit l'interrompre, soit même y renoncer" [the lady could complete her work, pause it, or even give up on it altogether] (Renouard 1838: 120). The publishers were entitled to entrust the final four volumes to another translator but not to use the features that were the intellectual property of the first translator. Titles were now deemed an important means by which books found their readership: unique titles had monetary value since they lowered the risk of readers purchasing another book by mistake (*Annuaire* 1872: 62). Since Mesnier and Fournier jeune had published Adélaïde de Montgolfier's translation with Louise Swanton-Belloc's title and classification, they, like Ladvocat, Montémont, Aubrée, and Rignoux, were found guilty of counterfeiting. They paid a fine of 100 francs and a further 1,500 francs in damages. As in Bobée vs. Ladvocat, the offending books were pulped. Again, at least for the budding translator's career, the case was by no means the kiss of death: Adélaïde de Montgolfier went on to publish numerous works in collaboration with Louise Swanton-Belloc. The two women were buried alongside each other after death.

The final case in the initial cluster as publishers and translators wrangled to define the limits of intellectual property in translation came a year after Louise Swanton-Belloc's victory in court. The well-known doctor Étienne Pariset (1770–1847) sued his bookseller Augustin-Claude-François Méquignon-Marvis in 1832. As reported by the *Journal du Palais* on 28 November, the case hinged on whether, in the absence of a detailed contract stipulating the print run, payment for a translation – Pariset's *Aphorismes d'Hippocrate* in this instance – meant that the translator

---

10 In 1830, Louise Swanton-Belloc was mother of an eight-year-old, a two-year-old, and a newborn infant. She also published four translations in the period 1829–32, including the multi-volume Edgeworth.

Developing a Legal Framework 95

renounced ownership of his intellectual property in exchange for a lump sum payment. In effect, the case sought to determine whether work-for-hire contracts, as common in modern translation practice in the United States, were permissible in France. In practice, the publisher had paid Pariset 350 francs for his translation, then brought out a second edition. Pariset claimed he had not been paid for the second edition; Méquignon-Marvis produced documents to show he had, in fact, paid Pariset a further 500 francs. The court heard that at no point did either discuss, let alone set down in writing, who owned the translation or how many editions and copies the payment covered. The court decided that Pariset had seemingly had no intention of claiming ownership of his intellectual property, and that he had therefore not been entitled to sell his translation to a rival publisher, Ferra. Consequently, Méquignon-Marvis was entitled to print and distribute his second edition as outright owner of the text. He did lose the case on one point, however. The cover of his third edition bore a statement suggesting Pariset had revised the text, which was not the case (*Journal du Palais* 1841: 1596).

Interestingly, this case, like the Swanton-Belloc case outlined above, suggests a burgeoning awareness on the part of translators of the need to protect their financial interests by staking a claim to their literary reputations, seeking to defend what were later to be enshrined in law as moral rights – a point studied in greater detail below. The effect of the cluster of court cases, particularly Bobée vs. Ladvocat, was to establish translators as authors in legal terms, deserving of protection under intellectual property laws. By the latter half of the century, Renouard's view of translation as an international intellectual commons was no longer valid. As the legal theorist Édouard Calmels wrote in 1856, a translation "constitue un ouvrage nouveau ... en ce sens que le traducteur aura sur la traduction, le même droit que l'auteur sur l'œuvre originale, et en conséquence, pourra poursuivre les contrefacteurs de sa traduction" [constitutes a new work ... in the sense that the translator has the same rights over his translation as the author over the original work, and consequently can sue counterfeiters of his translation] (Calmels 1856: 155).

* * *

In 1838, French law was not to dispute the possibility of multiple, rival translations of the same text for a decade to come. Renouard's treatise on authorial rights makes this perfectly clear:

> Il est presque superflu de faire remarquer que le compilateur, l'abbréviateur, le traducteur, n'ont droit à leur propre travail, et n'ôtent qu'à personne le droit de compiler les mêmes matériaux, d'abréger les mêmes ouvrages, de traduire le même auteur original.

96 *Professional Translators in Nineteenth-Century France*

[It is almost superfluous to remark that the compiler, abridger, and translator only have the right to their own work and do not remove anyone else's right to compile the same materials, abridge the same books, or translate the same original author.]

(Renouard 1838: 100–1)

This had significant repercussions for translatorial labour, as translators of popular works had to race to market, as seen in Chapter 2. Popular books came out in multiple translations, sometimes within a matter of days, and the fastest translator clearly had an edge in cornering the market.

Yet Renouard could see the wind turning in favour of international copyright legislation to establish a regulated trade in translation rights, writing "la question … mériterait une attention particulière si un droit international venait à être établi" [the question … would be worthy of particular attention if an international law were to become established] (Renouard 1838: 40–1). He was in fact sitting on a commission to study the issue of international copyright at the time (Strömholm 1966: 164). Within a few years, in 1843, France began signing bilateral copyright agreements for translations with various European partners, the first being Sardinia, Portugal, Hanover, and Britain. The Rosa vs. Girardin case of 1845 made it clear that France needed an international framework for authorial rights. The case turned on whether an unauthorised Spanish translation of a chemistry textbook infringed the original author's property rights. The court of appeal in Rouen deemed that an unauthorised translation did indeed harm an author as it was "une atteinte de concurrence" [unfair competition] and the publisher Rosa lost his appeal (Dalloz 1846: 212). The outcome enshrined the author's right to control the circumstances of a translation. Foreign authors were eventually granted legal protection in France by decree on 28 March 1852: translation rights now needed to be acquired within a legal framework, leading to the development of the modern foreign rights market (Rideau 2008) (Figure 4.2).[11]

Some canny entrepreneurs seized the new business opportunity: Charles Bernard Derosne (1825–1904) set up agencies for the protection of British literary property in France and vice versa in 1865, advertising his "parfaite connaissance des deux langues, une grande expérience du goût Anglais [sic], et des relations suivies avec les principales maisons de librairie Anglaises" [perfect grasp of both languages, extensive experience of English taste,

---

11 It should be noted that the USA was not a signatory to international copyright legislation at this point, leading to absurd situations such as that of Harriet Beecher Stowe's international bestseller *Uncle Tom's Cabin* being published in 11 competing French translations in 1852–3 (Parfait 2010).

Developing a Legal Framework 97

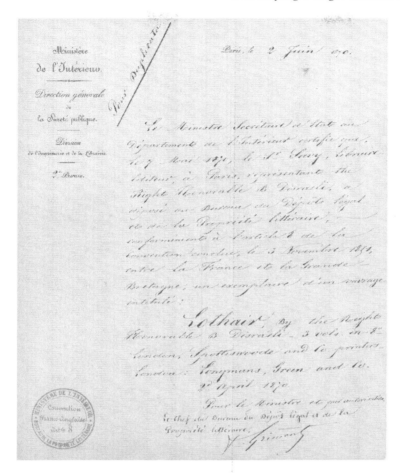

Figure 4.2 Bureau de la propriété littéraire registration ensuring the exclusive right to translate Benjamin Disraeli's *Lothair*, 2 June 1870. Image courtesy of Archives Hachette/IMEC.

and ongoing relationships with the leading English booksellers] (Derosne 1865: 2) (Figure 4.3).

He brokered the translation process for French publishers looking to bring their books to English audiences, charging a flat rate of 25 francs per book to record titles at Stationers' Hall in London – a key step in the copyright protection process – and an additional ten per cent of successful sales. Publishers were invited to sign an exclusive contract with him, filling in a form with the minimum amount they would accept for

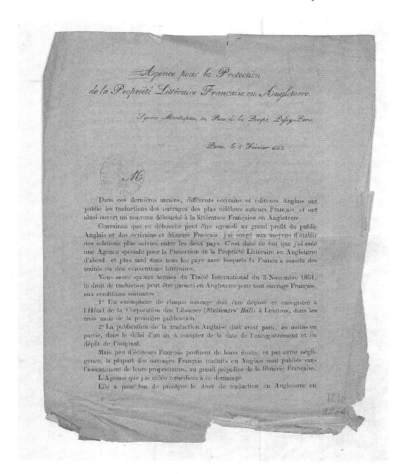

Figure 4.3 Prospectus for Charles Bernard Derosne's cross-Channel literary property agency, 5 February 1865. Image courtesy of the Bibliothèque nationale de France.

translation rights.[12] Back in London, he purchased translation rights to the works of authors such as Thackeray and Dickens, which he then sold on to French publishers. His innovative business service model predated A. P. Watt, generally credited with founding the first literary agency, by nine years (Hepburn 1968; Gillies 2007). Even prior to founding his agency, he achieved such a strong market position that his 1864 contract with Hetzel stipulated

---

12 The full document is available online at https://gallica.bnf.fr (accessed 4 January 2023).

Developing a Legal Framework 99

Si MM. Hetzel et Lacroix, pour ne pas mettre un trop grand nombre d'ouvrages signés par M. Derosne sur la place le jugeraient bon, il serait convenu entre eux et M. Bernard Derosne d'un pseudonyme pour ceux des volumes qu'ils jugeraient bon de ne pas publier sous son nom.

[If Messrs. Hetzel and Lacroix deem it necessary to avoid putting out too many books signed by M. Derosne, they will agree with M. Bernard Derosne on a pen name for the volumes they prefer not to publish under his name.]

(HTZ 2.11)

The emergence of international copyright agreements and the concomitant development of exclusive translation rights impacted translatorial practice in very real terms. While many translators still worked at speed, for instance when working on serial publications, at least they could now be broadly confident (unless working on an American author) that their efforts would not be undercut by a faster or less scrupulous colleague. It can be hypothesised that the legal recognition of translators as authors was a major driving force in the shift away from the discourse of translatorial labour outlined in Chapter 2, in which individual participants were highly fungible, towards an individualistic understanding of translatorial labour as the unique cast of the translator's creative spirit. As this section has shown, as early as the 1820s and early 1830s, some translators were keen to claim ownership of their intellectual property as a means of avoiding damage to their literary and/or intellectual reputations, thereby protecting their long-term financial interests. While the moral rights that protect literary reputations were not officially enshrined in French law for decades to come, their seeds were sown in the early decades of the century.

Translatorial Moral Rights

French *droit d'auteur* legislation currently enshrines four basic moral rights for authors:

1. *le droit de paternité*: the right of attribution/to be acknowledged as author of a work
2. *le droit du respect de l'oeuvre*: the right of integrity/not to have one's work altered without consent
3. *le droit de divulgation*: the right of disclosure/to decide when and if the work is ready for publication
4. *le droit de repentir* or *de retrait*: the right of withdrawal/to remove a work from the public sphere.[13]

---

13 See articles L121-1 to L121-9 of the *Code de la propriété intellectuelle.*

100 *Professional Translators in Nineteenth-Century France*

These perpetual, inalienable, imprescriptible rights are distinct from the author's patrimonial right to gain pecuniary advantage from his or her intellectual property, which is limited in time, currently expiring 70 years after the author's death. Moral rights are intended to protect literary reputation. Though only explicitly protected internationally since the Berne Convention was amended in Rome in 1928, they have long been a presence in legal debate. Their prehistory stretches back as far as antiquity, when plagiarism was already seen as a matter for moral censure, indicating a primitive form of ownership over intellectual output. In 1719, Daniel Defoe overtly compared the pirating of intellectual property to theft, challenging rogue publishers to "shew the Difference between [intellectual piracy] and Robbing on the Highway, or Breaking open a House" (quoted in Pickford 2011: 49).

Moral rights protect an author's non-economic rights – in other words, intangible forms of symbolic capital such as honour and reputation. The late-eighteenth-century debate over *le droit d'auteur* in France was shaped largely by playwrights such as Beaumarchais who argued that they should be entitled to a share of the profits from the Comédie Française (Boncompain 2001; Basalamah 2009). The *droit d'auteur* debate was closely bound up with notions of honour and reputation, reflecting a semantic slippage in the term *propriété littéraire* from propriety to property. As the Comédie Française was under the aegis of the *Gentilhommes de la chambre*, any playwright hoping to have his work put on there had to be "concerned with maintaining his honour and reputation in elite social circles" (Liemer 2011: 98). Failure to behave in a manner befitting *un homme honnête* could lead to the end of a career; conversely, the expectation that following the rules would pay off gradually crystallised into stakes worthy of protection. For example, playwrights who learned to influence when a play would be put on were essentially learning the *droit de divulgation*. Casting actors and being involved in staging was akin to a *droit de respect*: "a playwright's interest in displaying acceptable behaviour evolved into his interest in protecting his own creative decision-making processes and the non-economic values of his work, including his public reputation" (Liemer 2011: 104).

As Stig Strömholm (1966) convincingly demonstrates in his thesis on the genesis of moral rights in France, Germany, and Scandinavia, such rights began to crystallise as a legal concept in the early nineteenth century, since the process could only take place within a particular set of historical, social, and economic circumstances. Moral rights grew out of the *jurisprudence constante* of a cumulative body of cases judged in court, and therefore required the existence of a body of professional authors large enough and of sufficient social standing and economic clout to be able to take publishers to court. They also required a literary marketplace in which

Developing a Legal Framework 101

the financial stakes for authors were high enough to be worth the hassle of a court case. These conditions were met in the early nineteenth century as the literary marketplace expanded, driven by rising literacy rates and technological advances in the printing and distribution of reading matter. Strömholm notes that by the early nineteenth century, circumstances were ripe for non-economic interests in intellectual property to be fixed in law. As Pardessus wrote in 1814,

> La vente d'un manuscrit en pleine propriété ... n'a pas les mêmes effets que celles des propriétés ordinaires. Elle ne donne pas à l'acheteur le droit de disposer du manuscrit de la manière la plus absolue; il a le droit de le publier en tels formats et nombre d'éditions qu'il veut, mais il n'est pas le maître d'intercaller [sic] ou d'opérer des changemens de quelque que ce soit, sans le consentement de l'auteur ... L'auteur ... n'a pas aliéné l'espérance de réputation que la publicité de cet ouvrage peut lui procurer, parce que c'est une chose inévaluable.

> [The sale of full ownership of a manuscript does not have the same effect as the sale of ordinary property. It does not give the purchaser the right to do whatever he likes with the manuscript; he has the right to publish it in as many formats and editions as he likes, but he is not entitled to add intercalations or make any changes whatsoever without the author's agreement ... The author ... has not alienated the hope of reputation that advertising the book can afford him, because that cannot be evaluated.]

> (Pardessus 1814: 317–19)

Moral rights therefore emerged in France as a lengthy process of cumulative jurisprudence across the nineteenth century, crystallising into doctrine after 1880 (Binctin 2013: 305). Yet, as Liemer (2011) and Strömholm (1966) make clear, the issue was debated from considerably earlier in the century. The first court case recognising the author's *droit au respect*, Billecocq vs. Glandaz, was in 1814; the outcome was that printers and booksellers were legally obliged to print manuscripts in the state in which they received them (Strömholm 1966: 125). The question was also of political interest. A commission was set up in 1825 to put forward improvements to literary property legislation, though its recommendations were not implemented. Its president, vicomte de la Rouchefoucauld, opened the first session with a speech that gestured to the need to legislate for authors in light of "la considération due à sa personne", that is, consideration due to the author (Strömholm 1966: 165). The first explicit reference to moral rights came in parliament in 1841 in a discussion of Lamartine's proposed law on literary property, when the right to publish was defined as a "droit intellectuel, moral, personnel" [intellectual, moral, individual right] (Strömholm 1966: 177).

102 *Professional Translators in Nineteenth-Century France*

The concept of moral rights, then, was decades in the making before it was legislated into formal existence: perhaps swayed by the economic hardship faced by widows and orphaned children in the post-revolutionary climate, "early nineteenth century French courts applied the not-yet-named *droit moral* protections in ordinary legal disputes over intellectual property" (Liemer 2011: 115). The next section of this chapter turns back to the set of IMEC archival material used in Chapter 3 to study translator correspondence and contracts for evidence that translators were keen to protect the various aspects of their literary reputations that were eventually enshrined as the four types of moral rights listed above. It will also demonstrate that the extent to which translators were aware of, and in a position to leverage, what might be termed proto-moral rights maps to some extent onto the issue of translatorial agency. In short, translators with high agency in the terms laid out in Chapter 3 tended to be in a position to negotiate respect of their proto-rights from publishers; those with low agency were not.

The earliest evidence of a translator seeking to avail himself of a proto-*droit de divulgation* is to be found in some of the earliest surviving correspondence in the archive. Jean-Louis Burnouf (1775–1844) makes implicit claim to a *droit de divulgation* in a letter to Louis Hachette on 9 May 1831:

> je consens à vous tenir quitte et déchargé des six mille francs que vous me devez encore … à condition que vous ne me ferez plus aucune observation sur ledit retard, lequel, comme vous le savez très bien, provient de mes efforts assidus pour perfectionner l'ouvrage et en assurer le succès. [I consent to write off the six thousand francs you still owe me … on the condition that you will make no further remarks on the said lateness, which, as you very well know, has arisen from my assiduous efforts to perfect the work and guarantee its success.]
>
> (HAC 154.5)

At this point the project – a translation of Tacitus – was at least eight months overdue, as the letter further refers to previous correspondence on the matter the previous August.

Burnouf was a typically high-agency translator in terms of his position in the translation-for-publication field sketched out in Chapter 3. An exemplary instance of post-revolutionary meritocracy, he rose from humble beginnings to enter some of the most exalted intellectual institutions in the country. Born into poverty, the orphan son of a rural weaver, he received an education from the local priest and earned a scholarship to study in Paris. He was appointed to the chair of Latin eloquence at the Collège de France in 1816 and ended his career as librarian at the Sorbonne

Developing a Legal Framework 103

(Havelange 1986: 209). Added to his social and intellectual capital (not to mention the economic capital that let him write off a 6,000-franc debt) was the literary capital of the author and language pair he worked with, giving him an extremely strong position in negotiating terms with publishers – including determining when his work was ripe for publication, regardless of previous agreements with his publisher.[14]

Burnouf's case is similar to that of the philosopher, politician, and member of the Académie française Victor Cousin, whose translation of Plato was acquired at some point in the 1830s by the publishers Rey and Belhate.[15] Suffering from ill health, Cousin was unable to complete the contracted paratext for his translation. The publishers wanted to go ahead and print a second small-format edition without it; Cousin held out, asking the publishers to wait for his preface and print in a large format, requesting "que les éditeurs lui laissassent tout le temps nécessaire pour exécuter son travail selon les convenances de sa santé" [that the publishers give him all the time he needed to carry out the work when his health permitted] (HAC 5.15). Again, his social status, relative wealth, and the intellectual capital of his translation work let him dictate terms to his publishers to a certain extent.

A later contract reflects negotiations around issues of a proto-*droit de paternité*. Paul Lorain (1799–1861) was able to negotiate a clause ensuring his right of attribution in a contract signed in 1857:

la traduction des oeuvres de Sir Bulwer Lytton devant être publiée sous la direction de M. P. Lorain, il est bien entendu que le nom de ce dernier figurera, comme directeur de la publication, sur le titre et sur la couverture de la traduction de *What will he do with it?*

14 It is interesting to contrast Burnouf with another very early contract, signed in 1829 by Pierre-François Delestre (1793–1851), a headmaster in the rural towns of Tonnerre and later Cahors and an occasional author of books on religious and moral topics printed by minor regional presses in Toulouse. Delestre published a translation of the *Aeneid* with Hachette in a profit-sharing agreement from 1829 to 1832 that saw him stripped of any claim to translatorial recognition: "Le Sieur Hachette, s'il le juge à propos, substituera son nom à celui de l'auteur au cas du titre principal du premier volume, qu'il ferait alors réimprimer à ses frais" [If Mr. Hachette sees fit, he can replace the author's name with his own on the main title page in volume one, and reprint it at his own cost] (HAC 21.11). This was Delestre's sole translation, suggesting he did not develop sufficient professional translatorial identity to negotiate effectively with Hachette.

15 The correspondence is undated; the translation was eventually published in 1839. Belhate seems to have dropped out of the picture between acquisition and publication: the volumes were eventually brought out by Rey and Gravier. For a brief publishing history of the project, see https://www.textesrares.com/pages/philosophie/platon-ouvres-editees-par-v-cousin.html (accessed 8 November 2022).

104 *Professional Translators in Nineteenth-Century France*

[since the translation of Sir Bulwer Lytton's works is to be published under M. P. Lorain's direction, it is agreed that his name will feature as director of publication on the title and cover of the translation of *What will he do with it?*]

(HAC 43.37)

This was despite the fact that Lorain was not in fact the translator, but an editorial coordinator who subcontracted the translation process to underlings who went unnamed in the finished book.

Like Burnouf, Lorain was a typically high-agency actor, though the language pair and style of literature he worked with embodied less literary capital than Burnouf's Greek and Latin classics. Lorain's agency can be readily attributed to his social and institutional position as a former master of rhetoric at the Lycée Louis-le-Grand in Paris, rector of the Lyon *académie* (i.e. head of education for the Lyon region), and recipient of the *Légion d'honneur* (Condette 2006: 260–1). Such rights also occasionally extended to women. Elisa de Villers, author and translator of a number of titles in the 1870s and 1880s, signed a contract in 1871 for a translation of a children's book, *Les souliers de mon voisin*, which guaranteed that "cette traduction portera mon nom" [the translation will bear my name] (HTZ 9.35). What her work lacked in literary capital she made up for in social status as daughter of a baron, wife of a general, and a lifelong friend of literary luminaries such as Nodier, Lamartine, Victor Hugo, and Sainte-Beuve (Grenier 1888: 29).

Social capital certainly put translators into a stronger negotiating position, enabling some to enforce their *droit de respect*. In February 1886, François d'Albert-Durade (1804–6) wrote to the Paris publisher Victor Cherbuliez that he had permission to translate *Scenes of Clerical Life* not only from George Eliot, but also from her husband. After d'Albert-Durade's death in June of the same year, his son wrote to the publishers that "Aucune suppression ou modification ne sera faite au manuscrit du 2e volume des Scènes d'une vie ecclésiastique dont les épreuves doivent être soumises au signataire de la présente, avant le tirage définitif" [No suppressions or modifications may be made to the manuscript of the second volume of *Scènes d'une vie ecclésiastique* whose proofs must be shown to the signatory of the present letter, prior to printing] (HAC 4.2). Similarly, when in 1870 Pierre Hallays-Dabot (who made a point of including his status as *chef d'institution honoraire* and *chevalier de la légion d'honneur* in his contract) sold his rights to a translation of Cicero to Hachette, he authorised only minimal corrections (HAC 32.11).

The sole moral right that is not found in incipient form in nineteenth-century translator correspondence and contracts is the most rarely used of the four, the *droit de repentir*. This is unsurprising given that "ce n'est que dans quelques conflits peu nombreux et assez particuliers que ce principe a été affirmé" [the principle has been only affirmed in a handful of rather unusual cases] (Strömholm 1966: 121), none of which happened to involve translation. One modern legal theorist has in fact described the *droit de repentir* as "une fantaisie de théoricien" [a theorist's fantasy] (Recht 1969: 145), while Binctin (2013: 308) points out it is largely symbolic, has very rarely been used since its cost is prohibitive (publishers are entitled to be reimbursed for work withdrawn from the market), and could easily be abolished.

While the translators in the preceding paragraphs were able to bring various permutations of social, intellectual, and literary capital to bear on their contractual negotiations with publishers, many translators signed contracts that paid little or no heed to the developing legal discourse on moral rights or even, in some cases, actively flouted the law. Such contracts gave the lie to the legally established principle of translatorship as authorship, at least for those participants in the field unable or unwilling to leverage much translatorial agency. To give just a few examples, William Hughes, a prolific translator of authors including Dickens and Thackeray, signed a contract in 1857 that denied him both the *droit de respect* and the *droit de paternité*:

> Il a été parfaitement compris et convenu avec Messieurs Hachette … 2. Qu'il pourra modifier ma traduction comme il le jugera à propos; 3. Qu'il sera libre d'indiquer ou de ne pas indiquer ma collaboration sur le titre du volume et dans la préface qui sera mise en tête des *Oeuvres* de Dickens.
>
> [It is perfectly understood and agreed with Messrs. Hachette … 2. That he may alter my translation as he sees fit; 3. That he will be free to indicate or not to indicate my collaboration on the title of the volume and the preface to Dickens's *Works*.]
>
> (HAC 41.15)

The "he" in this instance was Paul Lorain, who, as we have seen, *was* able to ensure his own *droit de paternité* as editorial coordinator, usurping the translator's visibility.

Translators in those corners of the field most associated with low agency struggled to assert their rights even once France had signed the Berne Convention in 1886. Marguerite de Lahaye, a translator of children's literature who lived in Vannes, Brittany, signed away her *droit de divulgation* in 1893: "Il est entendu que M. M. J. Hetzel et Cie seront seuls juges de l'époque à laquelle cette publication pourra être faite" [It is agreed that M. M. J. Hetzel and co. will alone judge when the publication is to come out] (HTZ 4.1). Similarly, a Mlle J. Florimond was deprived of her

106 *Professional Translators in Nineteenth-Century France*

droit de paternité in 1901, unfairly stripping her of a source of income, as she wrote to Charles Bernard Derosne:

> Monsieur, En me présentant cette semaine à la librairie Hachette pour réclamer les droits résultant de la publication en volume de Jouets du Destin, j'ai été fort surprise d'apprendre que vous en aviez touché la totalité. Je pouvais croire, en vous allouant les 2/3 des droits d'auteur – sur un travail que j'ai fait en entier, qui n'a été accepté que sur ma présentation et dont je reçois encore aujourd'hui les épreuves à corriger – vous avoir fait la part assez belle pour éviter toute contestation.
>
> [Sir, When I came to the Hachette bookshop this week to claim the rights to the book publication of *Les Jouets du Destin*, I was very surprised to learn that you had been paid the full rights. I believed that by granting you 2/3 of the *droits d'auteur* – on a book I translated entirely, which was only accepted because I presented it, and whose proofs I received today – I had given you a fair enough share to avoid any challenge.]
>
> (HAC 21.2)

It is worth noting that Dorothea Gerard's *Les Jouets du Destin* is listed in the Bibliothèque nationale de France catalogue, but a search for J. Florimond returns no results. A search for Charles Bernard Derosne as author/translator, on the other hand, returns 275 hits.

While Marguerite de Lahaye and J. Florimond had the disadvantages of low status and low agency in gender, language pair, and literary genre, it is fair to say that social status did not always map neatly onto translatorial agency. Irish-born and French-raised William Hughes (1822–87), for instance, was chief clerk in the foreign press department at the Ministry of the Interior in Paris (Alger 1891: 191). As a prolific translator with over 70 books to his name, his seeming lack of concern for his moral rights may paradoxically reflect a highly professional outlook rooted in a business-minded attitude to translation practice rather than a more authorial identity. Conversely, the contract signed by Justin Corrard (1822–66), a teacher in Versailles, points to a more amateur, temporary presence in the translation field. Corrard was a friend of the literary critic Désiré Nisard, who later became *maître de conferences* [i.e. lecturer] at the *Ecole normale supérieure* (*Mémorial* 1877: 219). He signed a relatively well-paid contract to translate Schiller serially in 1857, but in so doing agreed that Hachette would retain the right to drop the publication whenever they saw fit, have a third party alter his work at will, and leave his name out of the book altogether (HAC 10.20). Like J. Florimond, Justin Corrard does not feature in the BnF catalogue, nor do the *Opuscules esthétiques* he was contracted to translate, suggesting the

Developing a Legal Framework 107

project came to naught.[16] Though Corrard was not low in agency *per se* in terms of social status, his fleeting presence in the field suggests he did not develop a translatorial self-image of the sort that would incite him to push for full authorial recognition.

* * *

So why were some translators in a better position than others when it came to asserting their moral rights? Or, to take a slightly different angle, why did some simply *care* more about them than others? On the first side of the equation, the response seems relatively straightforward: only authors in a relatively strong symbolic and social position were able to negotiate with their publishers over their implicit moral rights. The evidence on the other side of the equation – translators who were *not* able to avail themselves of incipient moral rights – is perhaps more complex, reflecting three distinct stances. First are translators such as Marguerite de Lahaye whose profile places them squarely in the low-agency, high-competition sector of the translation field. Then comes a figure like William Hughes, whose relatively high social capital and ongoing presence in the field are perhaps countered by the low literary and linguistic capital of the projects he worked on, and whose seeming lack of concern for moral rights despite his perennial presence in the field might hint at a highly professionalised "humdrum input" self-image of the sort explored in Chapter 5 (Caves 2000); translation was secondary to his primary professional identity as a civil servant. Then there is Justin Corrard, who worked on projects rich in literary capital from a position of high social status but who seemingly remained an amateur whose fleeting presence in the field meant he had no time to develop a translatorial self-image. He simply had no feel for the game.

Consequently, there seems to be a clear correlation between symbolic and social capital and the ability to impose moral rights, but less correlation between symbolic and social capital and the *failure* to impose moral rights. As the aforementioned examples show, the respect of the translator's moral rights was unequally distributed in line with the symbolic and social capital enjoyed by the individual translator, which impacted their agency in negotiating with publishers. All those who were able to induce publishers to respect their moral rights did so from a position of some strength, either because they brought some other form of intellectual consecration to bear on their translation work or because they were part of

16 The contract stipulates that Corrard's work was to be changed at will by Régnier, no doubt Adolphe Régnier whose name does appear on a number of Schiller translations in the latter half of the nineteenth century, though none under the title given in the contract.

108 *Professional Translators in Nineteenth-Century France*

a well-placed social network. On the other hand, those translators who were not in a position to defend, or were uninterested in, their moral rights seem to have enjoyed little in the way of symbolic or social capital, or perhaps lacked investment in the idea of translatorship as authorship. In some cases, nothing is known about them. We may rail against Charles Bernard Derosne's exploitative business practices at over a century's remove, but Miss J. Florimond's first name, let alone details of her translatorial career and self-image, remains a mystery.[17] History has its limits.

17 An Emelie Julia Florimond born in 1843 and a Jeanne Florimond born in 1867 are listed on http://www.familysearch.com (accessed 11 May 2023). The latter seems the more likely candidate though it cannot be confirmed. If it is Jeanne, she was born in Chissey-en-Morvan in rural eastern France to Joseph Florimond and Claudine Baroin. She left no other traceable records.

5 The Economic Lives of Nineteenth-Century Women Translators

The outbreak of the Covid pandemic in 2020 wrought economic havoc worldwide. The literary translation sector was no exception. In France, where the sector is relatively professionalised with around 6,000 practitioners paying into a specific social security regime on the basis of their literary translation income,[1] the *Association des Traducteurs Littéraires de France* (ATLF) conducted a survey of members in June and July 2020, shortly after the first lockdown. It revealed that to date, some 33 per cent of respondents had seen contracts delayed and 66 per cent had not signed any new contracts since the start of the outbreak:[2] the average loss to the translators was 5,400 euros, not including income from subsidiary activities such as readings and workshops.[3] In the longer term, respondents expressed concerns about declining rates of pay and proportional rights and losing visibility in a crowded marketplace as publications were delayed or cancelled and translators were forced to leave the field for other forms of employment. They were right to be concerned: a 2022 Culture Ministry report calculated that the translation for publishing sector dropped by as much as 33 per cent in May 2020.[4]

As was the case in many other sectors during the pandemic (OECD 2021), many of the workers in literary translation who were worst affected

---

1 The figure for 2010 was 5,880 translators known to the AGESSA social security system, with around 2,000 of those meeting the minimum income threshold for professional status: see https://www.sgdl.org/%20ressource/%20documentation-sgdl/actes-des-forums/la-traduction-litteraire/1519-les-chiffres-de-la-traduction-par-geoffroy-pelletier (accessed 17 April 2023). The social security system changed on 1 January 2020, meaning more up-to-date figures are currently unavailable.

2 See https://fill-livrelecture.org/wp-content/uploads/2021/05/ENQUETE-CRISE-SANITAIRE-2-copie.pdf (accessed 13 April 2023).

3 See https://atlf.org/wp-content/uploads/2020/06/ENQUE%CC%82TE_ATLT_CONFINEMENT_04_2020.pdf (accessed 13 April 2023).

4 See https://fill-livrelecture.org/wp-content/uploads/2022/04/CE-2022-1_Crise-sanitaire-dans-le-secteur-culturel-corpus-web.pdf, p. 31 (accessed 13 April 2023).

DOI: 10.4324/9781003173090-6

110 *Professional Translators in Nineteenth-Century France*

by the crisis were women. The sector is heavily feminised: 78.8 per cent of the 245 respondents to the ATLF survey were women. Of the 20 respondents who applied for government-mandated leave to look after minor children during lockdown, 14 were turned down, though it was ostensibly a legal entitlement.[5] However, some help was forthcoming as state institutions quickly began to take over from the market, and by June 2020, 80 translators had received emergency funding from the *Centre National du Livre* to the total tune of 165,549 euros.[6]

While the long-term impact of the pandemic on women's careers across the board, let alone in translation, will play out in the coming years and decades, the facts and figures of the initial crisis and government response do shed light on one under-explored aspect of translatorial experience: the *economic* lives of translators, particularly as they intersect with issues of professional status. The preceding chapters have drawn on a sociological definition of professionalism, outlined notably by Milan (2021). This chapter seeks to expand that definition by incorporating approaches inspired by cultural economics of the sort developed in Caves (2000), Benhamou (2003), and Menger (2006). As demonstrated in previous chapters, literary translator careers have never lain outside the market and have never been immune to economic mechanisms: a decision to specialise in the literary sector has always come with an opportunity cost, for instance, as translators would typically have been able to use their language skills more profitably in other business sectors.[7]

The economics of authorship has been the focus of scholarly and industry research since at least the 1930s (Davis 1940). William Jackson Lord opened his study of American freelance writers at mid-century with the (pessimistic but accurate) observation that successful writing careers require "freedom from concern about regular income" (1962: v) – a statement that will resonate with many contemporary practitioners. In recent years, book history has produced impressive studies by Batchelor (2005)

---

5 https://fill-livrelecture.org/wp-content/uploads/2021/05/ENQUETE-CRISE-SANITAIRE-2 -copie.pdf (accessed 13 April 2023).

6 See https://fill-livrelecture.org/wp-content/uploads/2021/01/Bilan-plan-durgence-CNL-au -30-juin-2020.pdf (accessed 13 April 2023).

7 Similarly, translators have tended to cluster in industry-specific locales such as London and Paris, not only to build the networks that are the bread and butter of sociological studies but also by the logic of economic agglomeration: when workers and related industries cluster together in urban centres, opportunities for cost savings and increased income arise (Bille and Schulze 2006: 1087). For instance, budding translators are potentially able to leverage their physical proximity to gatekeepers to speed up the apprentice stage and increase their chances of making it through the selection process (Caves 2000: 25).

The Economic Lives of Women Translators 111

and Sangster (2021), among others. However, the economics of translation, let alone translatorship, has drawn little attention.[8]

This chapter sketches out some facets of the artistic labour market of literary translation for women in nineteenth-century France. In so doing, it responds to two very different research traditions in translation while seeking to lay some of the groundwork for a third. It builds on a long-term body of research outside the academy into professional translator status in France, seeking to extend it diachronically; it also embraces the recent trend in (literary) translator studies of taking a holistic view of translators, who are viewed not solely through the lens of their profession but as rounded human beings with their own unique "being-in-the-world" (Kaindl 2021: 22). Looking at their individual or family income streams means digging deep into the archives to uncover details such as births, marriages, and deaths; it is therefore one way of responding to Anthony Pym's call to humanise translation history (2009). It invites further research into matters of money in translators' lives, past and present – contracts, passive income from rights, prize winnings, and so on. Understanding the economic lives of translators past sheds further light on the structures underpinning the literary translation field, as explored in Chapter 3. It also offers a means of studying the economic role of literary translation and translators within the business of French publishing (Chartier and Martin 1990b; Mollier 1988). As in Chapter 3, many of the structures explored in this chapter in the context of nineteenth-century France will chime with today's translators.[9]

---

8 Robinson (2023), whose own approach is on the economics of translatorial behaviour during the translation process itself, provides a brief overview of what little work has been conducted on the topic, including a handful of studies exploring descriptive studies of rates of pay, the economics of translation as a commodity, translation as a labour market, and signalling mechanisms in a market characterised by information asymmetry (Robinson 2023: 1). As Robinson's own book suggests, the topic is beginning to draw interest, with the publication of a 2022 special issue of *Translation Matters* on the topic of "Translation and Money" featuring articles on translation, money, and the ecological turn; the translation of Syrian banknotes; and translation as intimate erotic labour. The journal *Parallèles* also published a number of issues on the socio-economics of literary translation in 2023, with studies of translators in Hungary, Turkey, China, and elsewhere.

9 To take just one example, in 2021, the *Centre National du Livre* handed 24 French translators grants totalling 165,000 euros, subsidised French publishers of translations by a further 1,163,124 euros, and funded translations of French works into other languages to the tune of 635,737 euros. See https://centrenationaldulivre.fr/donnees-cles/bilan-des-aides-2021 (accessed 13 April 2023). Without such institutional cash injections, far fewer books would be translated and far fewer translators would be able to lay claim to professional status in the publishing sector.

112   *Professional Translators in Nineteenth-Century France*

The Tradition of Collective Translator Profile Research in France

As demonstrated in Chapter 2, literary translation was regularly framed as a form of labour until roughly the mid-nineteenth century – a strand of discourse that returned in the 1970s with the establishment of the ATLF in 1973. A body of industry- and ministry-sponsored research into collective literary translator profiles arose in response, beginning in the early 1980s. Such research is part of the long French tradition of state-sponsored cultural policy, reaching back to the establishment of such august institutions as the Collège de France in 1530 and the Comédie Française in 1680.

France has long imported and exported high percentages of books in translation. In terms of *extraduction* [translation out of French], it has been a leading language for translation in Europe for centuries: in the period 1770–89, some 400 works were translated from French to English, compared to around 625 original English prose titles (Gillespie 2005: 124).[10] In terms of *intraduction* [translation into French], according to Blaise Wilfert's detailed bibliometric study, translated novels accounted for 29.6 per cent of French output in 1816 and as much as 41.5 per cent in 1830. The percentages are lower than those quoted by Gillespie but the raw numbers were far higher, with a total of 495 translated novels in a sample taken every third year for the period 1818–39, reflecting a fast expanding (albeit fluctuating) marketplace (Wilfert 2012: 268).[11] This created a volume of work large enough to sustain a pool of translators who were aware of the advantages of the collective defence of working conditions as early as 1837, when the *Société des gens de lettres* [Society of men of letters] was founded to defend writers' interests collectively (Montagne 1889).

The series of membership surveys conducted by the ATLF spanning the period 1983–2020 can be read against this long-standing backdrop of the awareness of literary translators as a collective socio-professional grouping, explored in Chapter 2. The earliest survey, outlined in Heinich (1984), laid the groundwork for the subsequent enquiries by adopting an overtly Weberian approach to the definition of professionalisation, identifying a range of positions between the twin poles of art and waged employment, "dilettantisme" and "professionnalisme" (Heinich 1984: 265–6). The practitioners she surveys define themselves at various points along the

---

10 Around 400 French titles were published in the USA in 2022. See https://villa-albertine .org/professionals/2022-translation-sneak-peek-0 (accessed 24 May 2023).

11 It should, however, be noted that the figures fluctuated significantly from year to year. France currently imports around 18 per cent of foreign titles for its home market, around 12,500 titles annually, of which around 60 per cent are from English. See https://www .culture.gouv.fr/Thematiques/Livre-et-lecture/Actualites/Chiffres-cles-du-secteur-du-livre -2017-20182 (accessed 24 May 2023).

The Economic Lives of Women Translators   113

continuum from artists to what Caves (2000) prosaically terms "humdrum inputs". She focused on characteristics including sex, age, remuneration, and translation as a proportion of overall income. In 1983, the best part of a decade after the ATLF's establishment, 38 per cent of the 132 respondents earned over half their income from literary translation, with 29 per cent counting as "full-timers" earning 70 per cent of income from it – a few dozen individuals. Interestingly, the association was majority male (54 per cent) at this point, a proportion that has reversed significantly in more recent surveys as the profile of respondents expanded (Heinich 1984: 270). By 2020, women accounted for 79.5 per cent of members (Guillon 2020: 3), while 45 per cent of the 335 respondents counted as full-timers by Heinich's definition, a significant increase both proportionately and numerically. Of Guillon's 375 respondents – who can be presumed to be at the most highly professionalised end of the amateur/professional continuum – just 20 per cent derived their entire income from literary translation. For the clear majority, a diversity of income streams, mainly from teaching, research, writing, and other forms of translation, remains a necessity (Guillon 2020: 4). While it would be impossible to conduct such a fine-grained analysis of nineteenth-century translator cohorts at this historical remove, the patterns identified by these surveys are broadly similar to the findings of Chapter 3 based on translator archives, suggesting a deep-seated continuity in the place of literary translation within the artistic labour market, explored below.

The surveys, and the cohort findings outlined in Chapters 3 and 4, indeed tend to bear out the observations by Menger (2006). Artistic labour markets have a number of typical features:

> The now dominant project-based system of production, with its functional need for flexibility, relies on short-term assignments. Large parts of the business risk are transferred down onto the workforce in vertically disintegrated organizational settings. Artists and technical workers act mainly as contingent workers, freelancers and independent contractors; labor supply is patterned by repeated and discontinuous alternations between work and unemployment, and workers cycle between multiple jobs inside and outside the arts … On the supply side, the attractiveness of artistic occupations has to be balanced against the risk of failure that turns ideally non-routine jobs into ordinary or ephemeral undertakings. Learning by doing plays such a decisive role that in many artforms initial training is an imperfect filtering device.
>
> (Menger 2006: 766)

Many of the unsung nineteenth-century translators whose careers are outlined in the appendix would surely have recognised the description of a

114 *Professional Translators in Nineteenth-Century France*

typical career in the literary sector as characterised by instability, part-time, temporary, and fixed-term contracts, second jobs, and self-employment. Artists typically work discontinuously, on plural time-bound concurrent and/or subsequential projects. Reputation correlates strongly with employability; diplomas are relatively weak signalling mechanisms, with experience and reputation much more significant.[12] As a result, success in artistic careers is something of a lottery: the prospects of reaching the top are slim, and many entrants eventually leave the field for less risky, more stable careers. These features were recognised by Adam Smith in *The Wealth of Nations*, which notes that the wages and profits of given trades depend on five characteristics:

> first, the agreeableness or disagreeableness of the employments themselves; secondly, the easiness and cheapness, or the difficulty and expence [sic] of learning them; thirdly, the constancy or inconstancy of employment in them; fourthly, the small or great trust which must be reposed in those who exercise them; and, fifthly, the probability or improbability of success in them.
>
> (Smith 1776: 146)

All five characteristics are applicable to the translator cohorts described in Chapters 3 and 4 to some extent. The first leads to an oversupply of aspiring artists, bringing down remuneration levels, as experienced by translators in the crowded marketplace for popular English fiction in the nineteenth century. The second applies to translation, where the economic barrier to entry is low, more than to some other art forms, enabling women to enter the practice in significant numbers. The third is typical of artistic careers, though not necessarily an inherent feature: waged positions for artists, and indeed literary translators, do exist, though they are few and far between.[13] The fourth also applies given the information asymmetry inherent in the relationship between client and service provider in the translation market (Walker 2023). The fifth has been amply theorised as the "winner takes all" market model (Frank and Cook 2010). The risk inherent in such competitive careers may exclude naturally talented individuals from more

---

12 On signalling mechanisms in the translation market, see also Chan (2008), Chan et al. (2014), and Lambert and Walker (2022).

13 Orchestral musicians, for instance, often earn regular salaries (Menger 2006: 773). Literary translators were employed by the state in some Communist regimes: see Popa (2010). The London-based publisher Gallic Books also regularly hires literary translators who combine translation with in-house editorial duties: see https://belgraviabooks.com/diary -of-an-in-house-translator-or-5-things-ive-learned-about-translation (accessed 21 April 2023).

precarious backgrounds who cannot afford to wait for stability in their careers.

The Ministering Hand of the State

This chapter now turns to an examination of the careers of two nineteenth-century women translators briefly encountered in previous chapters, Louise Swanton-Belloc and Emma Allouard, seeking to determine the extent to which their economic lives echo those of their twentieth- and twenty-first-century colleagues in the ATLF. The next sections draw on institutional and personal archives to try to flesh out a description of these two nineteenth-century translators as workers in a two-speed artistic labour market – one subject to state intervention, the other left to the free hand of the market. The life of the first of the two translators, Louise Swanton-Belloc (1796–1881), is relatively well documented, particularly in Lepouchard (1994). Her work has been studied most recently by Ingelbien (2020), studying her role in the diffusion of Irish writing in nineteenth-century France. This section will focus on what we can glean from the archives about her economic role within her family and her life as a worker in the translatorial labour market.

In fact Swanton-Belloc and her husband, the artist Jean-Hilaire Belloc (1786–1866), were both active within the nineteenth-century French arts economy, each occupying different positions. Jean-Hilaire was born into a wealthy family with money from the sugar trade; as a man of independent means, he was able to shoulder the risk inherent in attempting to enter the artistic labour market outlined above. Accordingly, he started his career as an independent arts worker, choosing a ticket in the "lottery prize" artistic labour market (Caves 2000: 57). He did in fact enjoy some success, producing prize-winning genre paintings of historical and religious subjects. However, as Benhamou (2003: 72) points out, the propensity for risk-taking is higher at a younger age, when economic uncertainty is easier to face for many people. By the 1810s, the Belloc family faced financial ruin from the British sugar blockade in the West Indies (Lepouchard 1994: 20), doubtless making the prospect of an economically risky career less palatable. He eventually married Louise Swanton – after a lengthy delay for financial reasons, among others (Lepouchard 1994: 21) – in June 1821, and the couple had three children, born in 1822, 1828, and 1830. His new-found family responsibilities doubtless had a hand in altering his attitude to the economic risk inherent in genre subject painting – a typically discontinuous, project-based undertaking highly predicated on individual reputation – as he sought a more stable source of income, taking on a teaching role at the imperial drawing school. He eventually became its director in 1831, appointed by Madame Adélaïde, the king's sister, after Louise was presented to her (Lepouchard 1994: 36). This provided the family with a

116 *Professional Translators in Nineteenth-Century France*

steady income and free lodgings in the heart of Paris, at 5 rue de l'école de medecine (Beecher Stowe 1861: 486). Art school administration was regular but not spectacularly lucrative work, and though devoted to his students by Beecher Stowe's account, he did not die a wealthy man, leaving his three children 895 francs – around 4,250 euros in today's money – in his will in 1866.[14]

Accordingly, Louise's income from translation was no doubt a welcome addition to the household budget, as was her unpaid labour in caring for various members of the extended family – not only her own children, but also her aunt, her chronically ill brother, and her sister-in-law Jenny (Lepouchard 1994: 168–9). As seen in Chapter 4, Louise began translating at a young age. She, too, came from a family of former wealth that now found itself in relatively straitened circumstances as a result of the Revolution; her father had only a small military pension, and she was married without a dowry (Lepouchard 1994: 16, 21). Translation was thus a useful source of income in a family beset by financial worries: an undated letter on headed notepaper dating from the 1820s to her close friend Adélaïde de Montgolfier refers to an ongoing claim against her for rent she claims not to owe (GCPP Parkes 17a|1|2|2).[15] Clearly, as a woman, the options for entering the workforce were limited for Louise. Living by the pen and, specifically, translation was one of the handful of choices a woman could make without moral censure (Williams 2010). As a derivative, ancillary form of creativity, it escaped the censure that came with, as Adam Smith put it,

> some very agreeable and beautiful talents of which the possession commands a certain sort of admiration; but of which the exercise for the sake of gain is considered, whether from reason or prejudice, as a sort of publick [sic] prostitution.
>
> (Smith 1776: 156)

Translation may have been considered a suitably feminine occupation, but as Chapter 3 demonstrated, Louise developed a hard-nosed business attitude to her practice: in Heinich's terms, she took up a position that was closer to the pole of an "idéologie professionnelle" (Heinich 1984: 278) than of *diléttantisme*, with its pursuit of symbolic rather than economic

---

14 See https://www.historicalstatistics.org/Currencyconverter.html (accessed 17 April 2023).

15 The in-text archival references are to the Bessie Rayner Parkes archive at Girton College, Cambridge. In particular, see "Papers of Louise Swanton Belloc, 1654–1993", which is available at https://archivesearch.lib.cam.ac.uk/repositories/19/archival_objects/371175 (accessed 6 March 2023). Bessie Rayner Parkes was married to Louise Swanton-Belloc's son Louis; she was the mother of the poet Hilaire Belloc, Louise's grandson.

The Economic Lives of Women Translators   117

capital. There is evidence, for instance, that she tried to increase her own productivity by studying shorthand (letter to M. Lucas de Montigny, dated 11 June 1833) and negotiated her income based on her own labour time and reputation:

> [j]e viens d'écrire directement à M. Buckingham, et joins ici ma lettre que je vous prie de bien vouloir parcourir avant de la lui envoyer. Vous y verrez que j'ai fait un changement dans les conditions; en y réfléchissant, je l'ai jugé indispensable ... Mon premier calcul avait été basé sur la traduction entière, dont il me parlait dans sa lettre. Quelques feuilles seulement exigeraient tout autant de dérangement et de recherche que pour traduire l'ouvrage entier: de plus, c'est nécessairement <u>un ouvrage sans nom</u>, il y a un manuscrit à déchiffrer, un sujet à approfondir et à étudier car je ne sais pas, même comme traducteur, aborder des questions sans y avoir pénétré un peu avant; enfin, je crois pouvoir dire que la conscience que j'apporte à mes travaux me les rend plus difficiles et plus compliqués qu'ils ne le sont pour la plupart de mes confrères. Je ne sais pas me contenter d'à peu près, et c'est une disposition dont je dois me méfier en affaire d'argent et qui m'a souvent rendu onéreux des marchés fort beaux en apparence.

> [I have just written to M. Buckingham directly and am enclosing my letter: please read it before forwarding it. You will see I have changed the conditions: thinking it over, I found it indispensable ... My initial calculation was based on the whole translation discussed in his letter. A few sheets would require as much effort and research as the whole book: and since it is necessarily a work without a name, there is a manuscript to decipher, a subject to look into and study, since I cannot, even as a translator, talk about issues without researching them beforehand a little; and what is more, I think I can say that the pains I take with my work makes it harder and more complicated than for most of my colleagues. I cannot be satisfied with slapdash work, a characteristic I must mistrust in matters of money and one that has often cost me dearly in deals that looked highly appealing.]

> (Undated letter to Jullien *père*, emphasis in the
> original)

Like the majority of Guillon's respondents, translation was not Louise's sole source of income. She combined it with a range of authorial practices including writing, criticism, and editing. She was a prolific contributor to the *Revue encyclopédique* and in 1836 launched a pioneering distance learning magazine for children, *La Ruche*. She also wrote a number of books for children. This portfolio of different activities, a typical artistic bet-spreading strategy to maximise income streams, proved crucial to the

118 *Professional Translators in Nineteenth-Century France*

long-term stability of the family's finances. Where income from translation was project-based, with no provision for ongoing royalties, her authorial practice as a writer of moral works for children brought her valuable attention from the authorities in two ways. First of all, she had contacts at the Ministère de l'Instruction Publique to whom she could pitch projects that would, if accepted, bring her guaranteed sales. For instance, on 1 February 1833, she wrote to an unnamed ministry contact offering to produce French versions of Harriet Martineau's *Ella of Garveloch* and *The Hill and the Valley*, framed in her description as useful works of political economy. If the project were to be accepted by the Ministry, she goes on to ask, how many copies would the university take? If the order were sufficiently large, she could find economies of scale in the printing process.

Secondly, and more importantly, she was able to benefit from targeted funding for creatives deemed worthy of government support, providing the family with a significant passive income stream that smoothed the peaks and troughs of income from translation contracts, allowing Louise to maintain her place in the field where others without recourse to state funding were forced out. Over the longer term, this enabled her to benefit from the process whereby job allocation is distributed unequally according to the accumulation of skills and reputation: "experienced and network-building artists and workers are frequently hired and face less discontinuous employment than beginners and individuals only loosely connected with the most active entrepreneurs" (Menger 2006: 778) (Figure 5.1).

Annual stipends for artists were a relatively recent development in French state cultural policy, reflecting a shift from the purely individual patronage model of the *ancien régime* towards a more institutional model of state support for the arts in what has been called "sans doute l'un des tous [sic] premiers gestes de la puissance publique en matière de culture" [doubtless one of the very earliest actions of the public authorities in terms of culture] (Négrier 2017: 1). When Louise first received her stipend in 1832, the move towards transparency and accountability in state spending on the arts was a recent innovation: the "indemnités littéraires" in the king's gift had been made public in the budget of 1830. Questioned in a parliamentary debate about the secretive nature of royal spending on the arts, a government representative acknowledged the need for transparency and stated that under 24,000 francs went to "[des] littérateurs âgés qui se trouvent dans l'infortune" [elderly men of letters fallen on hard times], though as it turned out most were being rewarded for supporting the monarchy (Roch 1830: 357 and 286).

The archives in fact show that both Louise (then in her mid-30s) and Jean-Hilaire were among the so-called "littérateurs âgés" to benefit from this funding stream. A little over a decade into her lengthy career, she began receiving an annual "indemnité littéraire", or stipend, of 500 francs,

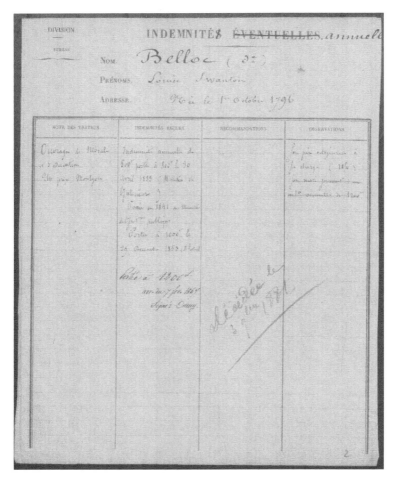

Figure 5.1 Official record of Louise Swanton-Belloc's literary stipend, noting her death in 1881. Image courtesy of the *Archives nationales*, Pierrefitte-sur-Seine.

gradually rising over the decades to reach 1,200 francs in 1867.[16] Jean-Hilaire also received 1,200 francs annually before his death (F_17_3116_Belloc_2). At 2,400 francs,[17] the couple's combined income from stipends in the 1860s was well over the amount Hilaire bequeathed his family on

---

16 See file F_17_3116_2_Belloc at the *Archives nationales*.
17 According to https://www.historicalstatistics.org/Currencyconverter.html, 500 francs in 1832 is equivalent to 3,688 euros, and 2,400 francs in 1865 is equivalent to 11,704 euros in 2015, the most recent year for which conversion is available (accessed 12 June 2024).

120 *Professional Translators in Nineteenth-Century France*

his death in 1866. It also compared favourably with an average working man's wages: in 1862, farm hands typically earned a daily wage of 2.77 francs (Levasseur 1909: 414), while an iron puddler would bring home 90 francs a month (Chevallier 1887: 59).

The archives record that Louise's grant was renewed annually in recognition of her contribution to society by writing educational works. Yet paradoxically, the funding was linked to the family's overall income, in which her financial contribution via her writing labour was overlooked. In a statement that reveals much about attitudes to women's labour at the time, a police report into the Belloc family finances as "pensionnaires de l'état" [recipients of a state grant] concluded that they lived comfortably but had no other income than "les émoluments attachés à la place de M. Belloc" [the emoluments from M. Belloc's position, i.e. his headship at the art school] (F_17_3116_2_Belloc 16) (Figure 5.2).

Louise was required to present a "certificat de vie" signed at her local town hall every year, attesting that she had no other waged income or pension. Earnings from writing were apparently not taken into account in evaluating the family's need for support, presumably because of their inherent instability as an income stream.

The grant lasted until Louise's death at the age of 85, in late 1881: her family wrote on 28 April 1882 to inform the ministry of her passing the previous November (F_17_3116_2_Belloc 3). At the time of her death, she had enjoyed just under 50 years of financial support from the state for her writing career. The longevity of this support reflects – and no doubt shaped – the nature of her writing and translation work. As the author and translator largely of morally improving works for young readers, her work represented no threat to the state in an age of political turmoil. This in turn indicates the ambiguous nature of such funding for authors and translators in the nineteenth century: while it was moving away from the patronage model dependent on the individual whim of the purse-holder towards a state-led, cultural policy-driven model of greater accountability and transparency, the process was still subject to the vagaries of ministerial approval. Funding was ostensibly granted on grounds of need but could also be withdrawn if the recipient's political views were deemed unsuitable. Another translator who found this to her cost was the Saint-Simonian and early feminist Eugénie Niboyet (1796–1883), whose dates almost exactly coincide with those of Louise Swanton-Belloc. Niboyet, a translator of Dickens and Maria Edgeworth, was granted an "indemnité littéraire" in 1837 after a marital separation left her impoverished: she lost it in 1848 when she began printing the feminist daily *La voix des femmes* [*The Voice of Women*]. Though the publication was soon forced to close, leaving her with heavy debts, her indemnity was never reinstated despite her multiple appeals (Sullerot 1966: 91).

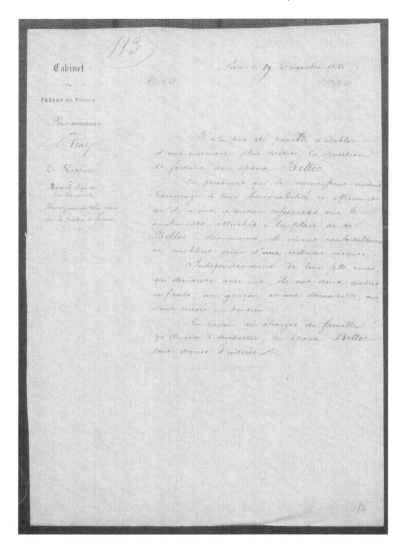

Figure 5.2 Police report into the Belloc family finances, 19 December 1856. Image courtesy of the *Archives nationales*, Pierrefitte-sur-Seine.

Keeping in the ministerial good books and receiving a literary stipend was a way for translators to achieve significant passive income, particularly if they combined their translatorial practice with other higher-profile forms of authorship as part of a portfolio career strategy. Yet it came with its own constraints in terms of state surveillance of family finances and, as Eugénie Niboyet found to her cost, acceptable political opinions and

122 *Professional Translators in Nineteenth-Century France*

topics. It did not work for everybody. For those who failed to attract positive ministerial attention through their writing (or perhaps chafed at the constraints it implied), the open marketplace offered more freedom – but less financial stability.

The Free Hand of the Market

This section turns to the career of a second, and less well-known, translator, Emma Allouard (1836–1918). Forty years younger than Louise Swanton-Belloc, she has vanished from literary history altogether. If she is remembered at all, it is by art historians who admire the portrait by her friend John Singer Sargent (c. 1882), on loan to the Metropolitan Museum of New York, showing a dark-haired woman in her forties, dressed in deep black with hooded eyes and a faint smile. Since so little is known of her, I will begin by outlining the coordinates of her life, gleaned from various archival sources including the genealogy websites ancestry.com, geneanet .org, and familysearch.org, the Paris city archives, and a file of her correspondence at the *Département des arts du spectacle* at the BnF.[18]

Emma Allouard was born Emma Cadiot in Autun on 1 February 1836. Her father Louis-Florian Cadiot was the town's *sous-préfet* and a journalist who regularly contributed to *Le National* (Schor 2022: 59).[19] Though little is known of Emma's early life, it may have borne some similarity to that of her older sister Marie-Noémi, later a well-known sculptress and early feminist better known by her adopted name of Claude Vignon. Marie-Noémi is known to have attended an exclusive boarding school near Paris, from which she eventually absconded with a teacher; she later became a member of Eugénie Niboyet's *Club des Femmes* and eventually married Maurice Rouvier, a minister in Jules Ferry's government (Schor 2022: 60). Emma married a bank clerk by the name of Pierre Allouard (1820–88) in Paris on 5 May 1859, when she was 23. He was 16 years her senior and had been married previously (to a woman named Elisabeth Chedeville in 1851). The couple's early married life was struck by tragedy as their two-year-old son Emile died in 1863, followed by the arrival of a stillborn child a year later in 1864. The death certificates for the children describe Emma as "sans profession". The couple moved regularly around Paris as Pierre Allouard regularly came into conflict with the courts over rent disputes. This was the period studied in more detail below, when Emma was in fact

---

18 The biographical note in the file of her correspondence at the *Département des Arts du Spectacle* at the BnF is inaccurate in a number of particulars. It gives a wholly incorrect date of birth, making her some 15 years younger than she was, and misattributes her family relationships: the sculptor Henri Allouard was her nephew by marriage, not her son.

19 See https://www.familysearch.org/ (accessed 26 April 2023).

The Economic Lives of Women Translators 123

earning a fairly regular income from translation: the first dated publication attributed to her in the BnF catalogue is from 1865, though we know from the evidence of the IMEC archives that she had begun her career a couple of years earlier.

There are few traces of Emma's private life in the archive through the 1860s and 1870s. A key event that no doubt shaped her life significantly is not recorded at all during this period, coming to light only in her husband's death record in 1888 and her own in 1918. When Pierre Allouard died in his late 60s, having risen to an eminently respectable position at the Banque Diplomatique, his death certificate recorded that he and Emma were divorced – a highly unusual event in nineteenth-century France, illegal until just four years before.[20] The exact date and cause of the couple's separation are not known, many of the relevant records having been destroyed in the Paris Commune. Tracing Emma's descendants in the archives, it seems likely that they had split up by the mid- to late 1860s: Emma's daughter Marguerite Eliette, traced via the birth certificate of Emma's grandson Jacques Feller,[21] was born in Lyon in August 1867. Though the story is somewhat murky at this point, it seems clear that Pierre Allouard was not the child's father. Nor, in fact, was Emma Allouard her birth mother, it seems: according to her birth certificate, Eliette (who went by her middle name) was born to an Emma Oberthal. She used her birth mother's surname until she married. No father was mentioned on her eventual marriage certificate to Paul Feller in 1889.[22] Even more confusingly, the only other trace of an Emma Oberthal is an 1849 death certificate, and

---

20 Divorce was outlawed in France for much of the nineteenth century. It was legalised in 1884, and the couple's official dissolution was registered at the 10th arrondissement town hall on 22 November 1886. It was an unusual choice: official statistics point to a divorce rate in 1885 of 14 per 1,000 marriages, with just 73 cases recorded in Paris between 1886 and 1900 (Yvernès 1908: 102). The grounds for divorce were all fault-based, including adultery, "peine afflictive ou infâmante" (cruel or degrading treatment), and "excès, sévices, injures graves" (outrageous behaviour, violence, and serious insults) (Bertillon 1884: 59). Statistically, it is highly likely that Emma, not Pierre, instigated the divorce, since 86 per cent of cases in 1884 were at the request of the wife (Brée 2022: 80). Interestingly, Emma's 1888 novel *Après...*, jointly authored with Marguerite Belin under the shared pseudonym Jouan-Rolland, was a moralistic tale of female adultery – a theme her sister also wrote on (Allen Harvey 2004: 568).

21 Emma's daughter is mentioned but not named in her correspondence in BnF Mn-1050. Emma's grandson, Jacques, was named repeatedly in her correspondence. He was born in 1890. See Jacques Feller's obituary at https://bbf.enssib.fr/consulter/bbf-1968-07-0325 -001 (accessed 1 May 2023).

22 Intriguingly, Emma Oberthal's own mother, Marguerite de Monbarron, had a surname that was very close to Emma Allouard's mother's maiden name, Zoé de Montbarbon, raising the spectre of a recording error in the archive and possible kinship.

124 *Professional Translators in Nineteenth-Century France*

Eliette had also married a Louis-César Charpillon in 1888.[23] Though legal adoption of Eliette as a newborn would not have been possible (Mignot 2015), informal adoption among family and friends was relatively common. Still, the precise nature of the relationship between Emma Allouard, her daughter Eliette, and her grandson Jacques (regularly named in her correspondence) remains somewhat mysterious. Nor is it known exactly at what age Eliette entered Emma's life, though it is clear that she was on the Paris social scene by the time she turned 20 at the latest, her first marriage being announced in *Le Figaro*.

On balance, it seems likely that Emma gave birth under an assumed name or took on an adoptive mothering role in the mid- to late 1860s. Whether or not this was the case, within a couple of years of her daughter's birth, she moved on from translation to become a novelist and playwright, often working in collaboration with other well-known writers and pitching her work to the Comédie française and Sarah Bernhardt. As early as 1873, she was using the double-barrelled surname Allouard-Jouan, though in the mid-1870s she was also still using Allouard on its own (for instance in her SACD application, discussed below). She also used Emile Jouan as a pen name. While Emile may have been inspired by the son she lost as a toddler, I have been unable to trace the source of the name Jouan: it does not appear to come from her own family tree. It can perhaps be hypothesised that it was the name of a partner.[24] Her correspondence reveals she lived alone in her later decades, spending much time in Aix-les-Bains; it also reveals a liaison with the author J. H. Rosny *aîné*. Interestingly, separation and divorce do not seem to have affected her social standing: when in Paris, Emma was clearly a society figure, as her Singer Sargent portrait makes clear. In 1885 she made the press for suing the clothes designer Charles Frederick Worth for publishing her name on a list of bad payers: she was awarded 1,000 francs in damages (*Petite Presse 1885*: unpaginated). By 1901, she was listed in the Paris address book as a "rentière", that is, living on unearned income (*Paris-Adresses* 1901: 104). Sadly, her correspondence, particularly

---

23 The marriage was listed in *Le Figaro* on 19 March 1888. Louis-César (1859–1925) was the son of Louis-Etienne Charpillon (1814–94); his mother Marie-Catherine was said to be an illegitimate daughter of Alexandre Dumas. See https://fr.wikipedia.org/wiki/Louis-%C3%89tienne_Charpillon (accessed 5 May 2023). Eliette was granted a pension as "veuve Feller" in 1915, listed in the Journal Officiel de la République Française. Louis-Paul-César Charpillon remarried Marie-Alice Dislère in 1891, as announced in *Le XIXe siècle* for 10 February: it is likely his marriage to Eliette was annulled.

24 The Cadiot family was no stranger to marital scandal: Emma's sister Marie-Noémi had absconded from school with a teacher she was forced to marry by her father, then left her husband for Alexandre de Montferrier in the early 1850s and had a son with the architect Hector Lefuel in 1859. See https://en.wikipedia.org/wiki/Marie-No%C3%A9mi_Cadiot (accessed 28 April 2023).

The Economic Lives of Women Translators   125

with the essayist Jacques de Boisjolin (1840–1914), suggests her declining years were difficult: she was plagued by illness, had a challenging relationship with her daughter and her son-in-law, received mysterious poison pen letters, and almost lost her grandson Jacques to tuberculosis. She maintained an interest in feminism and women's issues to the end of her life: in the 1890s, Rosny *aîné* poked fun at her "manie de pièces féministes" [mania for feminist plays], while in the early 1910s, she pitched articles on marriage in France since 1830 and women's suffrage to Boisjolin.

It is not known how Emma obtained her first translation contract: it may have been through her brother-in-law Antoine-Ignace Allouard (1815–91), a Paris bookseller. The fact that she began translating early in her married life when the couple were in financial trouble, as evidenced by her husband's multiple rental disputes and their repeated house moves, suggests the income was sorely needed to keep the household afloat. However she got her foot in the door, her first contracts translating children's adventure books and Wilkie Collins's *Armadale* proved the start of an income stream that lasted for the rest of the decade, albeit with wild fluctuations (Table 5.1).

Unlike Louise Swanton-Belloc, Emma Allouard's translatorial output (and indeed her later writing) was not of a nature to attract government support. Accordingly, she was at this early stage in her career entirely at the whim of the marketplace. In a crowded market for translators from English, outlined in Chapter 3, this was a vulnerable place to be, putting her in a less favourable negotiating position than Louise Swanton-Belloc. The 29 December 1867 contract for *The Adventures of a Griffin*, for instance, included a clause to the effect that missing her deadline of 29 February would cost her 100 francs a fortnight – out of a total pay packet of 300 francs (HTZ 1.4). Compared to the male translators in Chapter 3 who completed their projects *decades* late, this punishment for failing to keep up with a highly intense labour schedule seems draconian indeed. As it happens, the payment records in the Hetzel archive make it clear she did hit the deadline: she was paid in full on 20 March 1868. This is an

Table 5.1 Emma Allouard's Total Income from Translation in Francs, 1863–69

Year	Total Income from Translation (Francs)
1863	700
1864	1,800
1865	4,785
1866	1,980
1867	300
1868	1,300
1869	500

126 *Professional Translators in Nineteenth-Century France*

impressive achievement, especially considering that she may have been the sole parent of a four-month-old infant when she signed the contract. It is perhaps no coincidence that her income in 1867, the year her daughter was born, fell significantly and never recovered to the level it had been prior to motherhood.

The details of the Hetzel payment records shed further interesting light on Emma Allouard's position in the marketplace. She typically signed away her full rights to the projects she worked on, as was customary. Her 1863 contract for an unidentified text entitled *Les Petits échappés* stated that she was to receive 300 francs for selling the literary property in her translation to Hetzel outright (HTZ 1.4). Yet the Hetzel accounts show not a series of spaced lump-sum payments corresponding to the completion of individual projects, but an ongoing pattern of regular small payments (Figure 5.3, Table 5.2).

The monthly income for *Armadale* in 1864, corresponding to ongoing serial publication in English, reflects a model of payment akin to a monthly salary. Similarly, for *Les Nègres marrons*, she received six separate payments spaced from 30 September 1863 to 21 May 1864. This placed her closer to the professional "humdrum input" model of ongoing service provision rather than a typical arts economy model of the one-off contribution. Yet, as the fluctuations in annual income show, translation was hardly a reliable revenue source, particularly for a woman who may have been suffering marital difficulties and was undoubtedly grieving the loss of two children while perhaps parenting a very young third. In these circumstances, the "psychic income" (Menger 2006: 777) of enjoyable work may not have been enough to make up for fluctuating payments reliant on working under pressure at a breakneck pace. Marital difficulties would have exacerbated the difficulty of her financial position. As Menger further points out,

> [A]rtists may improve their economic situation in three main ways which are not incompatible and may be combined: artists can be supported by private sources (working spouse, family or friends) or by public sources (subsidies, grants and commissions from the state, sponsorship from foundations or corporations, and other transfer income from social and unemployment insurance); they can work in cooperative-like associations by pooling and sharing their income and by designing a sort of mutual insurance scheme; and finally they can hold multiple jobs.
>
> (Menger 2006: 794)

Again, the data is telling. There is a clear pattern of regular payments from 1863 to late 1866, pointing to a flourishing early career with plenty of ongoing work. Then in late 1866 comes a huge gap, with no income

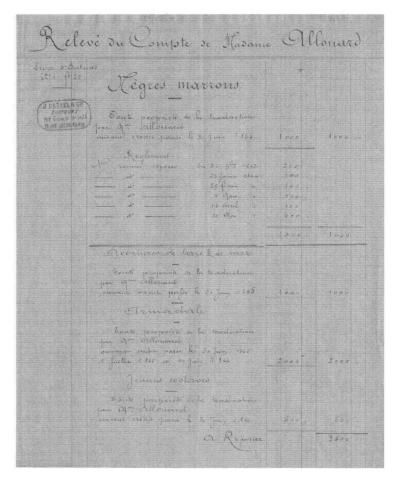

Figure 5.3 Hetzel account book for 1866, showing details of translation payments to Emma Allouard. Image courtesy of Archives Hetzel/IMEC.

from translation recorded for over a year. As seen above, the latter part of this period may correspond to Emma's early months of motherhood: late 1866 or early 1867 may correspond to her move from Paris to Lyon, where Eliette was born in August 1867. This suggests not only the impact on women's careers of motherhood (as experienced by the ATLF members denied leave to look after their children during the pandemic), but also possibly the risk of stepping away from the logic of agglomeration. The French literary publishing industry was heavily Paris-centric: by moving to Lyon, Emma may well have simply been dropped from the publishers'

128   *Professional Translators in Nineteenth-Century France*

Table 5.2 Monthly Breakdown of Emma Allouard's Translation Payments from the Hetzel Accounts, 1863–9

Date	Sum Received in Francs	Details of Project Where Known
15 June 1863	300	*Petits échappés*
30 September 1863	200	*Les Nègres marrons*
23 January 1864	100 + 100	*Aventures de terre et de mer*, Thomas Mayne Reid + *Les Nègres marrons*
29 February 1864	100 + 100	*Armadale*, Wilkie Collins + *Les Nègres marrons*
4 March 1864	100 + 100	*Armadale* + *Les Nègres marrons*
16 April 1864	100 + 100	*Armadale* + *Les Nègres marrons*
21 May 1864	400	*Les Nègres marrons*
30 September 1864	200	*Armadale*
2 January 1865	200	
February 1865	200	
March 1865	50	
18 April 1865	200	
2 June 1865	35	
30 June 1865	1000	*Aventures de terre et de mer*
30 July 1865	200	
18 August 1865	200	
16 September 1865	200	
17 April 1866	600	*Maisons de la Jamaïque*
20 July 1866	500	
12 September 1866	200	*Égarés dans la forêt*, Thomas Mayne Reid[25]
20 September 1866	180	
22 September 1866	200	
23 September 1866	100	
20 October 1866	200	*Afloat in the forest*, Thomas Mayne Reid
31 January 1868	100	
4 February 1868	100	
7 March 1868	100	
17 March 1868	300	
20 March 1868	300	*Adventures of a Griffin*, Harden S. Melville
12 May 1868	100	
8 September 1868	300	
28 April 1869	500	*Armadale*

25 This and the following are presumably the same title: no book is listed under the French title in the BnF catalogue.

regular roster of collaborators for practical reasons. Before the advent of electronic communications, it cost time and money to correspond with a translator several hundred kilometres away, which explains why as recently as Heinich's 1984 study, just 20 per cent of literary translators lived in the provinces (Heinich 1984: 279), compared to over half in 2020 (Guillon 2020: 3).

Working in popular fiction for children and adults and with a family set-up liable to fail government-mandated moral scrutiny, Emma had no recourse to public funds of the sort on offer to Louise Swanton-Belloc. Her complicated family circumstances meant she may not have had much access to private sources either. Logically enough, she turned to the second main way outlined above, apparently bringing her translation career to a close in the late 1860s and turning to other, more remunerative forms of authorship, writing novels, plays, and journal articles. These let her stake a claim in the "winner takes all" economy of successful authorship while also letting her apply to join a "cooperative-like association": the *Société des auteurs et compositeurs dramatiques* (SACD), founded in 1777 by Beaumarchais. While author-translators were admitted to the society, translators for the stage were not universally popular and their claim to share in the economic spoils of successful authorship not uncontroversial. The stage magazine *Le Ménéstrel* described them harshly in 1884 as "parasites de lettres qui vivent du bien d'autrui" [parasites on literature who live on other people's goods], going on to outline a recent instance in which the composer Camille Saint-Saëns had been forced to protect his international rights by reluctantly taking on the extra labour of issuing some ten translations; the SACD, *Le Ménestrel* concluded, "pourra sans doute intervenir dans bien des cas pour corriger, par des arrangements particuliers, les inconséquences que nos diplomates n'ont pas su éviter" [will doubtless be able to intervene in many cases with private arrangements to correct the illogicalities that our diplomats were unable to avoid] (*Ménestrel* 1885: 363).

Emma Allouard signed up to the SACD in June 1873. In the same session she was admitted, the committee appointed a working party to settle the long-standing issue of theatre contributions to a writer's *caisse sociale* [social support fund] once and for all (*Bulletin* 1876: 118). This opened up the possibility for her to benefit from a common feature of collective action in the arts economy: "income transfers and redistributions that may allow workers to adapt to more flexible and more unbalanced artistic labor markets" (Menger 2006: 797). In the longer term, the sort of sociability fostered by SACD membership proved key to her greater longevity in the field of authorship and playwriting, working in collaboration with others, as her correspondence amply demonstrates.

130 *Professional Translators in Nineteenth-Century France*

Conclusion

From the surviving archives, even at this historical remove, we can glean that the government-supported career of Louise Swanton-Belloc perfectly matches the definition of artists in the workplace: "Individuals learn to manage the risks of their trade through multiple jobholding, occupational role versatility, portfolio diversification of employment ties, and income transfers from public support, social insurance and social security programs" (Menger 2006: 766). As a result, she was able to maintain her position in the translation field for decades, in combination with other forms of authorship. Emma Allouard, on the other hand, seems to have left the field relatively soon, perhaps unable to negotiate the financial instability of an early career and preferring to invest her time and energy in an alternative form of authorship that would provide her with equal psychic income while increasing her chances of success in the "winner takes all" model but still offering the safety net of mutual insurance.

Louise Swanton-Belloc and Emma Allouard's divergent paths in the literary translation field point to the importance of further research into how economic circumstances dictate careers in this small corner of the arts economy. Alper and Wassall (2006: 815–18) offer a classification scheme for studying artists' careers, covering theoretical models of artistic career processes; exploiting extant anecdotal or quantitative data on a group of artists from a range of sources (the model used in this chapter); surveying artists to glean a retrospective view of their careers from interviews or questionnaires (the Heinich and Guillon model); and building a longitudinal body of panel data. The field of literary translation is almost wholly untilled from these four perspectives, whether through a historical or contemporary lens: much work remains to be done to add to our knowledge of what translation careers look like, diachronically, individually, and collectively, and of the economic models that underpin them and the field as a whole. There is abundant scope for data-based research in sources such as the Société des Gens de Lettres archives, with its dozens of files on individual translators.[26] There is much to do: marrying cultural economics and translation history gives us a new road map to explore with.

---

26 See the list of "Dossiers nominatifs des membres de la Société dont les droits ne font plus l'objet d'une exploitation (décédés depuis plus de 50 ans) et collections d'autographes: Traducteurs", shelfmarks 454AP/1 and following, at the *Archives nationales*.

6 The Life and Career of Auguste-Jean-Baptiste Defauconprêt, Inventor of the "Lingual Steam Engine"

Type "Defauconprêt" into the Bibliothèque nationale de France online catalogue, and it will give you an astonishing 690 hits. Filter the results to take a close look at his translatorial output in the 1820s, and you will find 135 references across the decade. Even taking multiple holdings of individual titles into account in the BnF catalogue, the numbers are impressive: Michaud (1855) attributes a total of 500 individual titles to him. His prodigious output has been noted by a number of commentators, from Valéry Larbaud's foundational *Sous l'Invocation de Saint-Jérôme* (1946) to Agnès Benani, who describes his oeuvre as "colossal" (Benani 1993: 189), and Patrick Hersant, who refers to him as "le plus prolifique des traducteurs de son temps" [the most prolific translator of his day] (Hersant 1999: 83). Vladimir Nabokov and George Steiner both lamented the way literary historians overlooked the importance of his translations of Walter Scott, the source for most other European translations in his day (Barnaby 2011: 6–7). Most recently, his extraordinarily prolific career has been noted by Fiona MacIntosh-Varjabédian (2019). Not only was his output staggeringly abundant, but also remarkably enduring. Narrow the results down to the twenty-first century, and the extraordinary longevity of Defauconprêt's translations becomes apparent: his versions of James Fenimore Cooper and Walter Scott are still being reprinted as recently as 2019, some 200 years after they first hit the market. Defauconprêt's translatorial career is an extraordinary one by whatever yardstick you choose.

* * *

Suspiciously so, in fact. Most seasoned twenty-first-century translators would agree that translating 500 or so full-length books across their career would be difficult. Well-established leading professional literary

DOI: 10.4324/9781003173090-7

132 *Professional Translators in Nineteenth-Century France*

translators today top out at around 100 titles.[1] So should Defauconprêt's output be taken at face value? Was there simply not much else for a keen translator to do on long winter evenings in Regency London? Was he, like some factory workers, working a 90-hour week (Gilmore 2021)? Or is there perhaps something else going on?

Well, as Chapter 2 demonstrated, it is not much of a mystery: Defauconprêt promoted his translation team in one 1825 publication. It was an open secret in its day: the *London Saturday Journal* reported in 1842 that "There is … a translation factory from the English kept pretty briskly at work. The lingual steam engine is driven by M. Defauconprêt". Yet this in itself raises intriguing questions: at what point did he switch from translatorship to translation foremanship? How did the process of slicing and dicing texts for translation work in practical terms? And why have modern-day scholars been so ready to overlook the overtly collaborative nature of his translation practice and believe one man capable of such a tidal wave of publications? This chapter investigates the career of Auguste-Jean-Baptiste Defauconprêt using the methods of book history and approaches made feasible by the mass digitisation of print material unavailable to earlier generations of scholars to dig down deep into the details of his career.

Auguste-Jean-Baptiste Defauconprêt (1767–1843): A Brief Biography

This chapter began with a short biography of Defauconprêt. While the basic coordinates of his life have been a matter of public record since Michaud (1855) devoted an article to him in the *Biographie universelle*, mass digitisation projects and their metadata have given scholars easy access to a wealth of details. The main source on Auguste-Jean-Baptiste Defauconprêt's career is Jacques Bereaud's very detailed 1964 PhD thesis *Auguste-Jean-Baptiste Defauconprêt: Agent de liaison franco-britannique, 1767–1843*, held in a single fragile typescript at the university library in Lille. However, Bereaud probably did not know that a photograph of his subject existed in the Bibliothèque nationale de France, showing an honourable-looking gentleman of advancing years, posing behind a curtained frame flanked by two putti (Figure 6.1).

The image creates a *mise en abîme* effect, chosen perhaps to mimic his own status as a writer of other people's writings. His hand rests on a

---

1 Ros Schwartz has translated around 100 fiction and non-fiction titles in her career, according to her website: https://www.rosschwartz.co.uk/ (accessed 9 January 2023). Similarly, Frank Wynne's website lists 75 titles he has translated: https://www.terribleman.com/translations/ (accessed 9 January 2023).

Auguste-Jean-Baptiste Defauconprêt 133

Figure 6.1 Photographic portraits of Auguste-Jean-Baptiste Defauconprêt (bottom left) and his son Charles-Auguste Defauconprêt (bottom right), *Portraits d'écrivains et hommes de lettres de la seconde moitié du XIXe siècle* vol. 2. Image courtesy of the Bibliothèque nationale de France.

small pile of books, their titles unfortunately unreadable. Bereaud would also have found it difficult to locate the small ad Defauconprêt placed in a London newspaper early in 1816, advertising his services as a French tutor, now easy to find with a simple keyword search. The ease and scope of online tools allow us to put more flesh on the bare bones of Michaud's dry paragraph-long description than would have been possible even ten years ago. Here is what we can now piece together about his life.

134 Professional Translators in Nineteenth-Century France

Auguste-Jean-Baptiste Defauconprêt was born in the parish of Sainte-Catherine in Lille on 7 July 1767. His rarely used full surname, Defauconprêt de Thulus, indicates his family's aristocratic status: several variant spellings are found, such as de Faucompré (Magny 1894: 10). Auguste-Jean-Baptiste's father Jean-Baptiste-Ernest (1737–sometime before December 1797) was a magistrate and *conseiller secrétaire du roi*; his mother was Félicité Defauconprêt, née Macquart de Saisseval (1749–1826). The young Defauconprêt was selected as one of 60 young men of noble birth to be given a free education at the highly prestigious Collège des Quatre-Nations in Paris, founded by Cardinal Mazarin: former students included such luminaries as D'Alembert, Lavoisier, Coulomb, and Jacques-Louis David. He was an outstanding student, winning four first prizes in the *concours général* in 1785 for Latin and French eloquence and Latin and Greek translation (Bereaud 1964: 8). He was also awarded the *prix d'honneur de l'université*. He studied law with a view to following his father into the magistrature, taking a job as a notary's clerk for a Maître Gasche (*Bulletin* 1904: 186). He began writing in the 1790s. His earliest works include essays dating from 1789 on the causes of emigration to urban centres and how to pay off state debt without burdening the people (Bereaud 1965: 386; 1966: 309); translations of Latin poetry; and, more unexpectedly, what seems to have been a one-off attempt at theatre in the anti-clerical comic opera *La Papesse Jeanne* [Pope Joan], performed at the "théâtre de Molière" on 22 February 1793. His early writing career was not a roaring success: he struggled to find a theatre willing to put the play on, as the preface makes clear (Defauconprêt 1793).

At this point, mid-Revolution, he was calling himself "le c. [i.e. citoyen = citizen] Fauconpret", dropping the aristocratic "de". He married Marie-Céleste Béville (1777–1838), daughter of a Saint-Denis notary, in 1794: by then he had revolutionary responsibilities in the town, renamed Franciade between 1793 and 1800, as district secretary.[2] However, his revolutionary leanings seem to have died down relatively quickly. By 1802, he was parish administrator in Saint-Germain-des-Prés, where his name is carved on the organ installed in 1810 (*Bulletin* 1904: 187). In 1802 he printed a reference work entitled *Nouveau barême, ou Tables de réduction des mon-*

---

2 The French archives have a record for a sizeable bequest of land north of Paris left by Céleste Béville, who died on 13 December 1838, to the couple's two children. Bereaud gives the incorrect date of 1854 for her death (1964: 27). Defauconprêt then married Mary (or Marie) Ellison Voysey on 12 February 1840, as announced in the *Court Magazine and Monthly Critic* (1840: 278). It seems likely that he and Marie-Céleste had long been separated and Mary Ellison Voysey had long been his partner: Defauconprêt's *Londres en 1819* mentions the death of his old friend Mr. Voysey. Mary, born in Salisbury in 1791, was Mr. Voysey's daughter, 24 years Defauconprêt's junior. The Voysey family were descended from John Wesley.

naies et mesures anciennes en monnaies et mesures républicaines analogues [Tables of Reductions of Ancient Currencies and Measures into Analogous Republican Currencies and Measures], which proved useful in business and went through eight editions (*Bulletin* 1904: 186). He was well-known as a host of regular weekly dinners for literary types (Besnard 1880: 203) and was generally interested in intellectual pursuits: his name appears, for instance, in a list of subscribers to Lavater's *Art de connaître les hommes par la physiognomie* [Art of Studying Men by Physiognomy] in 1807. His son Charles-Auguste was born on 19 December 1797, his daughter Félicité in September 1804. He took over Gasche's notary business in June 1800 (*Bulletin* 1904: 186), acting as an early sales agent for Paris real estate: a list of premises he was selling features in the *Journal de Paris* for 26 February 1805 (p. 1105). Scans of a number of his notarial transactions are available online.[3]

The financial difficulties that shaped the latter half of his long career seem to have begun in 1809, when he was in his early 40s. His house in the rue de Buci was slated for demolition without compensation (*Bulletin* 1904: 187), and he was forced to move to the nearby rue de Seine. This was a major financial blow and unfortunately timed, since Napoleon brought in a law on 8 March 1810 to compensate such cases.[4] Furthermore, based on a careful comparison of his notary registers in the Seine *département* archives, Bereaud notes that compared to other notaries of the time, his approach to business was rather risky: rather than basing his practice on issuing notarised certificates, much of his income was derived from money lending. This proved unwise. In February 1814 he lent 12,000 francs, charging a fee of 120 francs for the transaction (Bereaud 1964: 12). Later that same year, he was forced into bankruptcy, was sentenced to a hefty fine, and fled to London to avoid the shame of conviction. Bereaud quotes a letter written by Defauconprêt to his recently widowed son in 1836 explaining why he could not consider returning to France. His debts were not due to gambling or a taste for luxury, but to the fact that most of his clients were émigrés returning to Paris after the revolution who sought 18 per cent interest on their investments and withdrew their funds when he could not guarantee such a high rate. When his brother-in-law, Marie-Céleste's brother, went bankrupt, he lost the confidence of his own clients completely. He sold a house in Paris, a farm, his business, his library, and his furniture to pay his creditors 300,000 francs, leaving him with 100 louis to start over in England. Ironically, a rumour later spread that he had become wealthy on the back of his Walter Scott translations, and he

---

3 See https://www.siv.archives-nationales.culture.gouv.fr (accessed 25 January 2023).
4 See https://fr.wikipedia.org/wiki/Expropriation_pour_cause_d%27utilit%C3%A9_pub-lique_en_droit_fran%C3%A7ais (accessed 10 January 2023).

136 *Professional Translators in Nineteenth-Century France*

was once again harassed by his creditors (Bereaud 1964: 14–17). Though he never succeeded in repaying all his debts he did return to France occasionally in the 1820s, eventually moving back permanently around 1840 (Bereaud 1964: 28): perhaps not coincidentally, this was around the time of the death of his first wife in December 1838. He married his second wife, his long-time companion Mary Ellison Voysey, in Paris in February 1840 (*Court Magazine* 1840: 278), leaving her a widow three years later when he died in Fontainebleau on 7 March 1843.[5] As late as October 1840, he was still writing to Gosselin to suggest new translation projects (Bereaud 1964: 29). Movingly, his will, dated 7 March 1842 and addressed to his son, bears witness to his thankfulness for his translation career: "j'ai ... à remercier le Ciel de m'avoir donné du goût pour la carrière que j'ai suivie depuis trente ans ou à peu près, et de m'avoir fait trouver du plaisir au genre de travail auquel je m'étais soumis par nécessité" [I must thank heaven for giving me a taste for the career I followed for thirty years or so, and for letting me enjoy the kind of work I subjected myself to out of necessity] (Bereaud 1964: 30).

Defauconprêt in London: Launching a Mid-Life Career in Translation

In 1807, the pastellist Henri-Joseph François[6] penned a poem entitled *Discours à M. Defauconprêt sur la carrière des lettres* [Discourse to M. Defauconprêt on the Literary Career], which warned against the temptations of a writing career: literary glory was a fickle mistress (François 1807). Literary *entrepreneurship*, however, was a different game. There were fortunes to be made in the publishing business: the Frankh brothers, booksellers in Stuttgart, sold 30,000 sets of Walter Scott's complete works, profiting to the tune of 100,000 gulden in 1828 (Fullerton 2015: 56). When Defauconprêt fled Paris for London in his late 40s, he was forced into a mid-life career change. He chose translation. Was it a surer path than poetry? Was there a way of making a career in writing more entrepreneurial, to reap a greater share of the publisher's vast profits? Or was it purely a creative calling?

In some ways, translation was a wise choice: he already had a literary background, demand was plentiful, and start-up costs, overheads, and barriers to entry almost non-existent – vital conditions, given his lack of capital. It turned out to suit him very well and within a handful of years, in

---

5 She eventually returned to London, where she died in Hackney in 1868 (Clarke 1886: 217).
6 The author is identified only as Henri-J. François, artiste, in the printed poem but the details match the pastellist and poet: see http://www.pastellists.com/Articles/FrancoisH.pdf (accessed 10 January 2023).

1819, he was confident enough to defend his professional vision in a letter to the *Journal des débats*:

> Je crois qu'en faisant passer un roman d'une langue dans une autre, le premier devoir d'un traducteur est de le mettre en état de plaire aux nouveaux lecteurs qu'il veut lui procurer. Le goût des Anglais n'est pas toujours conforme au nôtre.
> [I believe that in transferring a novel between languages, the translator's first duty is to put it in a position to appeal to the new readers it hopes to find. English tastes do not always correspond to ours.]
>
> (*Journal des débats* 1819: 4)[7]

This section sets out to examine Defauconprêt's path into translation, starting with his arrival in England. It examines the evidence for his mastery of English as a fledgling translator and the strategies he used to build up a network of publishing contacts. In general, as seen in Chapter 3, information on early careers and how aspiring translators entered the profession is heavily under-represented in nineteenth-century archival sources: it is therefore intriguing to read Defauconprêt's writings with an eye to gauging his knowledge of English at the outset of his translatorial practice. The key sources here are his own accounts of his early stays in London, published as an annual series of reports on current affairs in the city, beginning with *Quinze jours à Londres, à la fin de 1815* and concluding with *Londres en 1824*.

On arriving in London, Defauconprêt wrote (somewhat disingenuously, though understandably so) that his main reason for travelling was to further his knowledge of English literature, "à laquelle je ne suis pas tout à fait étranger" [with which I am not wholly unacquainted] (Defauconprêt 1817a: 7). He claims to know no one in the city but comes bearing a letter of recommendation from a member of the Académie française for a Lord A. of the Royal Society. On page 13, he claims to speak decent English but cannot understand the Kent accent of a local servant on arriving in Dover. On page 61, he cannot understand a sermon. This raises the question of what knowledge of English he had on arrival and how he could have learned the language. As seen in Chapter 1, modern foreign languages were not on the curriculum at most French schools until the late 1820s. There were, however, private language tutors – the *Almanach du commerce de*

---

7 The letter was in response to a critique of his heavily domesticating translation of Sydney, Lady Morgan's *La France*, which toned down or outright removed many passages critical of the restored Bourbon monarchy and the Catholic Church. Lady Morgan was outraged and commissioned a second, unexpurgated translation, publicly disowning Defauconprêt's version. For a full account of the affair, see Barnaby (2011).

138 *Professional Translators in Nineteenth-Century France*

Paris for 1811 lists tutors by the name of Niell, Davies, Bousie, Martinet, Frenck, and Carré, for instance – and plenty of self-teaching materials in bookshops. He had won prizes for Greek and Latin translation at school decades earlier and now began to apply that knowledge to English, translating an extract of John Scott's *Visit to Paris in 1814*. What he lacked at this point was knowledge of British culture and idiomatic language. He was stumped by hot cross buns in the shops (Defauconprêt 1820: 48) and a satirical print of Queen Charlotte entitled *Throwing the Stocking*: "Une chose qui me surprit encore, c'est quoique je connusse tous les mots employés par les divers personnages de cette scène, le sens de certaines phrases m'échappait" [One thing that surprised me again was that I knew all the words used by the various characters in the scene, but the meaning of some of the sentences escaped me] (Defauconprêt 1817b: 193). He lodged with English families, read two newspapers a day to improve his vocabulary (Defauconprêt 1820: 55), and used John Walker's *Critical Pronouncing Dictionary* to work on his accent (Defauconprêt 1817b: 48).

Above all, his accounts give a lively sense of just how enmeshed French was in the life of the capital at this point, making it relatively easy for a newcomer to the city to build a network in his own language while acclimatising to the foreign one. His 1819 *Une Année à Londres* includes references to French street singers, evangelists distributing French (and German) religious pamphlets in cafés, French as the universal language of sociability, and indeed an entire chapter on the presence of the French language in the city. London was home to an extensive French community, though precise figures are hard to come by for the 1820s. There were some 40,000 émigrés in the city in the 1790s (Carpenter 1999: 217); many had returned home, but equally many had put down roots. Flora Tristan's 1840 *Promenades dans Londres* records that "On m'a assuré que plus de quinze mille Français habitent Londres" [I am assured that over fifteen thousand French people live in London], which Bédarida considered a significant underestimate based on the 1851 census (Cross 2013: 147). Travel guides to London from the period list plentiful amenities for French visitors, including coffee houses such as Saulieu's on Nassau Street and Tom's on Cornhill (Feltham 1807). More significantly for our purposes, London offered no fewer than four French bookshops: de Boffe in Gerrard Street, de Conchy in New Bond Street, Dulau in Soho Square, and Boosey in Old Broad Street.[8] The first three were within a 10- or 15-minute stroll from Defauconprêt's first lodgings in Great Titchfield Street. Dulau and Deboffe were central meeting points for the city's French community, which had its own rich print culture, producing newspapers such as the *Courier de*

---

8 Reboul (2014: 228) notes at least 34 booksellers, publishers, print sellers, and stationers in the French émigré book trade network.

Londres, which ran from 1776 to 1826 (Burrows 1999). The French book market in London was also newly vibrant after years of restrictions: as the *Monthly Magazine, or British Register* wrote in 1811, not wholly impartially,

> The merciless Assassin of the Tarragonese and Spaniards has condescended to allow an importation of French books into London, intended, perhaps, to dazzle the English barbarians with these sacrifices of art and genius at the bloody shrine of his vanity. Some months ago, he licenced a Paris bookseller to come to London, and negotiate exchanges of English against French books. The English government having liberally participated in the plan, the French books, amounting to fifty thousand volumes, are just arrived at the shops of Messrs. Deboffe, Dulau and Deconchy.
>
> (Anonymous 1811: 158)

Leading British publishers published books in French and language resources. Henry Colburn – who may have had French ancestry himself and possibly set up a branch in Paris at one point (Melnyk 2002: 36–7) – launched an English and Foreign Circulating Library, which featured around 50 books in French on topics of French interest, also available in circulating libraries (Saglia 2013; Shaw 2002). Conversely, Dulau printed books in French on British topics of interest, including an 1809 *Effets du blocus continental sur le commerce, les finances, le crédit et la prospérité des Iles Britanniques* [Effects of the Continental Blockade on the Trade, Finances, Credit and Prosperity of the British Isles] (Shaw 2002: 114).

All these resources, combined with his natural intelligence, put Defauconprêt on the path to translation within a matter of months of arriving. He struck up an acquaintance with an English bookseller, as told in *Quinze jours à Londres,* who, "sachant que je m'occupe de littérature" [knowing I take an interest in literature], made him "la proposition la plus saugrenue dont j'aie jamais entendu" [the most outlandish proposition I ever heard]: to take up translation (Defauconprêt 1817a: 109). He describes his first brush with his new career: as he browsed the shop one day, the bookseller approached him.

> Je viens, me dit-il en tirant de ses poches deux énormes volumes in-8°, vous proposer une spéculation fort avantageuse. Voici un ouvrage que je viens d'imprimer: il est traduit de l'allemand; c'est un livre très-ancien, d'un auteur très-estimé, et qui cependant n'a jamais été traduit en anglais ni même, je crois, en français ... je crois qu'une traduction française de celui que je vous apporte y [i.e. in France] aurait beaucoup de succès. Je viens donc vous proposer de me donner trente livres (720

140 *Professional Translators in Nineteenth-Century France*

fr). Je vous laisserai cet exemplaire, et je m'obligerai à ne publier cette traduction que quand la vôtre sera terminée, afin que vous n'ayez pas à craindre la concurrence. Je vous donne la préférence ... car je trouverais à Londres bien des libraires français qui seraient enchantés de cette affaire.

[I come, he said, pulling two vast octavo volumes from his pockets, to offer you a highly advantageous speculation. This is a book I have just printed: it is translated from the German; it is a very old book by a much-admired author, yet it has never been translated into English, nor even, I believe, into French ... I think a French translation of this book would be very successful there. I suggest you give me thirty pounds (720 fr). I will leave you this copy and undertake not to publish this translation until yours is complete, so you need not fear competition. I am giving you first refusal ... for in London I could find many French booksellers who would be delighted with such a deal.]

(Defauconprêt 1817a: 110)

The anecdote offers a fascinating glimpse into the hiring practices for translators. Perhaps most interesting in light of the modern literary translation economy is the suggestion of a pay-to-play model, a practice mirrored in such modern-day publishing practices as submission fees for literary journals, ticketed access to agents, and fee-charging manuscript incubators (Thompson 2022). These reverse the buyer-seller relationship between translator and publisher and potentially create an economic barrier to entering the profession.[9] In the event, he turned the offer down because he disapproved of the practice of relay translation; the bookseller offered to obtain the German original (there is no indication he checked whether Defauconprêt knew any German), but still wanted 30 pounds in exchange for giving him a foot in the door. Given the parlous state of Defauconprêt's finances on arriving in London, spending 30 pounds to launch his career in translation was probably not an option.

Though this project fell through, it apparently sparked something in Defauconprêt. On arriving in London, he had begun offering his services as a language tutor: the *Morning Chronicle* for 3 February 1816 contains a small ad in his name offering French lessons "by an easy and speedy method, without any of the provincial accents which disgrace it, by a French Grammarian who has lived thirty years in Paris". He was also active passing on banking information for friends and dealing with booksellers, negotiating with Jordan and Wilson for the sale of Mirabeau's letters (Bereaud

---

9 On the pay-to-play economy in the arts, see Coase (1979) and Caves (2000).

1964: 21).[10] However, he soon began to supplement his income with translations: 1816 saw the publication of no fewer than four translated novels in his name, all in multiple volumes. The titles that began his career were Amelia Opie's *Valentine's Eve* (*Catherine Shirley, ou la veille de la Saint-Valentin*), the anonymous *Cavern of Astolpho* (*La Caverne d'Astolpho, Histoire espagnole*), *Romantic Facts, or Which Is His wife?* (*Juanna et Tyranna, ou Laquelle est ma femme*), and Anna Maria Bennett's *Faith and Fiction, or Shining Lights in a Dark Generation* (*L'orpheline du presbytère, fiction et vérité*). And this was just the start. 1817 saw the publication of a further seven titles, 1818 another six, including his first Walter Scott novel, *Rob Roy*, and a number of travel narratives – a genre he worked in extensively early in his career.

This seems like a remarkably swift start to a career in literary translation, but it is doubtless in line with the factory line model explored in Chapter 2. Intriguingly, the BnF catalogue also lists 7 translations by Defauconprêt's son Charles-Auguste by 1819, the year he turned 21. Were the Defauconprêts prodigious translatorial talents from father to son? Or is this evidence that Auguste-Jean-Baptiste was engaging in literary entrepreneurship almost as soon as he set foot on British soil? The next section studies the evidence on both sides.

Exploring a Translator's Career

In 1828, Joseph-Marie Quérard wrote that Auguste-Jean-Baptiste Defauconprêt had given him an incomplete list of his translations, featuring 422 volumes, 47 of which were published that same year (Quérard 1828: II, 419). Though the list apparently made no mention of any co-translators, Quérard smelled a rat. It seemed unlikely to him that the *Biographie universelle et portative des contemporains*, published two years earlier, was correct in its article on Defauconprêt when it claimed that

> Le nombre d'ouvrages qu'il a fait passer dans notre langue, depuis douze ans qu'il habite l'Angleterre, est presque incalculable, ce qui fait supposer à quelques critiques qu'il avait à Londres un bureau de traductions. Nous pouvons assurer qu'il n'a pas d'autre collaborateur que son fils qui l'aide quelque fois dans ses travaux.

> [The number of books he has translated into French in the twelve years he has been living in England is almost incalculable, which has led some critics to suppose he ran a translation agency in London. We can affirm

---

10 The letter is dated 16 July in either 1822 or 1832: the exact year is frustratingly unreadable in Bereaud's faded typescript.

142 *Professional Translators in Nineteenth-Century France*

that he works with no-one other than his son, who sometimes assists him.]

(Rabbe, Vieilh de Boisjolin and Sainte-Preuve 1826: II, 1643)

Quérard concludes that the *Biographie* is incorrect in its claim and that Defauconprêt "a fait traduire [de nombreux ouvrages] sous sa direction" [oversaw the translation of numerous books] (Quérard 1828: 419). Yet the *Biographie* was later backed up by other sources, including an anonymous reviewer across the Channel writing for the *Monthly Review*:

We happen to enjoy the friendship of M. De [sic] Fauconpret's son, who is one of the senior professors in the College Rollin at Paris; and from him we learnt that his father translates English works with the most astonishing rapidity.

(Anonymous 1839: 544)

The *Biographie universelle ancienne et moderne* also claimed that "cette prodigieuse fécondité donna même à penser faussement qu'il avait à Londres un atelier de traduction" [his prodigious fecundity even made people wrongly think he had a translation workshop in London] (Michaud 1855: 269).

The *Biographie universelle and portative*, *Monthly Review*, and Michaud were clearly dissembling or mistaken. The question is not so much *whether* Defauconprêt *père* subcontracted to other translators, but how much and when. For the translation historian, the challenge lies in trying to pin down the point at which Defauconprêt the impecunious hack translator took the step to becoming Defauconprêt the literary translation entrepreneur.

There are several potential approaches to these questions. Patricia Bogé-Rousseau's 2018 PhD dissertation on the four translations of Scott's *Quentin Durward* attributed to Defauconprêt drew on retranslation theory to try to determine whether Defauconprêt worked on the three later versions alone and whether they were true retranslations or merely revisions. Her approach is based largely on internal evidence of the handling of footnotes and Scotticisms. She concludes that while there are clearly differences between the various versions, they were most likely due to editorial intervention rather than re-(co)translation (Bogé-Rousseau 2018: 310). In support of her conclusion, she quotes Barnaby (2006: 34) who refers to a letter from Defauconprêt to his publisher Gosselin stating that Scott's agents in London were insisting on absolute secrecy for the arrangement whereby Defauconprêt received proof copies of Scott's novels before they came out in Britain. The agreement implied that Defauconprêt was sole

Auguste-Jean-Baptiste Defauconprêt   143

translator for Scott's works prior to 1827, when Scott lifted his own anonymity and acknowledged his authorship of the Waverley novels. After this, Bogé-Rousseau argues, Defauconprêt could openly work with collaborators (Bogé-Rousseau 2018: 310).

While it is possible that Defauconprêt kept Scott for himself, we know that this was not his practice across the board. One key question is whether this was a new practice when announced in 1825, or whether it had been going on behind the scenes for years. I will assess the evidence for two hypotheses: did Auguste-Jean-Baptiste work mostly alone with occasional help from his son in the early years of his translation career, or did he regularly subcontract work out to ghost translators from the outset?

To begin with, we need to know more about his son. Charles-Auguste Defauconprêt (1797–1865) became a figure of note in his own right as a leading nineteenth-century educationalist, pictured alongside his father in the collection of author photographs in Figure 6.1. He had clearly inherited his father's brains: he studied at the most prestigious school in Paris, winning prizes in classics and Latin at the Lycée Napoléon (soon renamed Henri IV) in 1809, 1813 (*Moniteur Universel* 1813: 907), and 1814 (Jalabert and Sacré 2010: 231). He was a *préfet des études* (i.e. head of discipline) at the Collège Rollin from 1819 to 1829 and remained in teaching for the rest of his life.[11] He co-authored a French-Greek dictionary in 1824 that was reprinted throughout the century and published translations under his own name until the early 1830s. One of his classmates, Victor Duruy, later a major reformist minister of education, wrote that he "avait une activité infatigable qui lui valut le surnom du Furet" [his tireless activity earned him the nickname the Ferret] (Duruy 1901: I, 9). It seems from his schooling that he remained in Paris with his mother when his father fled to London: as an *épouse judiciairement séparée des biens*, Céleste Béville was not legally liable for her husband's debts and had no reason to leave. The question then is how much exposure would the young Charles-Auguste have had to English? Amazingly, the abundance of sources now available online gives us not only the name of his English teacher, but also a glimpse of the teaching methods he would have used.

While modern languages were not on the curriculum of most schools until considerably later in the century (Puren 1988), the *Loi générale sur l'instruction publique* [general law on public education] of 1 May 1802 stated that "il y aura près de plusieurs lycées des professeurs de langues vivantes" [several high schools will have modern language teachers].[12]

---

11 He also applied unsuccessfully for a post as librarian in Lille in 1828 (Asselineau 1861: 414).

12 See https://www.education.gouv.fr/loi-generale-sur-l-instruction-publique-du-1er-mai -1802-11-floreal-x-1646 (accessed 12 January 2023).

144 *Professional Translators in Nineteenth-Century France*

One of those schools was the Lycée Napoléon, where the English teacher was apparently a native speaker, a M. Roberts, author of a *General View of English Grammar*. Roberts also taught extramural classes with a programme described in some detail in the *Athénée de Paris* (1806: 13):

> M. Roberts commencera ce cours par les règles de la prononciation, ensuite il fera l'analyse exacte des principes, et pour rendre ce cours complet dans toutes ses parties, et applanir [sic] toutes les difficultés, il expliquera les meilleurs auteurs classiques en prose et en vers de la langue anglaise.

> [M. Roberts will begin this course with the rules of pronunciation, then he will give a detailed analysis of the principles, and to make the course fully rounded and overcome all difficulties, he will explain the finest English classics in prose and verse.][13]

The young Charles-Auguste would, then, have had a few years' grounding in English. Were *le citoyen* Roberts's teaching methods successful enough to allow Charles-Auguste to help his father get his fledgling translation career off the ground? Or was his name on the frontispiece a stand-in for subcontracted labour?

I will use two approaches to try and answer these questions, first applying a close reading of a sample translation attributed to Charles-Auguste to judge its competence, then drawing on book history methods to study the project's translatorial workflow. The work in question is the earliest solely attributed to Charles-Auguste on its title page, published in 1818 when he would have been 20 (he turned 21 in mid-December that year) and translated when he was 19. It is John MacLeod's *Narrative of a Voyage in His Majesty's Late Ship Alceste, to the Yellow Sea, along the Coast of Corea* [sic] *to the Island of Lewchew*,[14] titled in French *Voyage du capitaine Maxwell commandant "l'Alceste" ... sur la mer Jaune, le long des côtes de la Corée et dans les îles de Liou tchiou, avec la relation de son naufrage dans le détroit de Gaspar*.

A close-grained comparison of the first 60 pages of the translation sheds light on a number of interesting issues pointing to the translator's

---

13 Roberts had been teaching in Paris since at least 1792, appearing in the *Gazette nationale* as "le citoyen Roberts" in that year (*Gazette nationale* 1792: 1404). One anecdote about his classes survives. A crowd had turned up to hear André Chénier, but M. Roberts's class overran. Realising he had lost the attention of those present, he closed his book and apologised for keeping them. His words were met with a burst of applause and an old man called out that if he wanted to spark an interest in English literature he should choose a different time slot, as they had all come to see Chénier (*Spectateur* 1807: IV, 308).
14 That is Ryukyu, modern-day Okinawa.

Auguste-Jean-Baptiste Defauconprêt   145

professional reflexes. However, bearing this chapter's book history focus in mind, care must be taken in attributing shifts in translated texts to the translator alone, given the presence of other agents in the textual production process. Only some types of shifts in translated texts can be reliably attributed to translators rather than subsequent editorial intervention. For instance, the shift from Lewchew to Liou tchiou in the title might initially be thought to point to a sensitivity to the need to adapt the transliteration of toponyms, but in the absence of a genetic study of the translator's manuscripts, the shift cannot reliably be attributed to the translator alone. While this seems to be the first occurrence of this spelling in French, the shift was within the grasp of anyone, such as an editor, with some knowledge of English phonetics: Boyer's French-English dictionary regularly transcribes [tʃuː] as "tchiou" in words such as "voluptuous" and "fluctuate" (Boyer 1817). The same is true of the addition of content, for instance the footnote added to page 22 of the French edition adding the Chinese name of the White or North river, Pei-Ho – information most likely gleaned from earlier accounts of the region. Another strategy that can be potentially attributed to editorial intervention is the wholesale omission of paragraphs, such as the passages on the visit to the ship by Sir Sidney Smith and the harsh fate of the nuns of Saint Teresa (MacLeod 1817: 8). This content was likely deemed of little interest to a French readership – a decision that is editorial rather than translatorial in nature.

Other aspects of the French text are less likely to result from editorial intervention and can be more readily attributed to translatorial competence, or a lack thereof. These include the identification and use of specialist terminology, an aspect of the translation process that cannot be as easily substituted by an editor (Table 6.1).

A translation using specialist maritime vocabulary suggests, if not immediate fingertip knowledge of the specialist lexicon, at least access to research tools such as William Burney's *New Universal Dictionary of the Marine, with a Vocabulary of French Sea-Phrases*, which came out in a vastly expanded new edition in 1815. This points to relative instrumental

Table 6.1 Translating Specialist Maritime Vocabulary

Specialist Maritime Vocabulary in English (with Page References in MacLeod 1817)	Specialist Maritime Vocabulary in French (with Page References in MacLeod 1818)
Hoisting the colours half-staff high and topping the yards (7)	Carguant les voiles et abaissant les pavillons (8–9)
Refitment (17)	Radoubé (20)
Watering place (139)	Aiguade (162)
Carronade (252)	Carronade (285)

146 *Professional Translators in Nineteenth-Century France*

and strategic competence – though it is clear that the translator was far from a subject area specialist. Though the verb "carguer" is indeed a specific maritime term, it corresponds not to "topping" but to "clewing up" or "brailing in" a sail. Similarly, "abaissant" misses the mark for "hoisting the colours"; a more accurate translation would be "mettant les couleurs en berne et apiquant les vergues".[15]

While outright mistranslations are few and far between, this is perhaps because in some cases, elements that resisted straightforward translation were simply omitted. A careful reading reveals a few mishandled terms and omissions of exotic realia and wordplay that seem not to be obviously justified on editorial grounds (Table 6.2).

Interestingly, the lemma "mango" dips in and out of Thomas Nugent's bilingual French-English dictionary (as "mangou [sic], fruit des Indes Orientales"); it features in editions printed in 1797 and 1817, but not in between, including one printed in 1816. This suggests that the resources available to the translator were recent, but not entirely up to date. Nugent does not list "guava". The lemma is to be found in the 1817 edition of the other leading bilingual dictionary of the day, Boyer's *Dictionnaire anglois-françois et françois-anglois* [sic], but it is listed under the alternate spelling "guaiava" and may therefore have been passed over by a translator in a hurry. The rarity of both terms is apparent from the fact that they appear in a third source, Nicolas Gouin Dufief's 1810 *Dictionnaire nouveau et universel des langues française et anglaise, avec la prononciation figurée de chaque mot: contenant plus de cinquante mille termes ou noms qui ne se trouvent point dans Boyer, Perry, Nugent, Tocquot, et les autres lexicographes* – a resource our translator apparently did not have access to; unsurprisingly, since it was printed in a single edition in Philadelphia.

One final aspect of the text that hints at multiple translatorship is the issue of consistency of spelling of exotic realia. The English refers to "Ashantees" from West Africa (MacLeod 1817: 11). The French has "Ashantes" (p. 14). However, a year later, Thomas Bowdich's *Mission from Cape Coast Castle to Ashantee* (1819) came out in a translation again attributed to Charles-Auguste Defauconprêt. The translated title was *Voyage dans le pays d'Aschantie* (1819).

Based on internal evidence, then, the results are suggestive of multiple translatorship at this early stage. Some aspects of the text point to translatorial competence, but in many cases these are instances where editorial competence could substitute for it in the textual production process. Other aspects point to a lesser degree of competence and a strategy of omitting content that proved too challenging or time-consuming to tackle. It seems

---

15 With thanks to sailing translators Miranda Joubioux, Nikki Scott-Despaigne, Odile Legeay, and Ralph Houston for their assistance on this point.

Auguste-Jean-Baptiste Defauconprêt 147

Table 6.2 Treatment of Challenging Lexis and Cultural References

Original English Text (with Page Reference)	French Translation (with Page Reference)	Observations
This country produces all the various fruits of the warmer climates; such as pine-apples, oranges, limes, mangoes, guavas, melons, bananas, & c. (11)	On y trouve tous les fruits des pays chauds, comme ananas, orangers, limons, melons, bananes etc. (13)	Omission of mangoes and guavas, though both were attested in French, *mangue* since 1604 and *goyave* since 1643.[16] Botanically speaking, *limon* is a slight mistranslation of lime.
Here also we observed their clerks, or men of letters, distinguished by two enormous claws on their left hand, which render that limb in a great degree useless to them. (24)	∅	The observation is omitted, perhaps on grounds of the difficulty of visualising the handicap, doubtless a rare congenital form of cleft hand.
On our entrance a number of mandarins, (or, as the seamen termed them, *mad marines*) came on board to pay their respects. (40)	Plusieurs mandarins vinrent à bord nous saluer. (46)	Omission of challenging wordplay.
This morning, after sounding our way in, we came to an anchor in a most excellent harbour, named Murray's Sound; the two islands which principally form it, Shamrock and Thistle. (52)	… que nous nommâmes le Sund de Murray. Nous donnâmes aux îles qui le forment principalement, les noms de Shamrock et de Thistle. (61)	*Sund* is a geographically appropriate translation for "sound", attested in a number of early-nineteenth-century French travel accounts. However, the translator has apparently taken Shamrock and Thistle for surnames, like Murray.

16 See the entries for each term at https://www.cnrtl.fr/ (accessed 12 May 2023).

148 *Professional Translators in Nineteenth-Century France*

doubtful that a young man still in his teens with a few years of English under his belt could have produced the text, but given his obvious intelligence and drive – Duruy's "activité infatigable" – perhaps not impossible.

Applying a book history approach to the same project tells a similar story. There are two strands to this approach: one relying on tracking the print history of the books in French and English, the other exploring the publishing network behind the French title.[17] As was typical, publication of the book in English followed hot on the heels of the journey it recounted (Maclaren 2011). HMS *Alceste*, built in France in 1804 and captured in 1806, left Britain for China on 9 February 1816, arriving at the Formosa Straits on 28 July. The ship struck a reef in the Java Sea on the return voyage and was plundered by pirates. The stranded crew was picked up by the *Ternate*, transferred in Batavia (now Jakarta) to the *Caesar*, and arrived back in Spithead on 16 August 1817. Captain Maxwell was court-martialled for the loss of the ship but exonerated, rewarded, and then knighted in 1818. No doubt to capitalise on public interest in the event, the narrative by the ship's surgeon, John MacLeod (c. 1777–1820), was published within a matter of weeks, being announced as early as the October 1817 issue of the *British Critic*. The book must have come out in mid- to late October, as it was reviewed as a new title in the *Literary Gazette* for 8 November 1817.

Perhaps because the *Alceste* had once been French, interest in the events surrounding the ship was keen across the Channel. Writing in the *Annales maritimes et coloniales* for September 1817, a M. Langles translated an account of the *Alceste*'s fate from the *Asiatic Journal*, and the *Journal général de France* for 31 August 1817 reported on Maxwell's court martial.[18] Travel narratives were a hugely popular genre in general: as the *British Critic* had noted in 1800,

> The taste for these works, which was always very prevalent, is far from being now on the decline. Such, on the contrary, is the avidity of the public for a supply, and such the grateful zeal of publishers to gratify the wishes of their friends, that almost every foreign voyage is the parent of two or three English works, which start as rival translations.
>
> (*British Critic* 1800: xiv)

As such, speed was of the essence in translating to be first to market, and lengthy extracts from the *Alceste* narrative appeared in the French press by

---

17 For an outstanding study of the publishing context of the English original, see Withers, Keighren, and Bell (2015).

18 Presumably the Orientalist Louis-Mathieu Langlès (1763–1824), who translated a number of travel narratives in the very late eighteenth and early nineteenth centuries.

Auguste-Jean-Baptiste Defauconprêt 149

the year's end, for instance in the *Annales de physique et de chimie*, vol. 6 (1817). These extracts were not identical to the published book – the one in the *Journal des sciences médicales* (1817: 110) differs in some respects, for instance – suggesting either at least two rival translations or an ongoing editorial process.

Impressively, the *Bibliographie de la France* announced in December 1817 (1817: 639) that the translation was in press and would be published by Gide *fils* on 15 December 1817. This meant that were Charles-Auguste Defauconprêt to have been sole translator, his schoolboy English would have been enough to produce a polished translation of 71,190 words of relatively specialist content by hand in at most six weeks or so.[19] A slightly later work attributed in translation to his father, *Relation d'une expédition entreprise en 1816, sous les ordres du capitaine J. K. Tuckey, pour reconnoître le Zaïre, communément appelé le Congo* (1818), similarly printed by Gide *fils*, was announced as being translated from the English printer's sheets hot off the press, prior to binding and distribution; if the same were true of the *Alceste* narrative some months earlier, it meant there was a process in place to ship the printers' sheets to France more or less overnight to allow the young Charles-Auguste to get to work as fast as he could.[20] He would then have translated roughly 1,700 words of English a day, every day, for 6 weeks, counting from mid-October to the start of December, or some 2,300 words a day for a 5-day week – which, given a typical positive textual expansion rate between English and French, would come out to 10 or 15 per cent more text.[21] If he waited for the finished, bound book, he would have had to work even faster. As it happens, this period corresponds to something of a gap in the young man's biography: we know he was at the Lycée Henri IV until at least 1816, then working at the Collège Rollin from 1819 on. He may have devoted all his time to translation at this point; there is no absolute proof that he did not travel to London, though his father makes no mention of such visits in his annual accounts of London life.

19 Based on putting the Google Books PDF download through the online tool available at https://onlinecountword.com (accessed 16 January 2023).

20 "Le traducteur étant à Londres, et traduisant à mesure que l'ouvrage anglais s'imprime, nous serons à même de faire jouir le public français de cet intéressant ouvrage très peu de jours après sa parution en Angleterre" [The translator being London-based and translating the English book as it is printed, we will be in a position to furnish French readers with this interesting publication very soon after it comes out in England] (*Correspondant* 1817: 309).

21 Bogé-Rousseau (2018: 166) records that the word count in *Quentin Durward* expands from 197,000 words in English to 210,000 in French, an increase of 6.6 per cent. The relatively low rate of textual expansion suggests that some material has been omitted in translation.

150 *Professional Translators in Nineteenth-Century France*

Either way, in London or in Paris, this output seems rather too much for a young beginner. Solid data on translation speeds is hard to come by; around 2,000 words a day is often suggested as a rule of thumb. However, such claims rarely go into detail about whether source or target is being measured, language pair, expansion/shrinkage rate, subject matter, tools used, if proofreading time is included, and so on.[22] Nor is it clear that even if reliable productivity data were forthcoming that it could be unproblematically mapped onto working conditions in the early nineteenth century. Reference tools were less ergonomic, more cumbersome, and less readily at hand, doubtless lowering output; on the other hand, quality control was arguably looser, meaning translators could skate over difficulties at speed.[23] However, one source has been found that allows for a degree of triangulation of typical translatorial output prior to the mechanisation of the handwriting process and modern CAT tools. In the early twentieth century, the hugely experienced Russian-to-English translator Constance Garnett provided a point of comparison in a letter to her husband Edward, writing on 14 January (the year is not stated) that

> Tolstoi's letters are 300,000 words – and they want it done by March 15 – but if I couldn't do all I could do part ... Of course no one could do 300,000 in the time ... we could do 100,000 in 20 or 25 days.
>
> (Garnett 1991: 250)

This suggests a forecast output of 2,000 to 2,500 words per person per day for two highly experienced translators; she and Juliet Soskice in fact completed 24,000 words in ten days before the project was interrupted.[24]

---

22 Some modern-day translators claim productivity rates of up to 8,000 words a day using dictation software. See, for example, https://thetranslationguy.net/2021/06/23/how-many -pages-can-a-translator-translate-per-day/ (accessed 17 January 2023).

23 See, for instance, Marcel Clavel's 1938 assessment of the Defauconprêt Fenimore Cooper translations: "que dire ... d'une traduction qui supprime systématiquement les expressions difficiles à rendre, et qui, surtout dans les descriptions, saute des phrases entières, pour la seule convenance d'un traducteur pressé et qui est loin d'être toujours à la hauteur de sa tâche" [what is there to say ... about a translation that systematically suppresses challenging expressions and that, particularly in descriptions, leaves out entire sentences to suit a translator under time pressure who is not always up to the task] (Clavel 1938: 406–7). Examples he gives include "before the gray light of the morning was mellowed by the rays of the rising sun" > "dès le point du jour" (i.e. at daybreak) and "twenty times they thought the whirling eddies were sweaping [sic] them to destruction" > "vingt fois, ils se crurent sur le point d'être engloutis" (i.e. twenty times they thought they were about to be swallowed up) (Clavel 1938: 235–6).

24 My warm thanks to Cathy McAteer at the University of Exeter for bringing this reference to my attention. Nowadays, translators working on high-profile projects such as Prince Harry's *Spare* will work at high speed to enable the publishers to release the book in

Auguste-Jean-Baptiste Defauconprêt 151

However, this would have been using early twentieth-century technology. Karin Littau's media history approach to translation reminds us of the importance of taking technology into account (Littau 2011): it must therefore be borne in mind that all Charles-Auguste's work had to be written out by hand. He would have used a quill or an early model of fountain pen: modern mass-produced pen nibs were not available until the late 1820s. Using a quill, as was likely, would have meant dipping the pen in ink every three to six words or so, slowing him down. At a time when experienced clerks using nibbed fountain pens writing at the rate of 8 or 9 words a minute would copy 3,000 words a day (Gold 2009: 167), just transcribing the French text would have taken around 5.5 hours, not including research time and the intellectual labour of translation itself.[25] In terms of approximating early-nineteenth-century daily output, nowadays, French students with a degree in English sitting the *agrégation* are expected to handwrite a French translation of around 500 words from a challenging English original in around 3 hours.[26]

For the sake of completeness, two other possibilities must be mentioned in Charles-Auguste's favour. He could potentially have increased his output by using a shorthand writing system such as those developed in M. Clément's *La Sténographie, ou L'art d'écrire aussi vite qu'on parle* (1800) or Jean-Félicité Coulon de Thévenot's *Tachygraphie fondée sur les principes du language, de la grammaire et de la géométrie* (1802).[27] Translation and shorthand were seen as part of a similar skill set: one commercial London guide in 1818 lists four "short hand writers and translators of records" (Johnstone 1818), while Amédée Pichot's 1826 *Voyage historique et littéraire en Angleterre et en Ecosse* juxtaposes the two professions in British newspaper offices: "Les employés subalternes sont les traducteurs de nouvelles étrangères ... Mais les ouvriers importans [sic] sont les sténographes" [Translators of foreign news are subaltern employees ... but the important workers are the stenographers] (Pichot 1826: 197).

---

multiple languages on the same date, reaching extremely high daily outputs to meet the deadline. They will, however, tend to be unable to maintain such high output over the longer term.

25 The handwriting speed record was 30 words a minute in 1853 (Trubek 2016: 84).

26 See the text at p. 71 in the report on the 2015 examination for an example: https://saesfrance.org/wp-content/uploads/2014/08/rapport-agreg-ext-2015.pdf (accessed 17 January 2023). Students sitting the examination have six hours to produce two translations, one into French, the other into English, and can divide the time up as they like. No research tools are allowed.

27 Shorthand was in use in the Defauconprêt circle: John Hurford Stone, who printed Defauconprêt's translations in the 1810s, used it from the late 1790s on (Bayly Howell 1818: V, col. 1223).

152 *Professional Translators in Nineteenth-Century France*

Alternatively, he may have *dictated* his translation to competent stenographers: according to one 1855 author, Walter Scott's German translator G. v. Alvensleben worked so fast he dictated his translation to four high-speed scribes (Prinz 1855: 13; Bachleitner 1989: 17).

The second strand in determining Charles-Auguste's role in the project involves looking at his place in the translation production network in Paris, and again, there is evidence pointing both ways. As we have seen, Charles-Auguste became a *préfet des études* at the Collège Rollin, formerly the Collège Sainte-Barbe, in 1819. The history of this venerable centre of learning is long and convoluted (Quicherat 1860): after a period of upheaval in the Revolution, it was given a new lease of life by two brothers who took over the institution, Charles and Henri Nicolle. Charles (1758–1835) was a priest, while Henri (1767–1829) was a bookseller by trade. According to a biography of the former, Charles-Auguste was "un des hommes qui furent les plus aimés de M. Nicolle et de son frère" [one of the men most beloved of M. Nicolle and his brother] (Frappaz 1857: 220). This placed the young man and his father close to the heart of a significant Parisian publishing network. For much of the 1810s, Henri Nicolle was in a publishing partnership with Théophile-Etienne Gide (1767–1837, known in the trade as Gide *fils*): the two men published authors such as Charles Nodier together. Théophile-Etienne Gide was also a notable publisher of travel literature, bringing out the early translations attributed to Charles-Auguste and his father. Their offices were at 12 rue de Seine in Paris, while Defauconprêt's notary office was a few doors down the street at number 30. Some years later, when Henri Nicolle was busy taking over the college in the early 1820s, he passed the reins of his bookshop over to his nephew and apprentice, who was none other than Charles Gosselin (1795–1859) (Felkay 1987).[28] Both Defauconprêts, father and son, therefore had close direct connections to the publishers who gave them their big translatorial break. Gosselin seems to have made a point of hiring those close to him: one of Defauconprêt's later named co-translators on Scott's multi-volume *History of Scotland* was Rose Lattimore-Clarke, née Mame (1797–1866), who married Gosselin in 1830.[29]

This may explain why such a young man was able to become established in the translation field so fast, with seven books to his name by 1819. On the other hand, the Defauconprêt family's position within this publishing node can just as readily be understood as giving Defauconprêt leverage as

---

28 In 1852, Charles-Auguste gave Charles Gosselin's son the school prize in English translation (*Revue britannique* 1852: 494).

29 See https://gw.geneanet.org/ (accessed 24 January 2023). Rose Mame was a member of the Mame printing dynasty.

Auguste-Jean-Baptiste Defauconprêt   153

a budding literary entrepreneur, who used his son's name as a stand-in for projects sliced and diced for translation by subcontractors.

All in all then, the two-pronged book history approach suggests that while it is not *impossible* for Charles-Auguste to have carried out the work himself, it seems unlikely. It seems more probable that Defauconprêt *père* realised the business potential of subcontracting translations within a short time of starting his new career, either on his own – his background was in business, after all – or at the suggestion of the network of publishing entrepreneurs who were his former friends and neighbours in Paris. As a result, Charles-Auguste and his father began publishing collectively translated works under their own names as part of a highly efficient translation production process that saw books crossing the Channel to meet deadlines that individual translators could never hope to rival. This enabled Defauconprêt *père* to lay claim, in 1819, to 12 translations totalling some 1,885,098 words of English, or 628 days' worth of writing by a professional copyist.[30] In this sense, the attribution of individual translatorship to father or son was a somewhat moot point, and indeed the bibliography in Auguste-Jean-Baptiste's own 1829 novel *Robert Fitzooth* lays claim to the *Alceste* translation (Defauconprêt 1829: I, v). The next section of this chapter examines this process in greater detail, in a close study of how Walter Scott's novels were turned into French practically overnight.

Fast-Tracking Scott

In 1794, the Paris-based radical British printer John Hurford Stone (1763–1818), now best remembered as the printer of Thomas Paine and Thomas Jefferson, wrote to his brother with a request. "Be so kind", he asked,

> As to enquire of Gillet [i.e. the printer Thomas Gillet][31] whether the plan he prepared for literary translation from French into English cannot be inverted with respect to this country – whether he cannot furnish us with the means of getting books of merit which may come out, to

---

30 This would be a hugely impressive total for a modern-day translator. See, for example, the tweet by full-time professional translator and editor Eleanor Staniforth on 10 January 2022: "Here's how not to do work-life balance and why I felt on the brink of burnout at the end of last year … I hadn't realised what a ridiculous amount of work I was doing until I looked at my annual totals just now", together with a graph showing an output for the previous year of 1,103,172 words, three-quarters translated, one-quarter proofread: https://twitter.com/E_Staniforth/status/1480543434268098564 (accessed 24 January 2023). The responses by other professionals emphasised the impressive nature of the figures: Almudena Grau, for instance, replied that she never translated more than 500,000 words a year and the thought of doubling that exhausted her.

31 On Thomas Gillet, see MacDonald (2014).

154 *Professional Translators in Nineteenth-Century France*

translate from the English into French; a bookseller and a printer of eminence has been with me on this point; and knowing that I have many literary acquaintance [sic] among you, wishes to engage in procuring such books as ... would have a speedy sale: of this sort are travels ... If Mr. Gillet could procure the sheets of any such books as they come out, and send them over by post, he will receive the proportional profit.

(Stern 1980: 320–1)

While it is hard to tell if anything concrete came of Stone's plan, the letter demonstrates that printers and publishers were actively trying to set up fast channels to import promising works of literature from at least the late eighteenth century onwards. Suggestively, Stone's heir James Smith did print works translated under Defauconprêt's name, such as John Martin's *Histoire des naturels des Îles Tonga*, published by Gilde *fils* and Nicolle in 1817. Whether or not Stone's plan came to fruition, by 1806, the *Anti-Jacobin Review* noted in a review of Villers's *Spirit and Influence of the Reformation of Luther* that the translator

is evidently not to be confounded with the hack translators of the present times, whose numbers are constantly increasing, and must increase, so long as the booksellers ... are only solicitous to produce the *earliest* translations, not the *best*. A wholesale manufacturer in this way is applied to; he sets his subalterns to work, and a something is speedily produced, where not only the spirit of the original evaporates, but where the idiom of our language is lost.

(Anonymous 1806: 190)

By the time Defauconprêt became involved in translation in the mid-1810s, such channels were well in place for works such as MacLeod's *Alceste* narrative. The translator Jacques-Théodore Parisot (1783–1840) recorded that by 1821, Walter Scott's novels were being published on the same day in English in Edinburgh and London and in French in Paris (Green 1957: 40). This section seeks to shed light on the mechanisms by which the French publisher, Charles Gosselin – a newcomer to publishing, still in his mid-20s – achieved a feat that, according to one account, earned him 20,000 *livres* by 1825 (Legouis 1971).

How did print move so fast in the days before modern telecommunications? One answer was simply that it did so as a result of theft: one 1797 court case accused a workman of stealing newly printed sheets of seven plays (Maxted 2016). More honestly, authors agreed to sell proof sheets to printers keen to obtain preferential access. On 26 November 1826, Walter Scott visited Galignani in Paris, "where the brothers, after some palaver, offered me £105 for the sheets of Napoleon, to be reprinted at Paris in

Auguste-Jean-Baptiste Defauconprêt   155

English. I told them I would think of it" (quoted in Maxted 2016). In other instances, the author was left out of the loop entirely. One such is the agreement brokered, if not initiated, by Defauconprêt.

Green (1957) gives a detailed account of the events surrounding the establishment of a fast track to bring Scott's novels to France. In the spring of 1821, some six years into his translation career, Defauconprêt took a decisive step, perhaps seeking to take on a more active role as a publishing middleman. Seeking priority access to Scott's latest novel, he wrote – ill-advisedly, as it turned out – to the author, who at that point was still officially anonymous. Scott, annoyed at having his cover blown, shot back a denial on 15 April 1821, after which his publishers Constable and Cadell wrote directly to Defauconprêt:

> Your letter of the 9th inst. is before us. We have made no agreement of the nature mentioned by you with Mr Neville. We only talked on the subject as one of great difficulty and that the author must be consulted. You have taken upon yourself to apply to one who we have authority to declare is not the author of the book you allude to. We have done this for a series of years and it is rather too much for you to apply to anyone about a book without a name. The consequence is that we beg that no more communications be made on the subject either to us or to any other.
>
> (Quoted in Green 1957: 40)

This indicates that Mr. Neville, representing the London printers Black, Young and Young, had worked with Defauconprêt on a proposal to obtain advance proof sheets. A letter from him to Gosselin dated 4 October 1822 indicates that the translator was actively involved in the negotiations. It is worth quoting at length for the light it sheds on the timings and the process involved:

> Nous pouvons chanter "La victoire est à nous", mon cher Monsieur. Au moment où je vous écris, j'ai déjà entre les mains onze feuilles de Peveril du Pic … Je ne suis arrivé à Londres que mardi dernier. Le mercredi j'ai été chez M. Black que je n'ai pas trouvé … J'y suis retourné le jeudi à 9 [heures]. J'ai trouvé un grand jeune homme d'une figure prévenante et parfaitement honnête; il m'a fort bien reçu, et comme tout étoit à peu près d'accord entre vous, il n'a élevé aucune difficulté quant au fond. La chose sur laquelle il a le plus insisté, c'est un secret inviolable sur toute cette affaire, qui ne doit être connu que de vous, de lui et de moi. Si le bruit en arrivait à Edimbourg, il ne pourrait plus se procurer de la même manière les romans futurs de l'auteur de Waverley, et nous en serions privés par contrecoup. Je lui ai promis un silence absolu de votre part et

de la mienne ... Quand on verra paroître la traduction en même temps que l'original, ou [à][32] quelques jours près, si l'on vous interroge sur les moyens dont vous vous êtes servi, vous pouvez vous tirer d'affaire en disant que vous n'en savez rien, et que c'est le secret du traducteur.

M. Black avoit reçu, le mercredi, d'Edimbourg, un premier envoi de 11 feuilles. Les 2 1ers volumes lui seront ainsi envoyés par paquet de 8 à 10 feuilles, et le 3e feuille par feuille. La question était de savoir qui se mettait le premier en besogne, de moi ou du traducteur Allemand [sic]. J'ai demandé combien il traduiroit par jour: M. Black m'a répondu une demi feuille, et comme je lui ai dit j'en traduirois au moins une feuille dans le même temps, il a consenti à me laisser prendre l'avance, ce que je regarde comme important, attendu que le traducteur Allemand auroit pu retarder mon travail.

Tout va bien jusqu'ici, mais il reste un chapitre de contrariétés, [comme] on en trouve partout. On a commencé par imprimer le 2e volume, et le premier ne viendra qu'en second. Il est donc impossible que vous commenciez à faire imprimer la traduction, avant que j'aie en mains la totalité du 1er volume. Il y a deux raisons pour cela. La 1ere c'est que le commencement du 2e volume Anglois que je traduis en ce moment fera la fin du 2e volume françois; attendu que nous avons toujours divisé les trois en quatre; or la nécessité de la pagination ... rend impossible d'imprimer la fin d'un volume avant le commencement. La seconde raison, plus importante encore à mes yeux, c'est le désir que j'ai de rendre cette traduction aussi parfaite qu'il est en moi de le faire, de la soigner d'une manière toute particulière ... Or il peut se trouver dans le 1er volume des choses qu'il est nécessaire d'avoir lues pour bien entendre le 2d. Mr. Pichot, dans sa traduction du 3e vol: de Nigel, a fait, page 40, deux contresens qu'il n'auroit jamais faits, s'il avoit lu la scène passée à l'ordinaire de Beaujeu, à laquelle il est fait allusion dans ce passage. Je ne vois pas d'ailleurs que vous ayez besoin de tant presser l'impression. Le roman Anglois, m'a dit Mr. Black, ne sera mis en vente que dans le cours de Décembre [sic]; il attend la fin du 2d volume la semaine prochaine, le 1er viendra ensuite, et il croit qu'il l'aura reçu en totalité du commencement de novembre. Vous aurez donc tout le temps d'imprimer. Dès que j'aurai les premières feuilles du 1er volume, je vous enverrai 2 fois par semaine par la voie de l'ambassade, tout ce que j'aurai traduit, dès que j'aurai rejoint le 2e volume, je vous l'enverrai en totalité, et comme le 3e ira plus lentement, il sera plus facile à l'imprimeur de me suivre. D'ailleurs, il seroit peut-être d'une

---

32 Words between square brackets are suppositions, the words themselves being hidden by the manuscript binding.

Auguste-Jean-Baptiste Defauconprêt   157

bonne politique de ne faire paroître la traduction qu'une huitaine de jours après la mise en vente de l'original.

J'ai dit à Mr. Black que je serois chargé de lui payer la somme convenue volume par volume. Ne vous mettez pas en peine pour le premier, je puis l'avancer ... Je vous renvoie ce que j'ai revu de Nigel. Il me faut 4 jours entiers pour voir le reste, peut-être même 5. Dites moi si vous en êtes pressé, et à quelle époque vous désirez ce travail; parce que, si cela est possible, je voudrais employer les momens d'intervalle que Peveril me laissera, pour faire quelques feuilles de <u>Londres en 1822</u> pour M. Gide: travail pour lequel il me faudroit une dizaine de jours. N'oubliez pourtant pas que vous passerez toujours avant tout. Je vous écrirai toutes les semaines pour vous rendre compte de l'état des choses, relativement à Peveril.

[We can sing "Victory is ours", my dear friend. As I write, I am in possession of eleven sheets of Peveril of the Peak. I arrived in London only last Tuesday. On Wednesday, I went to see Mr Black whom I did not find. I returned on Thursday at nine. I found a tall, kindly and perfectly honest looking young man. He received me very well and, as almost everything had been settled between you, he raised no difficulty at all about the main issue. The thing he insisted upon most is inviolable secrecy about the whole business which must only be known to you, him and me. If Edinburgh got word of it, he would no longer be able to procure the future novels of the author of Waverley the same way and, as a result, we would no longer have access to them. I have promised him our absolute silence. When people see the translation appearing at the same time as the original, if you are questioned about the methods you employed, you can avoid the issue by saying that you know nothing about it and it is the translator's secret.

Mr Black had received a first set of eleven sheets from Edinburgh on Wednesday. The first two volumes will be sent to him in batches of eight to eleven sheets and the third, sheet by sheet. The question was who should get to work first, the German translator or me. I asked how much he could translate in a day; Mr Black said half a sheet and as I told him I could translate at least one sheet in the same time, he agreed to let me take the lead which I think is important since the German translator might have held me up.

Everything is going well so far but there is still one vexatious point. They have begun by printing the second volume and the first will come only after it. You cannot therefore begin printing the translation before I have the whole first volume, for two reasons. Firstly, the beginning of the second volume, which I am translating now, will be the end of the second French volume as we have always split three into four. The pagination means we cannot print the end of one volume before we

158 *Professional Translators in Nineteenth-Century France*

have the beginning. The second reason, even more important in my view, is my desire to make this translation as perfect as I can; to take special pains with it. But the first volume may contain things which are needed to understand the second properly. Mr Pichot, in his translation of the third volume of Nigel, made (p. 40) two mistranslations which he would never have made had he read the scene at the inn at Beaujeu, to which this passage refers. Furthermore, I do not think you need hurry the printing. The English novel, Mr Black told me, will not be on sale until some time in December; he expects the end of the second volume next week; the first volume will come later and he thinks he will have the whole novel by the beginning of November. You will have plenty of time to print as soon as I have the first sheets of the first volume. I will send you all I have translated twice a week, via the Embassy. I will send you the whole of volume two as soon as I have finished and, as the third will be slower, the printer can easily follow me. Besides it might perhaps be wise not to publish the translation until about a week after the original is put on sale. I have told Mr Black that I would be instructed to pay him the agreed sum volume by volume. Don't worry about the first; I can advance it. I am sending you what I have revised of Nigel so far. I will need four whole days, maybe even five, to go over the rest. Tell me if you need it in a hurry and when, because, if possible, I would like to use the time left over from *Peveril* to write a few sheets of *Londres en 1822* for M. Gide, which should take me ten days. But do bear in mind you will always come first. I will write to you every week to let you know how I am getting on with *Peveril*.]

(MS-3112: fols 180–1, underlined in the original)

This lengthy quote shines a rare spotlight on the translator's agency as an active stakeholder in the production process, shaping the workflow, arranging cross-Channel postage via the embassy, dictating the printing schedule, and even temporarily taking over the publisher's role as financial backer for the project. It demonstrates that the translator-editor relationship is – or can be – a labile process of negotiation involving fluid power dynamics and that the translator's role in the communications circuit or chain of command is far from being restricted to a straightforward process of linguistic transfer: as a highly professionalised translator, Defauconpret takes on multiple roles in the book production process. This suggests that Bachleitner's neat updated version of Darnton's communications circuit, incorporating the translator at a single point in the process between "mediators" and "editors" (Bachleitner 2009: 424), perhaps requires messifying with extra arrows to make it clear that translators can in fact take on multiple roles. Belle and Hosington (2017) make a similar point for the early modern period, pointing out that at this point in history, translation could be less neatly slotted in between production and distribution and

Auguste-Jean-Baptiste Defauconprêt 159

that the roles of printers and booksellers were not yet discrete (Belle and Hosington 2017: 10). Yet the point here is that even in the nineteenth century – and indeed even in the twenty-first – the role of translators extends far beyond the single step of linguistic transfer. Translators always have acted as agents, editors, book distributors, reviewers, and readers: they are enmeshed throughout the book production process, from inception to consumption.

A further point of interest in this letter is the light it sheds on issues of timing and productivity. The letter is dated 4 October 1822, a Friday; at this point Defauconprêt had 11 printers' sheets in hand and was planning to produce a sheet of translated text a day. Defauconprêt's exact address is not known at this point – at some point before 1827, he moved to Robert Street (*Kaleidoscope* 1827: 20) – but from either known address it would have been a half-hour walk for him to pick up the proofs at the Black, Young and Young offices in Tavistock Street. Looking at a first-edition copy of *Peveril*, this comes to either page 16 or page 32 – roughly 2,500 or 5,000 words a day – depending on whether the sheet was printed on one or both sides. The lower figure would be a decent individual daily rate today but would make the German translator noticeably slow; the higher figure is achievable with modern-day tools, but would be challenging to maintain in the long run. The figures can usefully be compared with Wilhelm Hauff's 1827 (obviously exaggerated) fantasy of a translation factory run on Fordist lines of maximum efficiency, where each translator was allocated half a printer's sheet to translate between eight a.m. and three p.m. and a further half-sheet to edit after an hour's break (Hauff 1827 [2015]: 11).[33]

33 Hauff's satire describes a translation factory in Scheerau which produces 15 translated sheets of Scott a day, drawing on modern print technology. It has 15 presses fed by a continuous paper machine – a technology patented in Britain by Louis-Nicolas Robert in 1803 – that streams paper into the basement like lava. There, it is machine-cut (though in reality this stage was still done by hand, as paper guillotines were not invented until the 1830s) and dried. The journey from pulp to finished book takes 30 hours. The 15 presses produce 20,000 offprints a day. The translation department is upstairs in 2 rooms, each of which holds 15 translators who produce rough drafts of 1 half-sheet every morning. Off the two rooms are four smaller rooms with a stylist and his secretary, tasked with polishing the first drafts. The stylists earn two taler a day but must pay their own secretaries. One stylist can polish the work of seven or eight rough drafters: they send each page through as they finish it. A fifth room contains a pair of poets working on poems and epigraphs. The site manager is working on a steam-powered translation machine that would automatically turn French and English into German, scrapping 34 jobs (Hauff 1827 [2015]: 10–12).

160 *Professional Translators in Nineteenth-Century France*

It should be noted that the letter refers to three volumes: at this point, Sir Walter Scott was still writing after a lull in August 1822[34] and eventually produced a fourth volume in a burst of speed, making this his longest novel. It totals 228,146 words based on the Project Gutenberg edition. Obtaining a word count for Defauconprêt's translation is no easy matter: a PDF version of a later edition is readily available on archive.org, but the quality of the reproduction does not lend itself to OCR word counting tools. The closest substitute is a Wikisource version of Albert de Montémont's translation in 1838 which, as seen in Chapter 4, heavily plagiarised the Defauconprêt version. This version totals 249,141 words, a slightly below-average expansion rate of 8.8 per cent.

The book was published in English on 7 January 1823. The French translation was then announced as one of the week's releases in the 25 January issue of the *Bibliographie de la France* for 1823. We know Defauconprêt cannot have worked steadily from October to January, since the book was still being written in early October and a whole extra volume was yet to come. Black told Defauconprêt he would have the whole book in hand by the start of November to publish in December. In the end, volume 3 was finished by 14 December and a start made on volume 4, which was completed by Christmas (Scott 2007: 498–505) – a staggering rate that led Scott to write "Peveril will, I fear, smell of the apoplexy" (Scott *Letters*: vol. 7). Furthermore, Defauconprêt was not able to give *Peveril* his undivided attention for the whole period. Fifteen days must be removed for edits to *Nigel* and *Londres en 1822*, which Defauconprêt did complete for Gide (the *Bibliographie de la France* lists it as a new publication in the week of 18 January 1823). This meant that even if Defauconprêt made a start on volume 2 as the sheets arrived from Edinburgh in around mid-October and volume one in November, he would still have been left with two volumes, some 125,000 words, to translate as the sheets came in between early December and mid-January. Counting generously, this leaves him with 45 days to complete the project, at a relatively manageable daily rate of 2,777 words if he never took a day off and the project met no delays – though transporting sheets from Edinburgh was liable to face weather disruption over the Christmas period: Walter Scott in Abbotsford wrote to his friend Daniel Terry in London on 9 January 1823 that "Peveril has been stopped ten days, having been driven back to Leith Roads by stress of weather" (Scott *Letters*: vol. 7). Translating under such time pressure must have been a stressful process, with all the issues raised by just-in-time translation of a text in the process of still being written and delivered to the translator sheet by sheet, described by Häring via Thomas de Quincey:

---

34 See http://www.walterscott.lib.ed.ac.uk/works/novels/peak.html (accessed 23 January 2023).

Auguste-Jean-Baptiste Defauconprêt 161

The sheets, dripping wet as they arrive by every post from the Edinburgh press, must be translated just as they stand with or without sense or connexion. Nay it happens not unfrequently that, if a sheet should chance to end with one or two syllables of an unfinished word, we are obliged to translate this first instalment of a future meaning; and by the time the next sheet arrives with the syllables in arrear, we first learn into what confounded scrapes we have fallen by guessing and translating at haphazard ... I shall content myself with reminding the public of the well-known and sad mishap that occurred in the translation of Kenilworth ... the sheet unfortunately closed thus: "*to save himself from these disasters, he became an agent of Smith-*". And we all translated – "um sich aus diesen trübseligkeiten [sic] zu erretten, wurde er Agent bei einem Schmiedemeister;" that is, "*he became foreman to a blacksmith*" ... next morning's post arrived, and showed that all Germany had been betrayed by a catch-word of Mr. Constable's. For the next sheet took up the imperfect and embryo catch-word thus: – "field matches, or marriages contracted for the sake of money".

(Häring 1825a: xxiv–xxvi)

Yet stressful does not mean impossible: after all, Scott had himself managed to *write* the text at an impressively fast pace.

Was Defauconprêt being honest when he swore the project would go no further than himself, Black, and Gosselin? Or did delays to the project and its unexpected length perhaps mean he started out intending to work on it himself but eventually ended up splitting the project with other translators?

A few clues point to the use of multiple translators for this project despite the need for secrecy. First of all, he would have had to start out slowly with the content he had in hand in early October, then speed up in the latter weeks and months as more and more unplanned material came in, while checking for consistency between the completed volume 2 and the incoming volume 1 and spending time on his other projects. Given the novel's historical setting, he would also likely have found the work slow going when confronted with archaic, dialectal, and other unusual language he was unlikely to have encountered in Regency London, such as "buff and bandoleer", "murrain", "wannion", and "there are rods in pickle to switch the Geneva cloak with".[35]

---

35 On the difficulties faced by translators without access to appropriate research tools, see this touching anecdote: "The French translator of Franklin's *Correspondence*, has made a truly French blunder. Upon an observation of the Doctor – 'People imagined that an American was a kind of Yahoo' – he makes the following note: '*Yahoo*. It must be an

162 *Professional Translators in Nineteenth-Century France*

Secondly, the letter alludes to (Amédée) Pichot's work on *Nigel*, published by Gosselin in 1822 under Defauconprêt's name long *after* negotiations with Black were underway to obtain advance proofs. If secrecy was paramount now, why not for *Nigel* a few months earlier? As the case of Captain Tuckey's narrative demonstrates, the practice of translating from advance proof sheets was well established by the early 1820s and was indeed something to be promoted in advertising. Defauconprêt had already approached Cadell about obtaining advance sheets, so when the translation came out within days of the original, it would surely have been no great leap for the printers to put two and two together. Though they did eventually break off the partnership with Gosselin, it took another three years and seems only to have come to an end when Galignani outbid him for the *Life of Napoleon* (Maxted 2016). Perhaps the need for secrecy was not so absolute after all – maybe there were only *some* people, like Gosselin's commercial rivals, it was imperative to keep in the dark.

Thirdly, the first volumes of the German translation by C. F. Michaelis, *Ritter Gottfried Peveril: Eine romantische Darstellung*, came out at the tail end of 1822 (*Halbjahr* 1822: 128). This suggests that Black may not in fact have let Defauconprêt always see the sheets before the allegedly far slower German translator, who was able to bring some volumes out before the French (and indeed before the full English version). The German publisher was paying £25 per volume for advance access (Green 1957: 42) and may well not have been happy to play second fiddle.

Finally, and perhaps most revealingly of all, Defauconprêt's name features on no fewer than 13 other translations in the period 1822–3, as well as on a two-volume novel of his own, *Masaniello, ou Huit jours à Naples*,[36] and his annual *Londres* series (he published further sub-Scottian novels of his own in 1824, 1825, and 1829). We know from the 4 October letter that he had at the very least editorial oversight over the translations that came out under his name. Given the hectic publishing schedule this implies, it is unlikely he could have devoted his undivided attention to one title from October to January. Based on release dates, he would have had the proofs to at least two further titles to handle over the period in addition to *Nigel* and *Londres*.[37]

---

animal. It is affirmed that it is the opossum; but I have not yet been able to find the word Yahoo in any dictionary of natural history'" ("Oliver Oldschool" 1818: 390).

36 The book is attributed to Defauconprêt in Girault de Saint Fargeau (1839: 164) but to Charles-Auguste in the May 1822 *Bibliographie de la France*.

37 According to the *Bibliographie de la France*, the translations came out as follows: Walter Scott's *Le Pirate* in early February 1822, *Guy Mannering* in late March 1822, *Halidon Hill* in mid-July 1822, *Rob Roy* in late July 1822, *L'Abbé* in mid-October 1822, *Le Monastère* in late February 1823, and *Quentin Durward* in late May 1823; Anna Maria Bennett's *Hélène, Comtesse de Castle-Howel* in late April 1822; Arthur Murphy's *Mémoires sur*

Auguste-Jean-Baptiste Defauconprêt 163

In the event, when the translation came out within a couple of weeks of the original, rumours immediately swirled about the use of multiple translators. Writing from London in mid-February 1823, Stendhal certainly suggested the project was sliced and diced: he began by describing the translated *Peveril* as seditious, then continued,

> Vous ne pouvez vous faire d'idée de la platitude des traductions françaises des romans de Walter Scott; on emploie quatre traducteurs pour chaque volume; trois au moins ne savent pas l'anglais; le libraire donne dix sous par feuille à un prétendu littérateur qui corrige le style.

> [You cannot imagine how flat Walter Scott's French translations are; four translators are hired for each volume; at least three don't understand English; the bookseller gives a would-be man of letters ten sous per sheet to correct the style.]

> (Stendhal 1908: 290)

Stendhal had been in London a matter of months at that point (Naugrette 1998): it would seem that despite the cloak-and-dagger business of obtaining advance proofs, Scott's multiple translatorship was more or less an open secret in French literary circles.

All this evidence, together with the tight timelines, makes Defauconprêt's single translatorship of Scott tenuous but not absolutely disproven. Where retranslation theory leads Bogé-Rousseau (2018: 310) to conclude that Defauconprêt worked alone on Scott's novels from 1822 to 1827, book history and a focus on the conditions of production of the translation as a material object suggest this was perhaps not the case.

Either way, within a handful of years, Defauconprêt was openly embracing his status as a literary entrepreneur. His 1825 translation of Häring's *Walladmor* boasts in its appeal to subscribers of Defauconprêt's crack team of experts in Paris who worked on the translation, revised the proofs, and provided the footnotes (Jenn 2013: 52: see fig. 3). The aim of this enterprise, the appeal continued, was to protect publishers from the downsides of competition which forced translators to place speed above accuracy. Turning the longstanding criticisms of cheap, low-quality, sweatshop-style translation factories on their head, multiple translatorship was now being touted as a closely monitored production process guaranteeing effective quality control: not without reason did one contemporary

---

Garrick et sur Macklin in late November 1822; John Galt's *Sir André Wylie* in mid-April 1823; an anonymous *Comédien ambulant* in early October 1823; Theodore Hook's *Pen Owen* in mid-September 1823; Fenimore Cooper's *Les Pionniers* in late August 1823 and *L'espion* in late 1823. If Defauconprêt had editorial oversight, he would have received proofs for *L'Abbé* and *Mémoires sur Garrick* while working on *Peveril*.

164　*Professional Translators in Nineteenth-Century France*

account call him "Defauconprêt et Cie" [Defauconprêt & Co] (Lacroix 1829: 14). Ironically, an 1837 call for subscribers for a new edition of Scott in French made the case that Defauconprêt outgunned his rivals due to the "sage lenteur qu'il est nécessaire d'apporter dans un pareil travail" [well-advised slowness required for such an undertaking], having worked on the translations for 15 years (Pichot 1837: 4). After decades of being accused of churning out fast, cheap French, Defauconprêt's commercial edge over his rivals turned out to be his longevity in the trade, framed as labour time compatible not with just-in-time manufacturing, but the careful honing of fine artisanry. Paradoxically, Defauconprêt's "lingual steam engine" let him claim to be the inventor of slow translation.

Conclusion

This chapter has sought to examine the nuts and bolts of an early-nineteenth-century translator's career. In focusing on the material details of how texts circulated in translation, it undermines often-repeated claims of Defauconprêt's extraordinary output. In so doing, it calls into question some arguments that have been made on the basis of his sole translatorship. For instance, the case made in Barnaby (2011) that Defauconprêt's political and aesthetic stance emerges in his Lady Morgan translations should perhaps be reassessed with an eye on traces of multiple translatorship, even at this early stage of his career. One broad question that remains to be explored in greater depth is why translation scholars have been so ready to accept productivity data that is immediately greeted with scepticism by practising translators: evidence, perhaps, of the gap between the ivory tower and the wordface or between the cultures of industry and research (Chesterman and Wagner 2002; Jemielity 2018).

This focus on person and process also opens up a range of new research avenues. What further innovative approaches could be applied to the oeuvre attributed to Defauconprêt to add to the evidence of multiple translatorship? Tactics could include a stylometric analysis along the lines of Rybicki and Heydel (2013), implementing stylistic authorship attribution methods based on a multivariate analysis of most-frequent-word frequencies to attempt to identify translators, or an embodied practice approach in which a human translator would attempt to recreate his output in similar conditions with similar tools. A social network map of the publishing nexus around Defauconprêt would likewise be an extremely useful venture, along the lines of the ongoing "ReConceptualizing Chinese-English Translator Networks in the Nineteenth Century" project at the Chinese University of Hong Kong. And who were the anonymous translators Defauconprêt worked with? While we will doubtless never know their names, a more in-depth study of the translation market in Regency London would certainly throw up some possibilities. A number of French translators advertised in the daily press and were listed in commercial gazettes. The official *London Gazette* records details of new translator businesses and insolvencies.[38] A detailed search of the 1841 census, the first to record occupations, would no doubt produce some names. Traces can be found in other historical sources, such as the Old Bailey archives. A keyword search for "translator" throws up some names: Auguste Gougenheim, assaulted by Jean-Jacques Courben in 1839; John Frederick (Jean-Frédéric?) Cobet, born in Belgium in 1791, a victim of manslaughter in a fight over a debt in 1845; Gustavus Westen, witness in a forgery trial in 1845.[39] All tantalisingly forgotten names for another dedicated translation historian to explore: "If we think of the history of translation as a mosaic, there can be little doubt that there are many small pieces or tesserae missing, as well as large empty spaces yet to be filled" (Santoyo 2006: 13).

---

38 See https://www.thegazette.co.uk (accessed 30 January 2023) for results from January 1800 to January 1850.
39 See https://www.oldbaileyonline.org/ (accessed 30 January 2023).

Coda

In mid-June 1981, some 300 literary translators across France received an unexpected envelope in the post. It contained a circular sent to every member of the *Association des Traducteurs Littéraires de France* (ATLF), then seven or so years into its existence, explaining the grounds for a mysterious rash of resignations among the board members. The ATLF, the circular claimed, was afflicted by "un malaise qui va croissant" [increasing unease].[1] The authors included leading figures from the world of translation such as Antoine Berman, Laure Guille-Bataillon, Claire Malroux, and Brice Matthieussent. Their dissatisfaction stemmed from the board's failure, as they saw it, to prioritise "la reconnaissance d'un véritable statut professionnel du traducteur littéraire" [implementing full professional status for translators]. The time had come, they believed, to push for unionisation. The issue had been bubbling under for a while: as early as 10 March 1975, in the association's first year of existence,[2] one AGM attendee, Roger Munier,[3] took the floor to argue that "le traducteur fournit une tâche et a droit, par conséquent, a un salaire" [the translator carries out a task and therefore has the right to a salary]. As the dissenters saw it in 1981, the ATLF was rooted in an "ambiguité fondamentale" [fundamental ambiguity] since the majority of board members were *not* full-time literary translators. The association was run by amateurs, sociologically speaking, whose main source of income and identity was academia. The crunch point had come in April 1981 with what they called "l'affaire du CNL". According to the timeline appended to the circular, the *Centre*

---

1 The quotations in this section are from uncatalogued and in many cases undated documents in the ATLF archive, photocopied by the author during her time as an ATLF board member from 2003 to 2013.
2 It split from the *Société Française des Traducteurs* in 1973 to defend the specific interests of literary translators. See https://www.sft.fr/fr/notre-histoire-3 (accessed 12 May 2023).
3 Roger Munier (1923–2010) was a writer and translator of Heidegger, Kleist, Rilke, and Paz, among others.

DOI: 10.4324/9781003173090-8

national du Livre had undertaken in 1978 to maintain specific translation funding for full-timers. In the April 1981 session, however, 3 full-timers had been turned down for funding, while of the 16 projects approved, 11 went to academics who translated as a sideline.

The dissenters' circular was met two days later by an official, and rather ill-tempered, response from the ATLF board loyalists, challenging their "arguments spécieux" [specious arguments]. The letter insisted that the "affaire du CNL" was "montée de toutes pièces" [a fabrication] and debunked the funding figures. An extraordinary general meeting was held on 18 June, the outcome of which was to establish a commission tasked with reporting on the potential for switching to trade union status. The commission put together a set of statutes for what, if approved, was to be called the *Syndicat des traducteurs de l'édition* [Union for translators in the publishing sector]. The proposal included a definition of professional literary translation status that insisted on the importance of maintaining an ongoing active presence in the field: full membership required having published at least three full-length books and publishing a translation at least every three years. The majority of the executive committee would be translators earning over half their income from the practice. This definition would exclude many amateur practitioners, including academics who dabbled in the field from time to time, particularly those whose translation practice was linked to their research interests. The union's main aim would be to campaign for legislation that would result in a collective bargaining agreement, full social security coverage, and salaried status for recognised literary translators. Suggestions were made for an accreditation scheme along the lines of a press card for journalists.

How realistic was the plan? Not very, according to Bernard Lortholary, the ATLF vice-president and senior lecturer in German literature at the Sorbonne. He pointed out that the majority of literary translators were part-timers – a fact borne out by the 1983 Heinich survey commissioned in response to the internal crisis – and were unlikely to agree to exclude themselves from the legal definition of their own profession. General secretary Jean-Pierre Lefebvre, professor of German literature at the Ecole Normale Supérieure, pointed out in turn that well under 50 individuals would qualify for union status. In any case, a vote was held on the issue on 3 December 1981. The *Bulletin d'Information de l'ATLF* 29 for January 1982 records the details of the heated debate – one member described the proposal as a "putsch" – and gives the result. Of 131 voting members, 125 votes were valid: 48 voted for the motion to unionise, 77 against.

The dissenters lost decisively. Yet by forcing the debate, they foregrounded the often unspoken issue of professional vs. amateur identity of translators. This debate has important repercussions for social justice, particularly in the field of literature. Much public-facing literary translation

168 *Professional Translators in Nineteenth-Century France*

discourse today focuses on who gets to translate.[4] To what extent does translatorial identity need to map onto authorial identity? To return to the introduction of this book, who should translate Amanda Gorman? Is it fair that men should translate key feminist works such as *The Second Sex* or, more recently, Caroline Criado Perez's *Invisible Women* and Chimamanda Ngozi Adichie's *We Should All Be Feminists*?[5] Can and should a straight translator translate a queer author? Should editors aim to seek out and hire neurodivergent translators for works about neurodiversity or by neurodivergent authors?

Less debated is the issue of who can *afford* to translate. Yet issues of professional status are closely bound up with issues of inclusion and exclusion, of which economic exclusion is part. For instance, irregularity of income can be a significant impediment to building a presence in the literary translation field, particularly since careers are largely built through postgraduate study and networking, at its most effective when it includes regular travel to translation events and attendance at translation residencies that can represent significant earnings penalties or opportunity costs for those in regular employment or with caring responsibilities. There are important issues of social representativity at stake in the way literary translation careers are currently structured.

As neural machine translation takes major strides forward, inching into the literary domain,[6] the assumptions about the creative nature of literary translation that have underpinned the practice for the past 300 or so years are facing an unprecedented challenge. This must beg the question of what future literary translation careers will look like, as wider social trends such as the emergence of tools like ChatGTP and changes to European competition law lead to shifts in the professional landscape.

In September 2022, the European Commission issued new guidelines allowing self-employed workers to engage in collective bargaining in some circumstances without breaching competition law. As I was writing the closing pages of this book, Finland's freelance audiovisual translators were quietly getting ready for court. On 24 April 2023, their industry body Kieliasiantuntijat, the Finnish Language Experts Association, reported that a collective agreement had been reached establishing minimum rates of pay for the country's 400 self-employed AV specialists. They can expect a six per cent pay rise as well as pension contributions and parental leave

---

4 See for example Bhanot and Tiang (2022).
5 The first English version of *The Second Sex*, by Howard Parshley, has been widely criticised: see Pickford 2019. Criado Perez was translated into French by Nicolas Dupin, while Ngozi Adichie was translated into Spanish by Javier Calvo. My thanks to Isabel García Aguilar for bringing the latter example to my attention.
6 On this fast-growing area of research, see Hansen (2021).

rights over the coming two years (Albarino 2023). While outright unioni-sation for literary translators seems as unrealistic a prospect today as it did to Bernard Lortholary in 1981, there is much in the collective agreement model that is appealing. Perhaps Wilhelm Hauff's 1827 proto-Taylorist fantasy of a high-tech, streamlined translation factory was not so far-fetched after all.

Appendix
Translators and Transactions in the Institut mémoires de l'édition contemporaine archives

This appendix adds to a growing set of bio-bibliographical sources[1] devoted to translators, including the Svensk översätterlexikon, the Dansk Oversaetterleksikon, the Germersheimer Übersetzerlexikon, the Norsk Oversetterleksikon, the Dutch Vertalerslexicon, and the Digital Lexicon of Polish Translators.[2] It offers an additional focus on evidence of publishing transactions that sheds new light on the collective economic lives of translators in the nineteenth century.

François D'Albert Durade (1804–86). Geneva-based curator and artist. George Eliot lived in his house in 1849–50 and he painted her portrait.[3] On 20 February 1886, he wrote to his fellow Genevan author Victor Cherbuliez that he was authorised to translate *Scènes de la vie ecclésiastique* not only by George Eliot, but also her husband. On 16 March 1886, Hachette paid him 800 francs for the rights to *Scènes de la vie ecclésiastique*, *Adam Bede*, *Le Moulin sur la Floss*, and *Romola*. On the same day, his son wrote that no changes were to be made to the manuscript of the second volume of *Scènes d'une vie ecclésiastique* and he was to sign off the proofs before printing. The title was to be George Eliot, *Scènes de la vie ecclésiastique*, Traduites avec l'autorisation de l'auteur par F. d'Albert-Durade. The rights to *Adam Bede* under the same conditions depended on Hachette buying the rights and plates for the extant edition from M.

---

1 Bio-bibliographical information on translators is drawn from https://catalogue.bnf.fr, https://data.bnf.fr, and the Oxford Dictionary of National Biography. Other additional sources cited in footnotes.
2 See https://litteraturbanken.se/%C3%B6vers%C3%A4ttarlexikon/, http://danskoversa etterleksikon.dk/, http://uelex.de/, https://www.oversetterleksikon.no/, https://www.ver-talerslexicon.nl/ respectively (accessed 21 March 2023). The Polish version is not online at the time of writing: see Lars Kleberg (2022) "Translators' Dictionaries in Sweden – and Europe". *Counterpoint* 8: 11.
3 See https://bge-geneve.ch/iconographie/personne/alexandre-louis-francois-d-albert-durade (accessed 2 December 2022).

172 *Appendix*

Georg. The only changes authorised were instances of Swiss French. Four days later, d'Albert-Durade's son wrote again to offer the rights to reprint the four novels for 3,500 francs. His father died a few months later, on 27 June (HAC 4.2).

Emma Allouard (1836–1918). Novelist (under the pseudonyms Emile Jouan and Jouan-Rolland) and prolific translator from the English, mainly of children's books, for a few years at mid-century. Her file in the Hetzel archive contains numerous payment details, some of which are listed in Chapter 5 (HTZ 1.4).

J. Anceaux (first name and dates unknown). A woman who authored and translated several children's books from the 1870s to the end of the century for Hetzel and for Delagrave. Hetzel wrote to her in 1874 to offer 400 francs for her translation of Holme Lee's *Vie et aventures de mon chien Match*. She had already received 100 francs for the project and was authorised to attend the accounting department on 8 January and 5 February 1875 to receive two further payments of 150 francs. I have been unable to locate a book by the title given in the letter; the BnF only has one French translation of a work by Holme Lee, co-authored with Ashford Owen. Her file also includes a payment of 100 francs on 3 September 1873 for a work entitled *Patins d'argent*, from an original by Mary Mapes Dodge, published by Hetzel under his own pseudonym P. J. Stahl in 1875 (HTZ 1.6).

J. Appert (possibly Jules Appert, 1835–1906?). On 5 July 1862, received payment of 100 francs for work on a translation of *The Arabian Nights*. The BnF catalogue lists a Jules Appert who wrote several works of local history on Normandy considerably later in the century. It seems unlikely to be the same individual, but no other candidate has been identified (HTZ 7.13).

Auguste Barbier (1805–82). Poet and memoirist elected to the Académie française in 1869. Translated from English and Italian. On 20 June 1876, he sold Hachette the right to reprint his translation of *The Ancient Mariner*, initially published in *Le Magasin Pittoresque*, for 500 francs. Hachette was free to choose the format and print run, but every edition had to feature Gustave Doré's illustrations. Barbier retained the translation rights in all other circumstances (HAC 7.24).

Jules Baytun (Bayntun) Gébelin (?–1864). A cosmopolitan figure who appears in various sources at mid-century as Julius/Giulio Bayntun Gebelin. A Piedmont gazette has him advertising English lessons as a native of London in February 1843. He was a doctor and English instructor in

Appendix 173

Italy and briefly edited the *Journal de Francfort* under the title *L'Europe* in 1862.[4] Early in 1856, he undertook to translate the Code Reynold for nautical signalling into Italian with the assistance of a Sardinian naval officer. The translation had to be approved by the Sardinian naval ministry and the translator agreed to make any changes they demanded at no extra cost. He was to be paid 1 franc per French page and a further 100 francs for the additional labour of cross-referencing and putting the manuscript into Italian alphabetical order. He was to be paid 50 per cent when he handed the work in and 50 per cent on ministry approval of the translation. On 30 April that same year, however, he wrote to say he had been forced to leave Paris at very short notice and would be unable to work on the project for two months, though it was due that week. He left orders with his concierge to hand over the work he had completed to date. Then on 23 May, he wrote to say the Messageries Impériales had lost the manuscript (HAC 7.39).

Mme de Beauchène (first name and dates unknown). The BnF catalogue gives D. as the translator's initial, but no further details. She received 500 francs on 5 September 1899 for *Les Nièces de M. Burke* based on an English work serialised in *Little Folk* in 1882. The translator's name in the published work was given as the masculine M. de Beauchène. In signing the contract on 18 August 1899, she gave away all her rights, though if the work were to fall out of print after a period of ten years, ownership of the translation would revert to her.

Frédéric Bellaguet (1798–1868). Classicist, headmaster, and educational administrator. On 7 April 1829, he sold Hachette the first edition of Sophocles's complete plays in a dual-language edition, with variants in footnotes and explanatory endnotes; he also undertook to read the proofs or have them checked by a third party. There was to be a print run of 1,000 copies in an octavo or in-12° format, whichever Hachette decided. Bellaguet was to receive 1,500 francs in three thirds, the first when the first volume went on sale, the second when the second went on sale, and the third within six months of the third going on sale.

On 16 April 1842, he sold Hachette the right to publish a prose translation of Sophocles and the right to print 250 copies of an octavo edition,

---

4 See https://books.google.fr/books?id=8Sd3vcLc4_wC&pg=PP2&lpg=PP2&dq=bayntun +gebelin&source=bl&ots=yLJQQQHwmb&sig=ACfU3U0M5HINA-jrwISBR7wAO q4sX9anrg&hl=en&sa=X&ved=2ahUKEwiWxZvqneL7AhVNsKQKHUPiAhMQ6AF 6BAggEAM#v=onepage&q=bayntun%20gebelin&f=false and https://docplayer.org /59056121-Geschichte-voll-franl-fllrt-aln-mahl.html (p. 120) (accessed 12 December 2022).

174 *Appendix*

100 of which would be for Bellaguet himself. He retained the right to publish the translation in any other format he liked. A little over a year later, on 16 June 1843, he authorised Hachette to print 500 copies in an in-12° format, of which he was to receive 150 rather than the 100 initially agreed. On 21 March 1864, he signed a third agreement, selling the translation outright for 500 francs: Hachette retained the right to alter his work to bring it into line with the most recent editions of Sophocles (HAC 1.4).

Thérèse Bentzon (pseudonym of Marie-Thérèse de Solms, 1840–1907). Noble-born journalist, essayist, and novelist, close friend of George Sand, and cultural intermediary between France and the United States. On 18 April 1899, she was paid an advance of 750 francs of a total 1,500 francs for translating *Les Aventures de Saint Rougemont*. On 30 April 1902, she sold the right to sell her translation of Bret Harte's short stories for as long as she and her descendants held the intellectual property to them. The stories were to be sold in the Meilleurs Romans Etrangers [Best Foreign Novels] collection at the cost of three francs. She was to receive a ten per cent royalty on all editions: the initial print run was 1,000 copies, with payment due when the contract was signed. See also the entry for Amélie Fliche (HAC 2.3).

François Berlay (dates unknown). Editor in chief of two journals, *Le Français* and *Le Journal des villes et campagnes*. On 17 May 1876, he signed a contract with Charles Bernard Derosne to serialise Mary Elizabeth Braddon's 1873 novel *Lucius Davoren*. The contract entitled Berlay to abridge the novel to no more than 40 serial episodes, making whatever changes he saw fit, and to alter the title. He was to pay Bernard Derosne 15 francs per issue as they appeared; if he went over 40 issues, he was to keep paying the same amount. No deadline was established: Berlay was free to publish when it suited his journal. The costs of registering the agreement were to be paid by Bernard Derosne, who guaranteed the work was not being translated elsewhere and that Berlay would not be attacked by Mary Elizabeth Braddon (HAC 21.2).

Charles Bernard Derosne[5] (1825–1904). Translator and literary entrepreneur, married to the celebrated actress Mademoiselle Judith. His files are by far the fullest in the archive. Below is a record of his Hetzel file; his file

---

5 Sources differ on whether Bernard was part of a hyphenated first name or his surname, though most agree on the latter. His portrait is available under "Derosne" in the same collection as the Defauconprêts father and son, a couple of pages further on, top left here: https://gallica.bnf.fr/ark:/12148/btv1b8438653k/f49.item.zoom (accessed 28 November 2022).

Appendix 175

with Hachette is far larger and as a result his interactions with translators, authors, and other literary figures in the file HAC 21.2 are listed under their names, not his own.

- On 22 January 1862, Hetzel purchased a five-year right to Bernard Derosne's translation of a volume containing *Guy Livingstone*, *Le jour et la nuit*, or a novel by "Wyte Melville" [Scottish novelist George Whyte-Melville]. Bernard Derosne was to receive royalties of 25 centimes per in-18° copy on sale at three francs within three months of the book going on sale. Royalties on further editions were fixed at 1/12 of the sale price. The first print run of 2,000 copies on sale at 9 francs netted the translator 500 francs. In this instance, Hetzel reserved the right to serial publication and the Belgian market.
- On 23 July 1863, he signed a contract with Hetzel selling the exclusive right to publish George Augustus Sala's *Les Sept fils de Mammon* and *La dame du Premier*, paying Hetzel 25 centimes per volume after the first print run of 2,000 and retaining serial rights for Belgium. Hetzel undertook to grant him first refusal on Sala translations.
- On 29 January 1864, Hetzel required him to demonstrate the legal right to translate for each volume he worked on. In this contract, "Bernard de Rosne" [sic] undertook to deliver one book a month in translation from a list supplied, in the order Hetzel and his then-business partner Lacroix chose. Hetzel and Lacroix were free to revise and alter the translations: if the work was not of sufficient quality, they would turn it down and have Bernard Derosne redo it. If there were too many works bearing his name on the market, they would choose a pseudonym together. Bernard Derosne would be paid 10,000 francs for the set of 12 works in monthly instalments of 833 francs and 33 centimes for serial delivery of the translations. Should Bernard Derosne fail to deliver translations for two months, the publishers were free either to break off the contract and turn to other translators or receive 1,000 francs from Bernard Derosne in damages. The list of novels is as follows (Article 6 in the contract):
  Alton Lock, par Kingsley
  Les aventures de Philippe de Tackeray [sic]
  O'Donoghu [sic] par Charles Lever
  Contes de Noël, nouveaux et intraduits en France par Dickens
  Guy Livingstone, déjà publié, par Lawrence
  Les New Coms [sic] de Tackeray
  Vive l'Occident de Kingsley
  Les Virginiens, de Tackeray
  L'Interprète de Melville
  Three forthcoming novels by Miss Bradoon [sic]

176 *Appendix*

The contract further stipulated that the aforementioned works must not have been previously published in France; otherwise Hetzel and Lacroix would be entitled to a total refund (HTZ 2.11).

Charles Berthoud (1813–94). Swiss clergyman and teacher who contributed to a number of (mainly Swiss) literary journals. He corresponded regularly with Ouida[6] and translated several of her works. On 5 May 1892, he received 750 francs for his translation of *Guilderoi*, signing away full ownership of the manuscript on a standard form. He had previously received the same payment for *Wanda* on 19 February 1884 and was again paid the same for *Syrlin* on 24 September 1891 – a lump sum rate that did not increase in nearly a decade. He also received 100 francs for translating a short story, *Don Gesualdo*, on 15 November 1887 (HAC 44.41).

Victor Bétolaud (1803–79). Teacher, grammarian, and translator of Greek classics. On 29 July 1858, he signed a contract with Charles Lahure for Plutarch's *Oeuvres morales*. The result was 5 volumes and around 5,782 pages in length, destined for an elegant society readership. Bétolaud undertook to write a faithful yet easy-to-read translation with footnotes. The entire project was to be completed by 30 September 1860. The publishers furnished him with a list of books he needed, including Ricard's earlier translation in five volumes of the same works. He was to be paid 3,500 francs for full ownership of the translation. If he was unable to complete the project for any reason, an outside party would be called on to judge the value of the work carried out and Lahure would pay him or his heirs based on their assessment (HAC 1.40).

Jeanne Bignon (dates unknown).[7] Not recorded in the BnF catalogue. She signed a contract on 27 September 1880 to translate a children's book by Stella Austin, *Boulotte*, for which she received 200 francs. Hetzel reserved the right to alter her work as he saw fit. At the time of signing, she lived in the small provincial town of Autun (HTZ 1.41).

Adolphe Bouillet (?1809–?1891).[8] Paris-based teacher, author of works on French history, and translator of Aeschylus. On 4 May 1865, he sold

---

6 See https://archives.bge-geneve.ch/archives/archives/fonds/ms_fr_00325_00344/n:89/view :all (accessed 28 November 2022).

7 A number of possible candidates can be found on http://www.familysearch.org (accessed 12 December 2022).

8 There are several possible candidates on http://www.familysearch.org; this one has the dates that seem the likeliest.

Hachette his Aeschylus translation for a first in-18° Jesus edition. He was paid the remarkable rate of 2 francs 80 centimes per page based on a page of M. Boyard's Aristophanes edition, with a minimum guarantee of 1,000 francs (HAC 3.2).

Mary Elizabeth Braddon (1835–1915). Prolific British novelist best remembered for her sensation novel *Lady Audley's Secret*. Her dealings with Charles Bernard Derosne are recorded in his Hachette file. On 2 May 1864, shortly before launching his own translation rights agency, he paid £24 per volume for the right to translate her works.

On 28 June 1867, he wrote to Hachette to remind them of his exclusive right to translate her novels into French: he pointed to his contract with Hachette of 21 October 1863, since when Hachette had published ten of her novels, paying Bernard Derosne 30 centimes per volume on each first edition. Hachette had turned down a further four novels. In this updated new contract, he passed full ownership of the ten novels published to date and a further four to come to Hachette, promising to complete the four by the end of 1867 and retaining serial publication rights to those titles. He received a lump sum of 4,800 francs. The contract makes it clear that the work was to be done by Bernard Derosne's wife, Judith, an actress now best remembered for her career with the Comédie Française. She translated *Lady Audley's Secret*, agreeing to give up all rights to the translation.

The file further includes an undated letter from Mary Elizabeth Braddon to Hachette: "To be read in France is one of the most earnest ambitions of my heart, and I am much indebted to the literature of your nation for any merit which you may be so kind as to attribute to me" (HAC 21.2).

Louis-Joseph Brossollet (?1823–?1898). It seems unlikely to be the navigator and explorer of the same name, on active service worldwide in the late 1850s, though married, presumably in France, in 1857. Given the theme of the novel, however, it is not impossible. On 10 May 1857, he signed a contract to translate Mayne Reid's *The Wreckers* for 1 franc 20 centimes per page in line with a sample attached to the contract. The project was to be completed and revised for 1 July. Hachette was able to revise the translation as he saw fit. The book was published under the pseudonym Louis Stenio. On 27 July, he was still waiting for the proofs but sent back a contract for another Mayne Reid novel, *The Quadroon*, at the lower rate of one franc a page, to be completed by 15 September (HAC 8.3).

Charles Brunel (dates unknown). A translation of Longfellow's *Evangeline* is the sole work ascribed to Brunel in the BnF catalogue. On 15 November 1872, the second edition came out in an octavo format print run of 2,000 illustrated with wood engravings. Hachette took all the income from sales

178   *Appendix*

until the cost of production and advertising were covered on copies sold at a discount of 35 per cent. Once costs were covered, profits were split 50-50 with the translator (HAC 8.9).

Edward Bulwer Lytton (1803–73). British parliamentarian and novelist. On 1 July 1857, he signed an agreement with Hachette covering 19 novels, some of which had previously been translated for other publishers without permission. The agreement gave Hachette exclusive rights to all his previous novels and all those to come within four years, which were to bear a statement on the title page that French rights were reserved. He received 4,000 francs for previous novels, whether Hachette decided to bring out an edition or not, and 1,000 francs for future novels equivalent in length to *The Caxton Family*. For future novels, Hachette had first refusal for a month, after which the rights reverted to Bulwer Lytton. Rights would be reduced proportionately for novels one-quarter shorter (HAC 8.23).

Mme Burée, B. (first name and dates unknown). Was paid 50 francs on 23 August 1871 for a translation of *Les Dons naturels* in *Le Magasin des Enfants* and 250 francs on 31 October 1871 for Mayne-Reid's *Les Naufragés*. She translated several Mayne-Reid titles and authored a report on the display of fans and decorative trinkets at the *Exposition Universelle* of 1878 (HTZ 1.67).

M. Burellier (first name and dates unknown). Administrator at the daily newspaper *Le Soir*. On 2 June 1870, he signed a contract with Charles Bernard Derosne for the translation of Disraeli's *Lothair*, to which the latter held all the rights. A date was fixed for the start of serial publication. Bernard Derosne undertook to keep the newspaper supplied with the translation so that it was always one volume ahead of readers. He was to receive two sets of proofs for checking two days prior to publication. The total length was not to exceed 25,000 lines. Bernard Derosne was to be paid 25 centimes per line – a potential total of 6,250 francs, far exceeding the going rate for novel translations.

Jean-Louis Burnouf (1775–1844). Classicist, professor, librarian, and translator. His file is among the earliest surviving material in the archive. On 3 October 1825, he signed an agreement with the bookseller Paul-Emile Bredif for 1,500 octavo copies on fine paper of a dual-language edition of Cicero. He was to be paid 1,000 francs and receive 24 copies of the book on 1 January 1826. Louis Hachette took over the Bredif bookshop in 1826. On 9 May 1831, Burnouf wrote to Hachette regarding his long-overdue Tacitus translation: if Hachette let him hand the work in when he

Appendix 179

was ready, he would forgive Hachette the 6,000 franc debt left over from his agreement with Bredif (HAC 154.5).

George Catlin (1796–1872). American adventurer and artist best known for his portraits of Indigenous Americans. In 1868, he sold the rights to *O-Kee-Pa* and *Last Rambles amongst the Indians of the Rocky Mountains and the Andes* to Hachette. They chose **Ferdinand de Lanoye** (1806–70) to translate the books, presumably on the basis of his experience as an author of travel narratives; he later translated several more travel accounts. The agreement stipulated that Lanoye was to combine the two books into one, altering and abridging the content as he felt necessary. Catlin included a note in the copy he sent over: "For the translator. As my little book was written for juvenile readers, the style has been chosen for their understanding; and the occasional change to interrogation – apostrophes &c. to break monotony, to keep up youthful attention – I would wish therefore, that the translation, both of the title page and the text, should be as literal as possible" (emphasis in the original) (HAC 9.3).

Paul Challemel-Lacour (1827–96). Parliamentarian, minister of foreign affairs, president of the senate, and member of the Académie française. On 29 May 1865, he sold Hachette the rights to an in-18° Jesus format edition of Valerius Maximus estimated at 400 pages and was paid 2 francs a page. At least 15 years later, at some point in the 1880s (the letter is dated 13 June), he wrote to apologise for the delay, asking if he could keep it in a drawer a while longer and suggesting it might need some revision (HAC 12.3).

Mme la Comtesse Gédéon de Clermont-Tonnerre (née Marguerite de Rigaud de Vaudreuil, 1830–1900). Translated a handful of works from the English beginning in 1869. On 30 September 1871, she received 800 francs for her translation of Wilkie Collins's *Moonstone*; Victor de Rély was paid 100 francs for revising her translation.[9] The file contains a series of letters in barely legible writing on notepaper bearing her coat of arms, complaining about the revision process (HAC 63.2).

Wilkie Collins (1824–89). Highly successful English novelist. On 22 August 1857, he sold Charles Lahure exclusive translation rights for three novels, receiving 750 francs for *The Dead Secret*, 500 for *After Dark*, and 100 for *Basil*. Lahure further agreed to pay 100 francs for novels published earlier and 750 francs for forthcoming titles, depending on the number of

---

9 He had already received 200 francs on the same date the previous year: see the reference at Victor de Rély.

180   *Appendix*

pages. Collins agreed to send Lahure a proof copy of each set of sheets as the books were printed. Five years later, on 6 March 1862, he sold Hetzel the translation rights to *The Woman in White* and *No Name*. The latter was shortly due to start serial publication in *All the Year Round*; Collins undertook to send Hetzel each issue as it came out so that the translation could track the English publication. He received 750 francs for each title (HTZ 9.45).

Justin Charles Corrard (1822–66). Son of a *chevalier de la légion d'honneur* who had a glittering academic career in Versailles and Paris until his early death: his first posting as a newly qualified *agrégé* in 1844 was taking over from Julien Girard, the expert who probably assessed Louis Judicis's Boethius translation.[10] At the time of the contract, he taught rhetoric at the lycée in Versailles. On 29 January 1857, he signed a contract to translate Schiller's *Opuscules esthétiques* for 1 franc 50 centimes per page – a sample page was attached – by 30 July. Hachette reserved the right to cancel the translation at any time, as long as they paid him for the work completed to date. The translation was to be freely edited by Hachette's representative M. Régnier, who could also choose whether or not to include Corrard's name on the title page and in the preface. He did not (HAC 10.20).

Mme Jean Darcy (pseudonym of Céline Chaverondier, also known as Nelly Carrère and Mme Jean Chaverondier-Carrère, 1859–1925). Novelist, journalist, translator from Italian, and literary entrepreneur. On 5 April 1902, she signed a contract with Hachette to scout foreign novels, write reader reports, obtain the rights, and place them in the French press. She was to source suitable translators, paid at a rate set by Hachette, and revise their work for a 5 per cent royalty on the catalogue price of the first 1,000 copies. The agreement was initially to cover six novels. The contract soon foundered when the rights to G. Rovetta's *Mater Dolorosa* were disputed. Mme Darcy claimed the novel was in the public domain but Hachette ended up paying Rovetta 200 francs (HAC 21.21).

Alice Decker (dates unknown, active in the first decade of the twentieth century). Received permission from the UK publisher Cassell to translate E. Hohler's *Jock's Legacy*. She signed a contract with Hetzel on 11 June 1903. Hetzel paid her 300 francs for perpetual ownership without reserve in all formats, including serially in the *Magasin d'Education et de Récréation*. She was to be sent the proofs but undertook to accept all changes required by the typesetting process. Should the work remain out

---

10 See   https://www.textesrares.com/pages/histoire/Corrard-Charles-1822-1866-maitre-de -conferences-a-l-Ecole-normale.html (accessed 16 December 2022).

Appendix 181

of print for a year, ownership of the translation and the translation rights would revert to the translator or her representatives. At the time of signing, she lived in Vannes, Brittany; like Marguerite de Lahaye, she was doubtless one of the women based in the town who inundated Hachette with translations of children's literature, as recorded in a 1924 letter in the complaints department (HTZ 2.7).

Pierre-François Delestre (1793–1851). Minor author on religious topics and headmaster in a number of small towns including Tonnerre and Cahors. In one of the earliest contracts in the archive, on 25 September 1829, he sold Hachette ownership of an *Aeneid* translation in 3 duodecimo volumes and a print run of 1,000. He paid for the paper of volume one and nine printing sheets of volume two, while Hachette paid for the remaining production costs. The books were sold at 2 francs 40 centimes per volume on a 50-50 profit-share basis. Hachette reserved the right to replace the author's name with his own on the main title of volume one, in which case he would take over all costs. For later editions, Hachette paid for all printing costs and Delestre received 1 franc per copy on print runs of between 1,000 and 1,500. For octavo format editions, he would receive 1 franc 50 centimes per copy (HAC 21.11).

Charles Dickens (1812–70) and **Benjamin Disraeli** (1804–81); see also **Wilkie Collins** (q.v.). Leading British novelists. An undated letter from Charles Bernard Derosne to Hachette gives some details of the transactions involving their works.

- *Le Mystère d'Edwin Drood* was listed in the *Journal Officiel*, thereby ensuring exclusive translation rights. Its estimated 20,000 lines at 25 centimes came to 5,000 francs. Bernard Derosne was to keep 2,000 francs for himself and split the rest 50-50 with Hachette.
- Wilkie Collins's *Le mari et la femme* was placed with the daily paper *Le Bien Public*. The estimated 40,000 lines at 15 centimes a line came to 6,000 francs, to be shared with Hachette.
- Wilkie Collins's *Pierre de lune* was to be serialised in *La Cloche*. The estimated 20,000 lines at 10 centimes per line came to 2,000 francs, of which Bernard Derosne would keep 25 per cent.
- Payments for Disraeli's *Lothair* amounted to 4,216 francs: Bernard Derosne had already paid Hachette 2,000 francs the previous July and therefore owed a further 108 francs.

The letter concluded by asking Hachette to think about the four novels by Mary Elizabeth Braddon he had in hand and other new works for translation, assuring the publisher that he worked as well, as fast, and at such

182 *Appendix*

advantageous conditions as anyone else and would place as many novels as possible in the press. Perhaps the most striking aspect of the letter is the wide range of payments and percentages depending on the project.

On 23 May 1870, Bernard Derosne wrote to a M. Templier, one of Hachette's editors, about Disraeli's *Lothair*, for which he had offers from two leading newspapers. However, he wanted to manage the translation, which another translator was already working on (presumably **M. Burellier**, q.v.). Bernard Derosne suggested it would be advantageous to entrust the project to him instead if they could find a way to do so. The title is recorded in the BnF catalogue as a translation by Charles Bernard Derosne (HAC 21.2).

Léon Dieu (1837–1919). Career soldier, badly wounded at the Battle of Gravelotte in 1870.[11] Translated a number of works from Italian. On 15 August 1877, he received payment of 400 francs for A. Caccianiga's *Le Baiser de la comtesse Savina*. On 11 August 1881, at which point he was living in the rural town of Montbéliard in eastern France, he earned 400 francs for the sale of full rights to his translation of Vittorio Bersezio's *Les Anges de la Terre*. He wrote to Hachette to point out that as a member of the *Société des Gens de Lettres*, he had to retain ownership of the right of reproduction. On 16 September the same year, he provided permission from Caccianiga to translate *Le Bocage de St Alipio*, and received a payment of 400 francs for the project on 1 March the following year. On 31 December 1884, he received the same payment for Bersezio's *Pauvre Jeanne* (HAC 19.20).

Marie Dupuy (dates unknown). Heiress of **Pier-Angelo Fiorentino** (1809–64), an Italian-born, French-naturalised author and journalist who regularly collaborated with Alexandre Dumas *père*. Dupuy may have been involved in the Dupuy bookshop on rue Saint-Sulpice, though it is a relatively common surname so it is hard to be certain. On 4 December 1867, she sold Hachette the rights to Fiorentino's much-praised *Divine Comédie* translation for 1,500 francs (HAC 20.36).

Louis Enault (1820–1900). Prolific journalist, novelist, and translator from German and English of works including Goethe's *Werther* and Beecher Stowe's *Uncle Tom's Cabin*. On 30 May 1853, he sold ownership of his version of *Uncle Tom's Cabin*, printed serially in *Le Pays*, for 500 francs. He guaranteed Hachette against any possible legal proceedings arising from their reprint of his translation. On 15 November 1855, he received

---

11 See http://military-photos.com/sthubert.htm (accessed 5 December 2022).

Appendix 183

400 francs for ownership of his *Werther* translation in the Bibliothèque des Chemins de Fer collection. As late as 1983, France Loisirs paid Hachette 8,400 francs for the right to reprint his translation of *Uncle Tom's Cabin* (HAC 4.4).

Alfred des Essarts (1811–93). Poet, playwright, journalist, translator. Des Essarts, son of a general, was librarian at the Bibliothèque Sainte-Geneviève in Paris and wrote for *La France littéraire*. A prolific writer, he was a *chevalier de la légion d'honneur*. He translated *The Old Curiosity Shop* and *Martin Chuzzlewit*, as well as the English manuscript of the memoirs of Catherine II of Russia's lady-in-waiting, Princess Dashkova. On 1 October 1856, he signed a contract with Hachette giving him three months to complete *The Old Curiosity Shop* and six for *Martin Chuzzlewit* (HAC 41.15).

Amélie Fliche, née **Chevalier de la Petite-Rivière** (1851–1934). Longstanding translator from English of popular women's novels and children's books. Born in Angers and died in Sens. The first trace of her in the archive is under her maiden name on 25 April 1884, when she was paid 300 francs for Annie Edwards's *A Vagabond Heroine* (HAC 10.48). She was still toiling away as an unsung translator nigh on half a century later, when on 24 April 1929, she wrote to Hachette to complain that their contract with Thérèse Bentzon for *Les Causeries de Morale* did not mention her or their longstanding 50 per cent profit-sharing agreement. Hachette had full knowledge of the terms since paying Bentzon for *Carrière d'Artiste*, which Fliche had translated entirely: the company had sent her the proofs and asked her to provide the sources of her quotations. She had even been praised for her style by an in-house editor. Thérèse Bentzon had made some minor changes to the manuscript to justify her participation. Fliche was angry not to have been paid for five out of seven editions or her half-share of royalties on one volume that did bear her name, though Bentzon's heirs had been paid their due. Hachette duly replied that she was not a signatory to the Bentzon contract; Thérèse Bentzon had indeed informed Hachette that Fliche was involved in the project and all responsibility for paying her collaborators was hers alone. An earlier letter dated 2 July 1925 makes the same demands with reference to a translation of Mrs. Humphrey Ward's *Diane Mallory*, which she translated alone. This must have been a longstanding grievance, since a letter from Hachette dated fully 15 years previously, on 29 December 1909, alludes to the same projects. When Amélie Fliche translated *Carrière d'Artiste* with Mme Bentzon, Hachette wrote, it was agreed that Hachette would pay her 500 francs, as recorded in a letter to Mme Bentzon on 18 August 1906. Bentzon's son was paid his half of the money on 3 June 1907 and Fliche on 15 June 1907, signing a receipt that granted Hachette full ownership of the translation.

184   *Appendix*

Hachette had agreed to double her remuneration for *Diane Mallory*, which she was requested to complete by early January (HAC 2.3).

J. (Jeanne?) Florimond (dates unknown). Translator of the romance novelist **Dorothea Gerard** (q.v.). Known only from one letter dated 10 November 1901, in which she complained that Charles Bernard Derosne had received full payment for a translation she had completed on his behalf, for which she should have received a one-third payment. She demanded immediate payment of 233 francs 35 centimes of a total 700 francs: if the sum was not forthcoming, she would be forced to place a lien on his future translation rights from Hachette. The accounts ledger shows she was paid within two weeks of sending the letter (HAC 21.2).

Félix Foucou (1831–70). Naval officer, science writer, fourierist, and fraudster. Born illegitimately in Guyana, he may have been of mixed race.[12] He signed a contract with Hetzel on 20 April 1866 to translate Tyndall's *Les Glaciers*. He was paid 125 francs for his ownership of the illustrations. The book was printed in 2,000 copies in in-18° format. The two volumes were on sale at 3 francs and 3 francs 50 centimes. The contract stipulated that the work was to be stereotyped for future editions. Hetzel was responsible for printing and advertising costs, after which all profits were to be divided on a half-share basis between Tyndall and Foucou, minus ten per cent for general costs and for Hetzel. They were to receive a sales statement every six months. Hetzel reserved the right to lower the sales price for rights for subsequent editions while Tyndall and Foucou reserved the right to check the proofs of each new edition. Foucou owed Hetzel first refusal of all Tyndall's subsequent books. He also undertook to write a preface and various additional paratexts, including two brief chapters from the *Saturday Review* which printed an annual account of Tyndall's Alpine adventures and a summary of Tyndall's recent debate with the renowned geologist Sir Roderick Murchison on valley formation (HTZ 2.57).

Henriette Fresneau (1829–1908) or possibly her daughter of the same name (1857–?). Daughter (or granddaughter) of the popular children's author the comtesse de Ségur, best remembered for *Les malheurs de Sophie*, she also wrote a handful of children's books in her own name in the 1880s and 1890s. Hachette paid her 300 francs on 14 December 1906 for a translation from the German of Agnes Harder's *Doktor Eisenbart*. She had written to him five days prior to inform him she had no intention of translating any more of Harder's work, and in fact preferred not to have her name on

---

12 See http://www.charlesfourier.fr/spip.php?article1658 (accessed 28 November 2022).

Appendix 185

the book at all. She suggested using her initials or a pseudonym instead. The book is not attributed to her in the BnF catalogue, which lists no works by Agnes Harder. I have been unable to trace it (HAC 23.11).

Gustav Freytag (1816–95). Popular German playwright and novelist. On 28 August 1856, Hachette purchased the rights to his Europe-wide hit, *Soll und Haben* [*Doit et Avoir* in French; *Debit and Credit* in English], for 500 francs. They had the right to abridge the work for periodical publication but cuts in the book had to be minimal. Freytag undertook to record the work's title in France at the Bureau de la Librairie at the Ministry of the Interior (HAC 22.34).

Elizabeth Gaskell (1810–65). British novelist. The Hachette and Gaskell families were close: when Mrs. Gaskell's daughter came to France, she stayed with the Hachettes. The Louise Swanton-Belloc file in the Hachette archive contains several items of correspondence between Gaskell and Hachette. First is an undated letter from Gaskell:

> every author of any note is anxious for a correct and faithful translation of what they do write; and although from the difference of literary taste between the two nations it may become desirable to abbreviate certain parts, or even to leave them out altogether, yet no author would like to have a whole volume omitted, and to have the translation of the mutilated remainder called an 'Imitation'. I ought perhaps to apologize for speaking so plainly about this; but, as I believe it to be your wish to enter into a very fair and liberal arrangement with the English authors of reputation, it is better to say frankly that I can not ask Mrs Nicholls [i.e. Charlotte Brontë] to give her assent to the present edition of the translation of *Jane Eyre* ... Mme Mohl will very willingly speak to Mme Belloc as you desire; but she thinks you are not aware that Mme Belloc is very poorly and seldom goes out. I do not know if *Cranford* will be one of my works which you will select for translation but if it were, I should be very glad as far as I am concerned, if you and Mme Belloc could come to any agreement, as I fancy she is well acquainted with the delicacies of the English language.

Highlighting the importance of personal connections and recommendations in the process of hiring translators, on 26 April 1855, she wrote,

> I am very glad to learn that you like the translation of Mlle Morel's better on further inspection. To me she was recommended by Mme Geoffroy St Hilaire, but when I became personally acquainted with her

186   *Appendix*

I became interested in her for her own sake, and I am very glad to learn from you that you approve of her translation of *Mary Barton*.

On 21 January 1856, a few years after the new international agreement on translation rights came into force, she wrote to thank Hachette for sending a copy of *Cranford* in French: she was "delighted with the grace and ease of the translation" and would write to Louise Swanton-Belloc directly to thank her too. She was also pleased with Pauline de Witt's *Ruth*. She added,

> I continue to receive letters from French ladies, requesting my permission to translate certain of my works; Mme Edmond de Pressensé is one, a friend of Mme George Sand's living with her at Nohant is another. I tell all that I have no longer any power, and I refer them to you.
>
> (HAC 29.3)

"Gem" (dates unknown). The mysterious pseudonym of the translator of Annie Edwardes's *Bluestocking* as *Le bas bleu* in 1879. A woman by the surname of Roberty purchased the translation rights from Edwardes for 100 francs and was paid 400 francs for the translation. On 2 October 1882, she wrote to Hachette with a copy of Annie Edwardes's permission, addressed to a "Dear Sir" since, the translator writes, she failed to recognise "à ma signature une plume feminine" [a feminine pen in my signature]. This was her second translation, the (unnamed) first having been well received by the publisher. She planned to send him Mrs. Henry Wood's *St Martin's Eve* for his consideration in the coming days, though the project seems to have come to naught: much of Mrs. Henry Wood's abundant output was translated, but not this particular title, it seems. The only possible candidate in the BnF catalogue is a Marie Guérin de Roberty (dates unknown) who published a slim religious pamphlet in 1838, though the discrepancy in the dates suggests it is unlikely to be the same individual – and without a first initial or dates, the trail runs cold (HAC 10.48).

Dorothea Gerard, a.k.a. **Dorothea Longard de Longgarde** (1855–1915). Scottish novelist and romance writer. On 9 February 1899, Charles Bernard Derosne signed an agreement to translate *An Arranged Marriage* for the woman's magazine *La Mode Pratique* for 15 centimes per line and per volume. He placed a number of Gerard's titles in the same magazine, including *Une reine des fromages*, *Un baiser sur la terrasse*, *Réputation sans tache*, and *Les Jouets du destin*, the last of which was translated by Miss **J. Florimond** (q.v.) (HAC 21.2).

Appendix 187

Marcel Girette (1849–1942). Functionary at the Ministry of Finances and playwright. He was a close friend of the composer Vincent d'Indy. Girette's wife also translated Israel Zangwill from English. On 27 June 1885, Marcel Girette sold Hachette ownership of Benjamin Farjeon's *Mystère de Porter Square* for 835 francs (HAC 18.15).

H. Gréard (dates unknown). A woman who translated a handful of works from English in the 1850s–1870s, including F. J. Smith's novel *Woman and Her Master*, published under the pseudonym Mme H. de L'Espine. Her other four recorded translations are religious in nature. She also used the pseudonym Henri de Cossoles. On 9 July 1857, she signed a contract with Hachette to translate Smith's novel by 1 October for one franc a page. A specimen page was included. In the terms of the contract, Hachette was free to alter her work at will; she was free to choose to sign the translation with her own name or her mother's. At the time of signing, she lived in Meaux, some 30 miles east of Paris (HAC 41.15).

Mme G. T. or **E. Guidi** (first name and dates unknown). Unusually, she features in two Hachette files. Having paid £5 (roughly 125 francs in 1880)[13] for the right to translate Maria Grant's *The Sun Maid*, she received 800 francs for outright ownership of her translation on 4 August 1882. No translations of Grant's novels feature in the BnF catalogue. A second file contains correspondence from a Mme E. Guidi – presumably the same person as, or related to, Mme G. T. Guidi – who claimed to have acquired the translation rights to Annie Edwardes's *Half a Million of Money* from Routledge & Sons. The file also contains a letter from Edwardes herself denying Guidi's claim: "I beg to say that I am unacquainted with even the name of M. Guidi, & that I never sanctioned his translation in any way". The BnF catalogue features a small number of translations of Edwardes's novels, but none that appear to match the title or identity of the mysterious translator – unless she used a pseudonym (HAC 16.12 and HAC 19.32).

Pierre-Victor Hallays-Dabot (1828–1918). Member of the theatre commission at the Ministry of Fine Arts and author of works on theatre history and censorship. On 27 March 1870, as heir to the translator Joseph Leclerc, he sold the rights to Leclerc's Cicero, approving only minimal changes. The editions were to bear Leclerc's name alone, as on the original editions of 1820 and 1823. He earned 4,500 francs and kept the right to produce an octavo edition of his own (HAC 32.11).

---

13 See https://www.historicalstatistics.org/Currencyconverter.html (accessed 16 December 2022).

188 *Appendix*

Ely Halpérine-Kaminsky (1858–1936). Renowned translator from the Russian and Polish of authors including Gogol, Turgenev, and Sienkiewicz. On 19 April 1886, he received a payment of 450 francs for Turgenev's *Un Bulgare*. The contract stipulated that the translator would check the proofs, but Hetzel retained the right to alter the translation to improve the book's chances of success or in line with requests by Turgenev's family (HTZ 3.16).

Gustave Hinstin (1834–94). Teacher of rhetoric now best remembered as the dedicatee of his former pupil Lautréamont's *Poésies*.[14] On 23 November 1880, he signed a contract for the complete works of Euripides in two in-16° volumes for 2,000 francs. In 1884 (the exact date is unknown), he signed a contract with Hachette to translate *Chefs d'Oeuvre des Auteurs Attiques* for 1,000 francs. The translation, intended for "les gens du monde", was contractually obliged to be a pleasant read.

Ferdinand Hoefer (1811–78). German-born science writer, doctor, and editor of the *Nouvelle biographie générale* and Victor Cousin's secretary. On 22 February 1843, he agreed to edit Terrasson's outdated translation of Diodorus of Sicily for the publisher Lefevre, rejuvenating it for a new audience. He had to hand his work in in quarters every three months: it was to be revised by an Aimé Martin. Lefevre was to have sole rights to the translation for six years, paying Hoefer a further 500 francs for corrections and improvements if a new duodecimo or octavo edition came out. He received 1,500 francs for his work. On 29 July 1863, he sold the rights to Lefevre's four-volume in-18° Jesus format edition of Diodorus of Sicily to Hachette. He declared the transaction was wholly separate from Lefevre's sale of rights to Gustave Charpentier and that he had not granted Charpentier or anyone else an extension or change to the terms of Lefevre's 1843 contract. He was paid 2,000 francs (HAC 31.1).

William Little Hughes (1822–87). Dublin-born Hughes moved to Paris as a young man and joined the foreign press department of the Interior Ministry in the late 1850s. He was a prolific translator of authors including Dickens, Bulwer Lytton, Poe, Twain, and Thackeray. On 7 March 1857, he signed a contract with Hachette for his debut translations (Hawes 2004), *Hard Times* and *Little Dorrit*. He undertook to deliver the completed translations to Paul Lorain within three days for *Hard Times* and six months for *Little Dorrit*, having already spent two months on the former. The contract stipulated Lorain was free to interrupt the contract

---

14 https://cahierslautreamont.wordpress.com/2020/09/05/hinstin-en-famille/ (accessed 16 December 2022).

Appendix   189

whenever he saw fit as long as he paid for the work completed to date at one franc a page; he was also free to edit Hughes's raw translation as he saw fit and leave his name off the finished book (HAC 41.15). Other than Charles Bernard Derosne, he is the only translator in the set to feature in two publisher archives: he also worked for Hetzel, who paid him 200 francs and 205 francs respectively for Michael Faraday's popular science works *Histoire d'une chandelle* and *Forces de la matière* in 1864. The latter is not in the BnF catalogue under that title. He further earned 300 francs for Margaret Gatty's *Contes de la tante Judith* in 1868 and 300 francs for *Histoire d'un rat et de deux petits orphelins* the following year. Again, the latter title is unlisted in the BnF catalogue (HTZ 3.26).

Jules Janin (1804–74). Celebrated journalist, author, and critic. The file opens with a lengthy rough draft of a letter from Hachette dated 7 July 1859 delicately informing Janin of the inadequacies of his Horace translation. On 27 July, he wrote to Janin that he had sent the translation to a M. Sommer for revision with a published copy of Horace. Sommer would soon be visiting Janin at home in Passy (a district in south-west Paris). Janin was to talk to Sommer to be persuaded of the importance of his role before deciding what he should be paid. Hachette then suggests revising the profit-sharing agreement to two-thirds in their favour since they would be paying for the revision process, indicating that Sommer would doubt-less be satisfied with 400 francs.

Then comes a letter dated 31 August, probably the same year, from a contributor whose name is illegible but is likely Sommer himself. He writes that he will immediately start revising Janin's translation of the odes, sat-ires, and epistles with a view to a new print run. He writes that, in accord-ance with Hachette's request, he will make a note of every aspect of the translation that runs counter to Horace's thought or intention. He requests 250 francs for revising 7,800 lines. The file further contains details of the profit share after costs: on 15 October 1860, Janin received a one-third share of 458 francs 55 centimes, and a further 1,349 francs 40 centimes on 1 March 1862 (HAC 29.18).

Adrien de Jassaud (1881–1937). A lawyer and occasional translator who used the pseudonym Vernoy. He began speculating on literary property as a young man: on 21 October 1904, he sold Hachette the rights to A. K. Green's *L'Affaire Leavenworth*, receiving royalties of 10 per cent and 400 francs for serial publication in the ladies' magazine *Mode Pratique* and a first edition of 2,000 copies. He also purchased the translation rights for Arthur Conan Doyle's *Hound of the Baskervilles* for £10 and was paid 300 francs for the translation. According to a historical currency converter, this

190   *Appendix*

gave him a profit of just 50 or so francs.[15] He made a better deal with Hall Caine's *L'Enfant prodigue*, purchasing the rights for £20 and being paid 750 francs, a profit of nearly 250 francs (HAC 29.16).

Louis Judicis de Mirandol (1816–93). Government administrator at the Seine préfecture (i.e. Paris), literary journalist, playwright, and novelist. On 11 June 1860, Hachette published his version of Boethius's *Consolation of Philosophy* on a 50-50 profit and loss basis. He would pay his half of the costs in cash and Hachette would pay itself back for its half of the costs on sales profits. If that took longer than three years, Judicis undertook to pay the remaining amount. His file also contains a letter from a certain Gilbert dated 12 May 1860 recommending Judicis through his former classmate, M. Breton, who happened to be Hachette's son-in-law. Gilbert warmly recommended Judicis in his own name and brought a new Académie française prize to Hachette's attention. The prize, worth 4,000 francs, was to be awarded for a Greek or Latin work. Judicis had not produced his translation with the prize in mind, as he had been working on it for several years, but had decided to enter with Gilbert's encouragement. The book therefore had to be printed and in the hands of the Institute by 1 January 1861. Judicis knew it was unlikely to sell, though it was not a title readily available on the market at that time, but hoped that winning the prize would boost its profile. Judicis was therefore open to whatever terms Hachette chose to offer. Gilbert further suggested having the translation assessed by an expert such as Julien Girard (1810–98, classicist and educational administrator). The final document in the file is an unsigned, undated assessment of the translation, possibly by Girard. The assessor sampled around one-third of the text, finding the translation extremely faithful and easy to read. The verse passages were generally good but sometimes showed a tendency to dullness and pomposity ("des longueurs, parfois un peu d'enflure"), though the latter was often Boethius's and the former forced by the rhyme. He concluded that the title would make a pretty little book that would sell fairly well. The book did come out in 1861, printed by Charles Lahure, though whether it made the 1 January deadline is not known. It seems to have only had one edition in the nineteenth century, though it was reedited in facsimile in 1981 (HAC 24.23).

Jules Kergomard (1822–1901). Minor poet and journalist better known by the pen name Gustave de Penmarch. An undated letter records that Hetzel paid him 300 francs for a translation of *Wuthering Heights* by "Ellis Bell", no trace of which can be found (HTZ 3.39).

---

15 See https://www.historicalstatistics.org/Currencyconverter.html (accessed 12 December 2022).

Appendix 191

Pierre Kropotkine, better known in English as **Peter Kropotkin** (1842–1921). Russian anarchist and scientist. Contacted Flammarion in 1888 to pitch his wife's translation of Korolenko, edited by himself. Wrote to Flammarion again in 1891 requesting the company not to charge an Italian printer, M. Fantuzzi, for translation rights given the crisis in Italian publishing. Flammarion agreed to waive the rights (FLM 8.5).

Albert Lacroix (dates unknown). Received 150 francs from Hetzel for full ownership of Mayne-Reid's *Fête des chasseurs*, which Lacroix had purchased from a M. Stark, who had in turn commissioned the translation from M. Flor O'Squarr (HTZ 3.49).

Ernest Lafond (1807–81). Author and translator. An undated agreement with Hetzel refers to his two-volume, octavo *Oeuvres de Johnson*. One thousand copies were printed for sale at six francs. The agreement is notable for the profit-sharing agreement that saw Lafond pay three-quarters of the publishing costs, quoted by a M. Claye at around 6,000 francs. Lafond would be entitled to three-quarters of any profits. Lafond and Hetzel were also to agree on publicity costs, split on the same lines as previously. A sample of the paper and print to be used were attached to the agreement (HTZ 3.52).

Marguerite de Lahaye (dates unknown). On 10 August 1893, she sold Hetzel the translation rights to Beatrice Harraden's *Master Roley*, which she had purchased for £10 10 shillings. She was paid 500 francs for her *Monsieur Roro* on 5 September 1893. The contract stipulated the publisher could alter the work and choose the date of publication as they saw fit. It was published under the pseudonym M. de Chateau-Verdun. At the time of signing, Marguerite de Lahaye lived in Vannes, Brittany. The 1924 letter of complaint from Hetzel referred to above in the entry on Alice Decker notes that *Monsieur Roro* proved a good project for him (HZT 4.1).

Charles Lahure (1809–87). Author, publisher, and printer. Signed a contract in September 1857 granting him exclusive rights to print translations of the Irish novelist Charles Lever (1806–72). Lahure was to pay Lever 25 centimes per page for works in the public domain and 1 franc per page for future works. A specimen page of the translation of Dickens's *Dombey and Son* was included in the contract, signed by both parties, as a point of reference: if the pages published differed substantially from the model, the rate of remuneration would be adjusted upward or downward. Lahure was free not to publish a translation but had to inform Lever of any refusals within six months in the case of previously published work and two months for future works; he further undertook to publish translations

192 *Appendix*

within a year. If he did not, the translation rights reverted to Lever (HAC 40.18).

The widow (name and dates unknown) of **Benjamin Laroche** (1797–1852). Benjamin Laroche learned English in exile in London as an opponent of the ultraroyalists and translated Shakespeare, Dickens, and Bentham, among others. In 1835, he signed a contract with Gustave Charpentier to translate Byron, eventually suing the publisher for failing to fulfil his obligations. The case came before the Paris court in 1846–9.[16] It was a valuable property: on 2 June 1853, his widow sold the publishing rights to Victor Lecou for 3,000 francs, and, on 4 February 1858, she sold Hachette the right to a four-volume in-18° edition on Jesus format paper (i.e. 56 × 72 cm) for 6,000 francs (HAC 36.26).

Ernest Lavigne (1845–80). Journalist and philosophy teacher, born in Naples. He signed a contract on 1 February 1870 for 1,000 copies of Lucretius's *De rerum natura*. The octavo books were to be sold at between five and seven francs. If the cost of printing was not covered by 1 April 1871, Lavigne was to pay. Any profits would be shared on a 50-50 basis. There were none: Lavigne eventually picked up 840 unsold copies (HAC 33.8).

Philippe Lebas (1794–1860) and **Théobald Fix** (1802–74). Lebas was a Hellenist and archaeologist, academic, and librarian at the Sorbonne who tutored Louis-Napoléon Bonaparte. Swiss-born Théobald Fix was a Hellenist, philologist, lexicographer, and librarian at the Conseil d'état. Both also translated from German. On 6 January 1843, they contracted with Hachette for one play by Aeschylus or Euripides a month, paid 120 francs per printing sheet for the Greek and dual-language editions and 100 francs for the French edition (HAC 34.16).

Pierre-Auguste Lemaire (1802–87). Publisher, grammarian, and professor of Latin poetry at the Paris Faculty of Letters. At the time of the contract, he taught rhetoric at the prestigious Collège Bourbon. On 29 August 1838, he signed away exclusive rights to his Lucretius edition (in Latin) in a cost-sharing agreement, with Hachette agreeing to pay 15 francs per unbound copy. Lemaire paid for newspaper advertising, while Hachette paid for catalogues and a sales prospectus. Hachette paid Lemaire 2,250 francs for 150 copies, with the possibility of ordering further ones in due course. A note in the corner of the sheet, presumably jotted later, adds that Lemaire paid Hachette 350 francs (HAC 31.10).

---

16 See https://catalogue.bnf.fr/ark:/12148/cb367961000 and https://catalogue.bnf.fr/ark:/12148/cb36796101b (accessed 14 December 2022).

Appendix 193

Albert Leroy (dates unknown). Received payment of 100 francs on 11 October 1871 for revising Victor de Rély's translation of Wilkie Collins's *Pierre de Lune* (HAC 63.2).

Antoine-Adolphe Lesourd (1799–1852). Journalist, high-ranking civil servant, and occasional translator.[17] On 25 April 1843, he sold the bookseller and publisher Abel Ledoux a translation by Charles Nodier of Goldsmith's *Vicar of Wakefield* together with the author biography and notes. He had previously published a large octavo bilingual edition of the same book in 1836 under the name Bougueleret. He formally declared Charles Gosselin only had the right to print a single duodecimo edition of the text. He received 500 francs for the translation (HTZ 2.78).

Paul Lorain (1799–1861). Education administrator, editor, and translator. Signed a contract with Hachette on 9 April 1856 to translate or oversee the translation of 12 Dickens novels and various short stories. The contract stipulated his role was to harmonise translations by his chosen team: the translators had to write on one side of the paper only and leave a half-page margin. The contract further stated the covers and title pages were to feature his name as editor. He was given 15 months to oversee print-ready translations of the 12 novels starting from the following July, starting with *Bleak House* and *Hard Times*. *Little Dorrit* was to be translated as the English text came out serially to be ready for print when the last English instalment came out. He was to be paid 250 francs per volume for his editorial work; the translators were to be paid 1 franc a page based on a specimen page attached to the contract. Lorain was not to be involved in paying the translators, which was Hachette's responsibility; the translations and Paul Lorain's contributions would be their sole property. If he missed the deadline, Hachette would call on another translator while paying for work completed to date. The contract covered all Dickens's forthcoming work and any other titles Hachette selected, with no obligation to entrust further contracts to Lorain.

On 16 January 1857, Lorain wrote to Hachette to introduce Alfred des Essarts, translator of *The Old Curiosity Shop*, which he planned to finish editing within a fortnight. Essarts received an advance (*à valoir*) of 500 francs upon presentation of Lorain's letter, which he had signed, "Mille compliments affectueux de ton bien dévoué P. Lorain". Lorain wrote again on 2 March 1857 to introduce William Hughes, who had just handed in his translation of *Hard Times*, which Lorain promised to finish editing within a fortnight (HAC 41.15).

---

17 See https://hal-normandie-univ.archives-ouvertes.fr/hal-02080590/document (accessed 28 November 2022).

194 *Appendix*

Francis Marion Crawford (1854–1909). American novelist. On 12 September 1893, Charles Bernard Derosne signed a contract to translate and rework *Three Fates* for the women's magazine *La Mode Pratique*. He was to receive royalties of 10 per cent on the cost of the volume for the initial print run of 2,000 copies and 15 centimes per line for the magazine version. The rights would revert to him six months after the book's publication so that he could publish a non-illustrated version.

On 27 April 1898, Bernard Derosne – by now in his early 70s, but apparently as active as ever – wrote to Hachette about the Hungarian translation of Francis Marion Crawford's *Three Fates*, from the French version *Insaissisable Amour*. He pointed out that Marion Crawford was a personal friend who had given him free rein in translating his books into French. The Hungarian version was based not on the original but on the French, which shortened the original by two-thirds: as a result, Bernard Derosne wished to be paid (HAC 21.2). As late as 1901, in his late 70s, Bernard Derosne negotiated a ten per cent royalty on Marion Crawford's *Haine de Femme* (HAC 21.3).

Nicolas Martin (1814–77). Born in Bonn to a French father and German mother. Later a writer, academic, and senior customs administrator in Calais. His uncle was the poet Karl Simrock. Martin translated a 300-page selection of *Contes allemands* (including tales by Simrock) for the *Bibliothèque rose*, a collection intended for young female readers. He was paid the unusually high rate of two francs a page (HAC 34.7).

Auguste Materne (1812–93). Philologist and *censeur* (i.e. school manager) at the Lycée Saint-Louis in Paris. Worked on several German translations for Hachette in the mid- to late 1850s. On 24 November, he was paid 600 francs for Hauff's short stories; on 15 May 1857 he received 1 franc 25 centimes per page for Otto Ludwig's *Entre ciel et terre*; on 17 July 1858 he translated Hackländer's *Boutique et comptoir*; and on 15 July 1859 the same author's *Le moment de bonheur*. In all cases, Hachette reserved the right to print the translation in whatever format they chose (HAC 33.40).

Ouida (Maria Louise Ramé, 1839–1908). Prolific British novelist. The Hachette archive contains a number of records of payment for translation rights from the late 1870s and 1880s. Ouida received 800 francs for the exclusive right to translate *Moths*, 800 for the right to translate and outright ownership of a collection of short stories, and a further 800 francs for the exclusive right to translate *Friendship*.[18] Further dated payments are as follows:

---

18 The title of the short story collection is unfortunately illegible.

Appendix 195

9 July 1878: 800 francs for *Signa*
May 1882: 800 francs for *In Marenna*
14 June 1883: 800 francs for *Wanda*
23 September 1883: 800 francs for *Fresques* and three further short stories
27 June 1884: 800 francs for *La Princesse Napraxine*
28 October 1885: 800 francs for *Othmar*
10 June 1886: 500 francs for *Don Gesualdo*, *La rose de Provence* and *Pepistrelles*
12 December 1886: 500 francs for *A House Party*
1 October 1887: 800 francs for *Ariadne* (HAC 44.41).

Adrien-Augustin Paulmier (?1813–?1869).[19] Arabist, Arabic-French lexicographer, and former advisor to the appeal court in Algiers. In 1850, Paulmier self-published a dual-language edition of the first book of Gil Blas for self-taught students of Arabic, revised by a Mouh'ammed R'oudja ben H'affaf. The book was printed by the jobbing lithographer Jacques Arbieu in Poissy, a small town to the west of Paris. Paulmier transferred ownership of the book to Arbieu to repay a debt of 4,000 francs, and Arbieu sold it on to Hachette (HAC 18.11).

Amédée Pichot (1795–1877). Novelist, historian, and translator, well known as a cultural intermediary between France and Britain from the 1820s onwards. Over the course of a long career beginning in 1819, he translated authors including Byron, Walter Scott, Sheridan, Dickens, and Thackeray. By the 1850s, he was extremely well established, as reflected in the quantity of surviving archival material in his file.

- On 28 February 1854, Hachette issued him a receipt for the purchase of the following translations:

La Mine d'Ivoire[20]	98
Contes d'Edgard Poë	148
Les Emigrés Français	194
Scènes de la vie maritime	315
Le mariage de mon grand-père	142
Pitcairn[21]	63
Total	960

---

19 For these dates, http://www.familysearch.org has an Augustin Adrien Paulmier, which corresponds to the author's chronology.

20 This seems to be *La Mine d'ivoire*, *voyage dans les glaces de la mer du Nord*, attributed in the BnF catalogue to Octave Sachot. Sachot is also recorded as the translator of the anonymous *Le mariage de mon grand-père* and *Le Testament du juif*, suggesting that Pichot, like Charles Bernard Derosne, may have been subcontracting some of his output.

21 Presumably T. Murray's *Pitcairn*, *nouvelle île fortunée dans l'Océan Pacifique*, published by Hachette in the Bibliothèque des chemins de fer series in 1853.

196 *Appendix*

- On 17 February 1854, he signed a contract for a number of volumes including *Les émigrés français dans la Louisiane*, *Le scarabée d'or*, and *L'aéronaute hollandais* by "Edgard Poë" [sic] and sundry works including *Le mariage de mon grand père*, *Le Testament du juif*, *La Mine d'ivoire*, and *Les scènes de la vie maritime* for 32 francs per in-16° printing sheet. A specimen was attached. The contract also covered a book called *Les Mormons* compiled by Pichot from English and American sources, for which he received 600 francs for a print run of 3,000 copies and 300 francs to cover all subsequent reprints. He undertook to update the subsequent editions and not to publish any other books with the same price or format on the same topic.
- On 1 April 1855, he sold the ownership of two Thackeray novels serialised in the *Revue Britannique* to Hachette for 400 francs. The works were to be published in book form in the Bibliothèque des chemins de fer series.
- On 18 May 1855, he wrote to Hachette about his translation of Thackeray's *Diamant de famille*, for which he was about to sign a contract. He pointed out that the book format had changed since he handed in the first part of his translation: a M. Templier had informed him that as a result he was to be paid two francs a page. This had clearly been forgotten in the contract he was sent. Pichot concluded the letter by saying that even if it was a mistake he would not push the matter, preferring not to talk money with a business like Hachette.
- On 1 July 1857, Hachette granted him permission to translate Bulwer Lytton's *What Will He Do With It?* at his own cost and serialise the translation in the *Revue britannique*, completing it within three months of the novel's serialisation in English in *Blackwood's Magazine*. For the publication in volume, he had to hand over all his rights to Hachette with no possibility of royalties. He was allowed to change and abridge the novel in serial form as he saw fit but had to guarantee the translation he provided for Hachette was accurate and complete. He was free to choose a pseudonym but had to agree that Paul Lorain's name would appear on the cover. Lorain was also entitled to alter Pichot's work as he saw fit (HAC 43.37).

Victor de Rély (or **Derély**) (1840–1904). Best known for his translations from the Russian, including Dostoievsky. On 30 August 1870, he was paid 200 francs for his work on Wilkie Collins's *Moonstone* (HAC 63.2).

Théodore-Albert Rey (dates unknown) and **Germain-Eugène Belha[t]te** (1812–84). In a letter that is undated but written between 1851, when Belhate took over from Gravier, and 1862 (see below), the pair wrote to Victor Cousin in their capacity as the new owners of his *Oeuvres de Platon*. He was well overdue in handing in the paratext for the translation, as a result of which the publishers had frozen an outstanding payment of 2,000 francs. He was to be paid 3,000 francs for the second edition, which was still not published, so the sum was not yet due. The publishers wanted to print a small-format second edition as soon as possible, but Cousin held out, preferring a large format with a full critical apparatus. They seemed to have come to an agreement, but all the contractual terms agreed were then struck through and replaced with a statement cancelling all prior agreements. Rey and Belhate sold the translation back to Cousin with the remaining 80 copies of the first edition, retaining the right to print the paratext to the first edition at their own cost. Cousin undertook to absolve Rey and Belhate of all the sums still owing to him, pay them 5,000 francs in cash, and pay 30 francs for the remaining first-edition copies.

On 9 July 1862, Cousin wrote to Hachette, who had purchased the remaining stock of the Rey and Belhate edition, promising to buy the remaining stock at the cost price of 30 francs (HAC 5.15).

Henri Richelot (1811–64). Economist, employed at the time of the contract (undated, c. 1862) at the Ministry of Agriculture. Wrote a number of works on economics and published a four-volume translation of Goethe's *Mémoires* at his own cost (HTZ 8.10).

Abraham-Auguste Rolland (1823–1905). Teacher and parliamentarian, also known as Auguste or Auguste-Abraham Rolland. Occasional translator from German. On 29 April 1893, J. Hetzel signed a statement that Rolland's *Lettres inédites de Mendelssohn* had been published on 20 May 1864, at which point he had already been paid for his work (HTZ 8.14).

Madeleine Rolland (1872–1960). English teacher, translator, and political activist, sister of the author Romain Rolland. On 4 June 1896, Thomas Hardy wrote to a Lady Lewis to grant Madeleine Rolland the right to translate *Tess of the Durbervilles*, as long as she could find a publisher to bring the novel out serially or as a standalone book by 30 June the following year. Hardy asked for £15 to cover losses on sales of the English edition in France and elsewhere. The translator was to retain profits on sales of her work. Hardy suggested she approach Calmann Levy in the first instance. On 18 December 1897 he agreed to waive the £15. In the end her translation was published by Hachette in 1901 (HAC 154.22).

David Soldi or **Soldin** (1817–84). Best known for introducing Hans Christian Andersen to French readers. On 15 November 1855, he was paid

198 *Appendix*

one franc per in-16° page for his *Contes d'Andersen* for the Bibliothèque du chemin de fer collection. Hachette owned the full rights to the translation. Soldi was paid an advance of 300 francs and received the outstanding sum due to him when the book went on sale. Hachette was still earning rights from ownership of the translation as late as 1976, when SAGEM paid 120 francs for the right to reproduce it (HAC 65.9).

John Hanning Speke (1827–64). British explorer in Africa. Hachette purchased the translation rights to his 700-page *Discovery of the Source of the Nile* (1863) and galvanoplastic plates of the many illustrations for 2,500 francs (HAC 2.2).

Louise Swanton-Belloc (1796–1881). French writer and prolific translator of Irish extraction, well placed on the Paris literary scene from a young age, beginning her writing career at 17. She was a keen advocate of women's education. Her circle included numerous leading authors, from Stendhal and Victor Hugo to Charles Dickens and Maria Edgeworth. Her Hachette file is one of the most abundant in the archive.

On 12 March 1855, Elizabeth Gaskell sold the exclusive rights to five novels and various shorter works to Hachette for 50 centimes per page, based on a sample attached to the contract. Alongside the contract is an undated letter from the Paris-based British writer and salon hostess Mary Mohl (1793–1883) to Hachette, who had spoken to her admiringly of Louise Swanton-Belloc. Mohl informed Hachette that Swanton-Belloc was starting a translation of *Cranford* and made the case that it was a particularly difficult work that Swanton-Belloc was best placed to tackle.

A letter from Swanton-Belloc to Hachette dated only "Saturday 31" (it must be March 1855, which was indeed a Saturday) states she has just learned he has a contract with Mrs. Gaskell and asks if he will let her translate either *Mary Barton* or *North and South*. She apologises for her indiscretion but adds that time is passing, she has no work on the horizon, and the people around her are so sad she wants to help them. In the end, *Mary Barton* was translated by a Mlle Morel and *North and South* by Mme Loreau and H. de l'Espine – presumably the H. Gréard listed above, who used the same pseudonym.

Hachette was a hard taskmaster: a note in the corner of a document dated 28 March 1855 records that on 9 April he offered her 500 francs to finish the work in three months at most. But Swanton-Belloc was having none of it. She wrote again on 12 April 1855, making it clear that she was still keen to translate *Cranford* at Mrs. Gaskell's request but that she could not judge the scope of the project from the serial publication in *Household Words* and requested a copy of the latest book edition. She also requested a sample page of print for payment, reminding Hachette that she had never

Appendix 199

translated a book for under 1,200 francs a volume. She said in this case she would make an exception and halve the rate, promising to complete the project in four months at most: it would have her full focus and she hoped to be finished sooner. She informed him that everyone she worked with would swear to her reliability but she preferred to negotiate an ample deadline just in case (HAC 29.3).

Auguste Teste (possibly 18?–1907). Possibly the prolific late-nineteenth-century composer of light songs of the same name recorded in the BnF catalogue, which has no record of the works contracted. Received 200 francs on 6 July 1874 for *De la poule parfaite* by a M. Marthowitz and 50 francs on 26 September 1874, for translating *Le petit pépé*, both from the Russian (HTZ 9.3).

William Makepeace Thackeray (1811–63). British author and novelist best known for his satirical pen. On 26 September 1857, he signed an exclusive translation contract with Charles Lahure, having lost money to pirate translations. The agreement stipulated payment of 50 centimes per page for novels in the public domain and 1 franc 50 centimes for new novels (HAC 10.48).

Achille Varembey (dates unknown) and **Gustave Ovrée** (dates unknown). Varembey – a half-Turkish Muslim[22] – was a history teacher and headmaster in Paris, while Ovrée was a headmaster who had previously taught with Varembey at the Lycée Charlemagne. On 4 August 1879 the pair handed Hetzel exclusive ownership of an unfinished translation of Thomas Wentworth Higgenson's history of the United States for children. The transfer was free of charge on the condition that Hetzel would have the work completed or redone entirely, publish by the following February at his own cost, and give the pair 50 copies of the in-18° edition. The agreement stipulated that whoever completed the work would not be named in the published book, which was to feature their names and social statuses on the title page. The published book does indeed bear their names (HTZ 9.28).

Xavier Verrier (dates unknown).[23] Not listed in the BnF catalogue. Granted sole translation rights by Wilkie Collins for his *I Say No* on 13 January 1885. The book is attributed to a Camille Valdy in the BnF catalogue,

---

22 See https://www.google.fr/books/edition/Mediterraneans/7bowDwAAQBAJ?hl=en &gbpv=1&dq=%22achille+varembey%22&pg=PA127&printsec=frontcover (accessed 14 December 2022).

23 A search on http://www.familysearch.org gives several possible candidates by this name.

200 *Appendix*

though Verrier is recorded as translator in various nineteenth-century bibliographies (HAC 63.2).

Elisa de Villers (18?–1888). Friend of Charles Nodier and Sainte-Beuve and occasional author and translator, mainly of English and German children's books. On 14 September 1871, received payment of 150 francs for translating Charlotte Maria Tucker's *Les souliers de mon voisin* (a second version was translated by a Mme S. Le Page). The contract stipulated she would be named in the book, as indeed she was (HTZ 9.35).

Elise Voïart (Elise Petitpain, 1786–1866). A well-known author and translator from English and German, mainly of children's books, beginning in 1817. By the 1860s she was very well established and able to negotiate higher rates than usual: on 6 June 1863, she earned 500 francs for Brentano's *Le coq et l'anneau de Salomon*. At the time of signing, she lived in Nancy (HTZ 9.40).

Léon de Wailly (1804–63). Novelist, playwright, and translator. He was a close friend of Alfred de Vigny. He translated numerous canonical British authors, including Swift, Sterne, Fielding, Thackeray, and Burns. On 11 May 1860, he agreed to translate Carleton's selected works for an in-18° edition with a brief biography of the author. He was to be paid a royalty of 20 centimes per volume, regardless of the cost of subsequent editions. He also gave Hetzel first refusal on subsequent Carleton translations while reserving the right to work with other publishers on more expensive illustrated editions. On 30 May 1861, he signed a contract agreeing to deliver a book of children's tales by the end of June to launch a new collection bearing his name as editor. The nine printed sheets were to be paid the high rate of 500 francs, though Hetzel – a personal friend of his – reserved the right to refuse any tales he felt were not a good fit (HTZ 9.42).

Bibliography

Archival Sources

Archives nationales, Files on Louise Swanton-Belloc, shelfmarks 20144790-130, F_1dII_V_7, F_17_3116_2, and F_21_1028.

File of Emma Allouard's correspondence, Département des arts du spectacle, Bibliothèque nationale de France, shelfmark Mn-1050.

Institut mémoire de l'édition contemporaine, translator files from the publishers Larousse, Hachette, Hetzel, and Flammarion.

Letter from Auguste-Jean-Baptiste Defauconprêt to Charles Gosselin (4 October 1822). National Library of Scotland, Walter Scott archive, MS 3112 fols 180–1.

Papers of Louise Swanton Belloc, Bessie Rayner Parkes archive, Girton College, Cambridge, shelfmark GBR/0271/GCPP Parkes 17a.

Primary Sources

Alexis, Willibald [W. H. Häring] (1824) *Walladmor: Frei nach dem Englischen des Walter Scott, von W*****s*. Berlin: Herbig.

——— (1825a) *Walladmor: Freely Translated into German from the English of Sir Walter Scott, and Now Freely Translated from the German into English*, trans. Thomas de Quincey. London: Taylor and Hessey.

——— (1825b) *Walladmor: Roman attribué en Allemagne à Sir Walter Scott*, trans. Auguste-Jean-Baptiste Defauconprêt. Paris: Charles Gosselin/Mame et Delaunay-Vallée.

Anger, Louis-Simon (1828) *Mélanges philosophiques et littéraires*. Paris: Ladvocat.

Annales de physique et de chimie, vol. 6 (1817).

Annales maritimes et coloniales (1817).

Annuaire de la Société des Auteurs et compositeurs dramatiques, vol. 2 (1872). Paris: Commission des auteurs et compositeurs dramatiques.

Anonymous (1805) "Almon's Correspondence of the Late J. Wilkes". *Anti-Jacobin Review* 20: 244–57.

——— (1806) "Viller's Spirit and Influence of the Reformation of Luther". *Anti-Jacobin Review* 22: 179–90.

——— 1811. "Varieties, literary and philosophical", *The Monthly Magazine* 217, September 1811: 158–165.

——— (1829) "Le secret des traducteurs: IIIe dialogue de Mercure et M. Chompré". *Le Mercure de France au dix-neuvième siècle* 27: 506–12.

——— (1830) "French Translation of Sir W. Scott's Novels". *Morning Post*, 22 January: 4.

202 Bibliography

—— (1833) "De l'art de traduire et des différens systèmes de traduction", *Revue britannique*, troisième série, t. IV: 31–50.

—— (1839) "Petite bibliographie biographico-romancière, ou Dictionnaire des romanciers". *Monthly Review* 3(4): 537–46.

—— (1855) *Paris Universal Exhibition, 1855. Catalogue of the Works Exhibited in the British Section of the Exhibition, in French and English*. London: Chapman and Hall.

—— (1855–90) *Recueil. Portraits d'écrivains et hommes de lettres de la seconde moitié du XIXe siècle*, vol. 2.

Asselineau, Charles (1861) *Mélanges curieux et anecdotiques tirés d'une collection de lettres autographes et de documents historiques ayant appartenu à M. Fossé-Darcosse*. Paris: J. Techener.

Athénée de Paris: Programme pour l'an 1806 (1806).

Aulard, François-Alphonse (1892) *Le Culte de la Raison et le Culte de l'Être Suprême (1793–1794): Essai historique*. Paris: Félix Alcan.

Balzac, Honoré de (1839) *Illusions perdues*. Paris: Hippolyte Souverain.

—— (2002a [1840]) *Revue Parisienne*, vol. 2. Paris: A la Revue Parisienne.

—— (2002b [1840]) *Les Journalistes: Monographie de la presse parisienne*. Paris: Le Boucher.

Barbier, Antoine-Alexandre (1872) *Dictionnaire des ouvrages anonymes*. Paris: Paul Daffis.

Bayly Howell, Thomas (1880) *A Complete Collection of State Trials and Proceedings for High Treason and Other Crimes and Misdemeanours*, vol. 25. London: Hansard.

Beecher Stowe, Harriet (1861) *Souvenirs heureux: Voyage en Angleterre, en France et en Suisse*, trans. Eugène Forcade. Paris: Michel Lévy frères.

Bernard Derosne, Charles (1865) *Agence pour la protection de la propriété littéraire français en Angleterre*. Advertising brochure printed in Paris.

Bertillon, Jacques (1884) "Le divorce et la séparation de corps dans les différents pays de l'Europe". *Journal de la société statistique de Paris* 25: 28–42.

Besnard, François-Yves (1880) *Mémoires de François-Yves Besnard: souvenirs d'un nonagénaire*. Paris: H. Champion.

Bibliographie de la France (1822–23).

Boutarel, Amédée (1885) "La propriété intellectuelle". *Le Ménestrel* 51: 18 October.

Boyer, Abel (1817) *Dictionnaire Anglois-François et François-Anglois*, revised by L. F. Pain. Paris: Lefèvre.

British Critic (June 1800 and October 1817).

Bulletin de la Société des Auteurs et Compositeurs Dramatiques, vol. 1: *Exercices 1872–1876* (1876). Paris: Commission des Auteurs et Compositeurs Dramatiques.

Bulletin des lois du Royaume de France, IXe série, vol. 28, issues 793–820 (1846). Paris: Imprimerie royale.

Bulletin du Ministère de l'Agriculture et du Commerce (1840). 1ere année. Paris: Imprimerie et Librairie administratives.

Bulletin du Ministère de l'Agriculture et du Commerce (1866). Paris: Imprimerie et librairie administratives de Paul Dupont et Cie.

Burney, William (1815) *New Universal Dictionary of the Marine, with a Vocabulary of French Sea-Phrases*. London: T. Cadell and W. Davies.

Calmels, Edouard (1856) *De la propriété et de la contrefaçon des oeuvres de l'intelligence*. Paris: Cosse.

Bibliography   203

Challamel, Augustin (1895) *Les clubs contre-révolutionnaires: cercles, comités, sociétés, salons, réunions, cafés, restaurants et librairies.* Paris: L. Cerf et C. Noblet.

Chevallier, Émile (1887) *Les salaires au XIXe siècle.* Paris: Librairie Nouvelle de Droit et de Jurisprudence/Arthur Rousseau.

'Chronique littéraire de la Revue Britannique et bulletin bibliographique' (1852). *Revue britannique,* vol. 10.

Clarke, Eliza (1886) *Susanna Wesley.* London: W. H. Allen.

'Clément' (1800) *La Sténographie, ou L'art d'écrire aussi vite qu'on parle.* Paris: Chez l'auteur.

Correspondance de Napoléon I, publiée par ordre de l'empereur Napoléon III, vol. 20. (1866) Paris: Imprimerie impériale.

Coulon de Thévenot, Jean (1802) *Tachygraphie fondée sur les principes du langage de la grammaire et de la géométrie.* Paris: Chez l'auteur.

Courrouve dit Pold, Léopold (1861) *Notice sur l'Athénée Polyglotte, agence universelle fondée en 1850.* Paris: à l'Athénée Polyglotte.

Court Magazine and Monthly Critic, vol. 6 (1840).

Dalloz, Victor (1833 [1846; 1857]) *Jurisprudence générale du royaume, recueil périodique et critique de législation, de doctrine et de jurisprudence.* Paris: Au bureau de la jurisprudence générale ou journal des audiences.

de Balzac, Honoré (1840). 'Révélations sur M. Havas, le Maître-Jacques des journaux?, in *Revue parisienne* 2. Paris: A la revue parisienne, 25 August, p. 245.

de la Grange, Edouard (1833) "Les traducteurs", in *Le diable boîteux ou Paris, ou le Livre des cent-et-un.* Stuttgart: Chez la Rédaction de la Collection d'oeuvres choisies de la littérature française, 240–51.

de la Tynna, J. (1815) *Almanach du commerce de Paris.* Paris: de la Tynna, Bailleul, Latour.

de Magny, L. (1894) *Recueil des généalogies de maisons nobles de France,* vol. 2. Paris: A la direction des archives de la noblesse et du collège héraldique de France.

de Quincey, Thomas (1851) *Literary Reminiscences; from the Autobiography of an Opium Eater.* Boston: Ticknor, Reed and Fields.

de Sainte-Beuve, Charles-Augustin (2013 [1839]) *De la littérature industrielle.* Paris: Allia.

Defauconprêt, Auguste-Jean-Baptiste (1793) *La Papesse Jeanne, opéra-bouffon, en vaudevilles, en trois actes.* Paris: Veuve Hérissant.

——— (1802) *Nouveau barême, ou Tables de réduction des monnaies et mesures anciennes en monnaies et mesures républicaines analogues.* Paris: Favre.

——— (1817a) *Quinze jours à Londres, à la fin de 1815.* Paris: Eymery.

——— (1817b) *Six mois à Londres en 1816.* Paris: Eymery and Delaunay.

——— (1820) *Une année à Londres en 1819.* Paris: Gide fils.

——— (1829) *Robert Fitzooth, surnommé Robin Hood, ou Le chef des proscrits.* Paris: Gosselin.

Dictionnaire du notariat, par les notaires et jurisconsultes (1857). Paris: A l'administration du Journal des notaires et des avocats.

Duruy, Victor (1901) *Notes et souvenirs (1811–1894),* vol. 1. Paris: Hachette.

F. D. (1832) "Compte rendu de *Demonology and Witchcraft* de Sir Walter Scott". *Revue de Paris* 36: 294–6.

Feltham, John (1807) *The Picture of London, for 1807.* London: Richard Phillips.

Féraud, Laurent-Charles (1876) *Les interprètes de l'Armée d'Afrique.* Alger: A. Jourdan.

204 Bibliography

François, Henri-Joseph (1807) *Discours à M. Defauconprêt sur la carrière des lettres*. Paris: Brasseur Aîné.

Frappaz, Zacharie (1857) *Vie de l'Abbé Nicolle*. Paris: Jacques Lecoffre.

Fréron, Elie (1774a) "Réponse de M. l'Abbé de Radonvilliers au discours de M. l'Abbé de Lille". *L'Année littéraire* 8: 293–9.

—— (1774b) "Lettre IV". *L'Année littéraire* 5–6: 73–92.

Gastambide, Joseph-Adrien (1837) *Traité théorique et pratique des contrefaçons en tous genres*. Paris: Legrand et Descauriet.

Gazette des tribunaux (1856), 1–2 September.

Gazette nationale (26 November 1792).

Girault de Saint-Fargeau, Eusèbe (1839) *Revue des romans. Recueil d'analyses raisonnées des productions remarquables des plus célèbres romanciers français et étrangers*, vol. 1. Paris: Firmin Didot.

Gouin Dufief, Nicolas (1810) *Dictionnaire nouveau et universel des langues française et anglaise*. Philadelphia: T. and G. Palmer.

Grenier, Edouard (1888) "Hommage à la mémoire de Madame Elisa de Villers", in *Mémoires de la Société d'émulation du Doubs*, vol. 3. Besançon: Dodivers.

Hackney, Iscariot [Richard Savage] (1732) *An Author to be let*. No publisher given.

Halbjahrsverzeichnis der Neuerscheinungen des deutschen Buchhandels erschienenen Bücher, Zeitschriften und Landkarten (1822).

Hauff, Wilhelm (1827 [2015]) *Die Bücher und die Lesewelt: Phantasien und Skizzen*. Berlin: Contumax.

Johnstone's London Commercial Guide and Street Directory (1818). London: Longman, Rees, Hurst, Orme and Brown.

Journal de Paris (26 February 1805).

Journal des débats politiques et littéraires (6 August 1810 and 8 February 1819).

Journal des sciences médicales (1817).

Journal du Palais, Répertoire général, contenant la jurisprudence de 1791 à 1845, l'histoire du droit, la législation et la doctrine des auteurs, vol. 8 (1848). Paris: d'Auvilliers et Giraudeau.

Journal général de France (31 August 1817).

L'Ami de la religion: Journal politique, littéraire, universel, vol. 8 (1861). Paris: Soye et Bouchet.

La Nacelle: Journal du commerce, des mœurs et de la littérature de la Seine-Inférieure (1823), 16 February: 4.

La Petite Presse (1885), 10 August.

Lacroix, Paul (1829) *Soirées de Walter Scott à Paris*. Bruxelles: August Wahlen.

Lantscheer, Hendrik Willem (1811) *Woordenboek der Fransche zee-termen, bijeen verzameld en in Hollandsche en gedeeltelijk in Engelsche kunstwoorden overgebragt*. Amsterdam: P. den Hengst en Zoon.

Lavater, Gaspard [Johann Kaspar] (1807) *L'Art de connaître les hommes par la physiognomie*. Paris: no publisher.

Le Correspondant, ou collection de lettres d'écrivains célèbres, vol. 3 (1817). Paris: Gide fils.

Le Spectateur français au XIXe siècle, vol. 4 (1807).

Ledru-Rollin, Alexandre (1841) *Journal du Palais: Recueil le plus ancien et le plus complet de la jurisprudence française*, vol. 24. Paris: F. F. Patris.

Les Cinq Codes de l'Empire Français (1812). Paris: Le Prieur.

Lescallier, Daniel (1777) *Vocabulaire des termes de marine anglais et français, avec un dictionnaire de définitions et un calepin de termes de commerce maritime*. Paris: Imprimerie royale.

Bibliography   205

Levasseur, Émile (1909) "Labor and Wages in France". *The Annals of the American Academy of Political and Social Science* 33(2): 183–95.

Literary Gazette (8 November 1816).

Locré, Jean-Guillaume (1819) *Discussions sur la liberté de la presse, la censure, la propriété littéraire, l'imprimerie et la librairie, qui ont eu lieu dans le conseil d'état, pendant les années 1808, 1809, 1810 et 1811.* Paris: Garnery and H. Nicolle.

MacLeod, John (1817) *Narrative of a Voyage in His Majesty's Late Ship Alceste to the Yellow Sea, along the Coast of Corea, and through its Numerous Hitherto Undiscovered Islands, to the Island of Lew-Chew, with an Account of her Shipwreck in the Straits of Gaspar.* London: John Murray.

——— (1818) *Voyage du capitaine Maxwell commandant "l'Alceste"*, trans. Charles-Auguste Defauconprêt. Paris: Gide fils.

Mainwaring, M. (1822) *Moscow; or The Grandsire.* London: A. K. Newman.

——— (1823) *Le grand-père, ou l'incendie de Moscou* [sic], trans. Pierre Dubergier. Paris: Masson.

Marchant de Beaumont, François (1818) *Le nouveau conducteur de l'étranger à Paris.* Paris: Moronval.

Masson, Frédéric (1877) *Le Département des affaires étrangères pendant la Révolution, 1787–1804.* Paris: Plon.

Mavidal, Jérôme, and Emile Laurent (1877) *Archives parlementaires de 1787 à 1860*, vol. 35. Paris: Librairie administrative de Paul Dupont.

Mémorial de l'Association des anciens élèves de l'Ecole Normale, 1846–1876 (1877). Versailles: Cerf et Fils.

Michaud, Louis-Gabriel (1855) *Biographie universelle, ancienne et moderne.* Paris: C. Desplaces.

Ministère du commerce et de l'industrie, Direction du commerce extérieur. *Annales du commerce extérieur: Situation économique de la France, exposé comparatif pour la période 1872–1886.* No place or publisher.

Ministère du commerce, de l'industrie, des postes et des télégraphies, Direction du travail, Service du recensement professionnel (1901) *Résultats statistiques du recensement des industries et professions*, vol. 4. Paris: Imprimerie Nationale.

Moniteur universel 250 (13 August 1813).

Monthly Magazine, or British Register 32 (1811).

Morning Chronicle (2 February 1816).

Muller, René (1858) *La fille de l'antiquaire.* Rouen: Mégard et cie.

Nicolai, Friedrich (1773–76) *Das Leben und die Meinungen des Herrn Magister Sebaldus Nothanker.* Berlin/Stettin: In der Nicolaischen Buchhandlung.

——— (1798) *The Life and Opinions of Sebaldus Nothanker*, trans. Thomas Dutton. London: Printed for C. Lowndes and sold by H. D. Symonds.

Nugent, Thomas (1797 [1816; 1817]) *New Pocket Dictionary of the French and English Languages.* London: C. Dilly/Mawman.

'Oliver Oldschool' (1818) "Anecdote", in *The Port Folio*, vol. 6, 390.

Pansner, Johann Heinrich Lorenz (1802) *Französisch-deutsches mineralogisches Wörterbuch.* Jena: C. E. Gabler.

Pardessus, Jean-Marie (1814) *Cours de droit commercial.* Paris: Garnery.

——— (1825) *Cours de droit commercial.* Paris: Nève.

Paris-Adresses: Annuaire général de l'Industrie et du Commerce (1901). Paris: Société Anonyme de l'Annuaire "Paris-Adresses".

P. B. (1833) "Compte rendu de *Mémoires d'un médecin, par le docteur Harisson* [sic]". *L'Artiste, Journal de la littérature et des beaux-arts* 5: 284–5.

206 Bibliography

Pichot, Amédée (1826) *Voyage historique et littéraire en Angleterre et en Ecosse*, vol. 2. Bruxelles: August Wahlen.

—— (1837) *Monsieur de l'Etincelle, ou Arles et Paris, roman moderne*. Paris: Gosselin.

Pouillet, Eugène (1879) *Traité théorique et pratique de la propriété littéraire et artistique et du droit de représentation*. Paris: Imprimerie et librairie générale de jurisprudence.

Prinz, August (1855) *Der Buchhandel vom Jahre 1815 bis zum Jahre 1843. Bausteine zu einer späteren Geschichte des Buchhandels*, vol. 1. Altona: In Commission im Verlags-Bureau.

Prudhomme, Louis-Marie (1804) *Dictionnaire universel, géographique, statistique, historique et politique de la France*, vol. 3. Paris: Baudouin.

Quérard, Joseph-Marie (1828) *La France littéraire*, vol. 2. Paris: Firmin Didot.

—— (1853) *Les supercheries littéraires dévoilées*, vol. 5. Paris: L'éditeur.

Quicherat, Jules (1860) *Histoire de Sainte-Barbe*. Paris: Hachette.

Rabbe, Alphonse, Claude-Augustin Vieilh de Boisjolin and Charles-Claude Saint-Preuve (1826) *Biographie universelle et portative des contemporains*, vol. 2. Paris: Au bureau de la biographie.

Regnault, Elias (1833) "L'éditeur", in *Les Français peints par eux-mêmes*, Léon Curmer (ed.), vols 1–2. Paris: Furne, 389–96.

Relevé de quelques omissions, contresens et additions de M. Defauconprêt dans sa traduction d'Ivanhoe (roman de Walter Scott) et qui ne se trouvent point dans la traduction nouvelle de M. Albert Montémont (1830). Paris: François Rignoux.

Renouard, Augustin-Charles (1838–9) *Traité des droits d'auteur, dans la littérature, les sciences et les beaux-arts*. Paris: Jules Renouard, 2 vols.

Roch, Eugène (1830) *Dictionnaire du Budget*, vol. 1. Paris: Sédillot.

Scott, Walter (1825a) *The Betrothed*. Edinburgh/London: Archibald Constable/Hurst, Robinson and Co.

—— (1825b) *Histoires du temps des croisades: Le Connétable de Chester*, trans. Auguste-Jean-Baptiste Defauconprêt. Paris: Charles Gosselin.

—— (2007) *Peveril of the Peak*, Alison Lumsden (ed.). Edinburgh: Edinburgh University Press.

'Scriblerus Secundus' [Henry Fielding] (1730) *The Author's Farce; And, the Pleasures of the Town*. Dublin: S. Powell.

Silvestre, Augustin-François de (1802–03) *Essai sur les moyens de perfectionner les arts économiques en France*. Paris: Madame Huzard.

Smith, Adam (1776) *An Inquiry into the Nature and Causes of the Wealth of Nations*, vol. 1. Dublin: Whitestone.

Stendhal (1908) *Correspondance (1800–1842)*, vol. 2, A. Paupe and P. A. Cheramy (eds). Paris: Charles Bosse.

The Kaleidoscope: Or, Literary and Scientific Mirror 7 (1827).

Tuckey, James (1818) *Relation d'une expédition entreprise en 1816, sous les ordres du capitaine J. K. Tuckey, pour reconnoître le Zaïre, communément appelé le Congo*, trans. A. J. B. Defauconprêt. Paris: Gide fils.

Ulliac-Trémadeure, Sophie (1899) *Emilie, la jeune fille auteur*. Limoges: E. Ardant.

Yvernès, Maurice (1908) "Chronique de statistique judiciaire. Les divorces et les séparations de corps en France depuis 1884". *Journal de la société statistique de Paris* 49: 101–3.

Bibliography 207

Secondary Sources

Agostini-Ouafi, Viviana, and Antonio Lavieri (2015) "Poétiques des archives". Special issue of *Transalpina* 18.

Alger, John (1891) "William Little Hughes", in *Dictionary of National Biography*, vol. 28, Leslie Stephen (ed.). London: Smith, Elder and Co, 191.

Allen Harvey, David (2004) "Forgotten Feminist: Claude Vignon (1828–1888), Revolutionary and femme de lettres". *Women's History Review* 13(4): 559–84.

Allen, Esther, and Susan Bernofsky (eds) (2013) *In Translation: Translators on their Work and What it Means*. New York: Columbia University Press.

Alper, Neil, and Gregory Wassall (2006) "Artists' Careers and Their Labor Markets", in *Handbook of the Economics of Art and Culture*, David Throsby and Victor Ginsburgh (eds). Amsterdam: Elsevier, 813–64.

Apter, Emily (2006) *The Translation Zone: A New Comparative Literature*. Princeton: Princeton University Press.

Assouline, Pierre (2011) *La Condition du Traducteur*. Paris: Centre National du Livre.

Atefmehr, Zahra, and Farzaneh Farahzad (2021) "A Microhistorical Study of the First Translators of Dār al-Funūn". *Iranian Journal of Translation Studies*, 19(73): 81–95.

Atefmehr, Zahra, and Farzaneh Farahzad (2022) "Microhistorical Research in Translator Studies: An Archival Methodology". *The Translator* 28(3): 251–62.

Azimi, Vida (2013) "La féminisation des administrations françaises: étapes et historiographie, XVIIIe siècle—1945". *Revue française d'administration publique* 145: 11–38.

Bachleitner, Norbert (1989) "'Übersetzungsfabriken'. Das deutsche Übersetzungswesen in der ersten Hälfte des 19. Jahrhunderts". *Internationales Archiv für Sozialgeschichte der deutschen Literatur* 14(1): 1–49.

——— (2009) "A Proposal to Include Book History in Translation Studies. Illustrated with German Translations of Scott and Flaubert". *Arcadia* 44: 420–40.

Bardet, Mary (2021) "Literary Detection in the Archives: Revealing Jeanne Heywood (1856–1909)", in *Literary Translator Studies*, Klaus Kaindl, Waltraud Kolb, and Daniela Schlager (eds). Amsterdam: Benjamins, 41–53.

Barnaby, Paul (2006) "Another Tale of Old Mortality: The Translations of A.-J.-B. Defauconpret in the French Reception of Scott", in *The Reception of Walter Scott in Europe*, Murray Pittock (ed). London: Continuum, 31–44.

Barnaby, Paul (2011) "Restoration Politics and Sentimental Poetics in A.-J.-B. Defauconprêt's Translations of Sir Walter Scott". *Translation and Literature* 20(1): 6–28.

Basalamah, Salah (2009) *Le Droit de traduire: Une politique culturelle pour la mondialisation*. Ottawa/Arras: University of Ottawa Press/Artois Presses Université.

Batchelor, Jennie (2005) "The Claims of Literature: Women Applicants to the Royal Literary Fund, 1790–1810". *Womens' Writing* 12(3): 505–21.

Belle, Marie-Alice, and Brenda Hosington (2017) "Translation, History, and Print: A Model for the Study of Printed Translations in Early Modern Britain". *Translation Studies* 10(1): 2–21.

Benani, Agnès (1993) "Auguste-Jean Baptiste Defauconprêt ou l'écrivain et son double", in *Traductions, passages: le domaine anglais*. Tours: Presses universitaires François-Rabelais, 189–201.

Bibliography

Benhamou, Françoise (2003) "Artists' Labour Markets", in *A Handbook of Cultural Economics*, Ruth Towse (ed.). Cheltenham: Edward Elgar, 69–75.

Bennett, Karen (ed.) (2022) *Translation Matters*. Special Issue of *Translation and Money* 4(2).

Bereaud, Jacques (1964) *Auguste-Jean-Baptiste Defauconprêt: agent de liaison franco-britanique, 1767–1843*, PhD dissertation. Université de Lille, France.

Bereaud, Jacques, and L. Machu (1965) "Un mémoire inédit de Defauconprêt (1789)". *Revue du nord* 47(186): 383–97.

——— (1966) "Un essai inédit de Defauconprêt (1793)". *Revue du nord* 48(190): 309–19.

Berthier, Patrick (2012) "Traduction de textes étrangers dans les périodiques français en 1830", in *Traduire en langue française en 1830*, Christine Lombez (ed.). Arras: Artois Presses Université, 21–34.

Bhanot, Kavita, and Jeremy Tiang (2022) *Violent Phenomena: 21 Essays on Translation*. London: Tilted Axis.

Bille, Trine (2020) "Artists' Labour Markets", in *Handbook of Cultural Economics*, third edition, Ruth Towse and Trilce Navarrete Hernández (eds). Cheltenham: Edward Elgar, 46–55.

Bille, Trine, and Günther G. Schulze (2006) "Culture in Urban and Regional Development", in *Handbook of the Economics of Art and Culture*, David Throsby and Victor Ginsburgh (eds). Amsterdam: Elsevier, 1051–99.

Binctin, Nicolas (2013) "Le droit moral en France". *Cahiers de propriété intellectuelle* 25(1): 303–61.

Bogé-Rousseau, Patricia (2018) *Traduire et retraduire au XIXe siècle: le cas de Quentin Durward, roman historique de Sir Walter Scott, et de ses traductions par Auguste-Jean-Baptiste Defauconprêt*, PhD dissertation. Université Toulouse II Jean Jaurès, France.

Boncompain, Jacques (2001) *La Révolution des auteurs: Naissance de la propriété intellectuelle, 1773–1815*. Paris: Fayard.

Borg, Claudine (2017) *A Literary Translation in the Making: An in-depth Investigation into the Process of a Literary Translation from French to Maltese*, PhD dissertation. University of Aston, UK.

Bouffange, Serge (1996) *Pro Deo et Patria: Casterman, librairie, imprimerie, édition (1776–1919)*. Genève: Droz.

Brée, Sandra (2022) "Deux siècles de séparations et divorces en France (1792–1975)". *Annales de démographie historique* 143: 73–114.

Bret, Patrice (ed.) (2016) "Louis-Bernard Guyton de Morveau, 'l'illustre chimiste de la République'". Special issue of *Annales historiques de la Révolution française* 383.

Brook, Orian, Dave O'Brien, and Mark Taylor (2020) *Culture Is Bad For You: Inequality in the Cultural and Creative Industries*. Manchester: Manchester University Press.

Brown, Hilary (2005) *Benedikte Naubert (1765–1819) and her Relations to English Culture*. Cambridge: MHRA.

Bruckmann, Denis (2018) "Bibliothèque nationale de France et grand public: Une longue marche". URL: https://bbf.enssib.fr/matieres-a-penser/bibliotheque -nationale-de-france-et-grand-public_68526 (accessed 13 June 2024).

Bulletin de la Société historique du VIe arrondissement de Paris (1904).

Burrows, Simon (1999) "The cultural politics of exile: French émigré literary journalism in London, 1793–1814". *Journal of European Studies* 29: 157–77.

Buzard, James (1993) *The Beaten Track: European Tourism, Literature, and the Ways to 'Culture', 1800–1918*. Oxford: Oxford University Press.

Bibliography 209

Buzelin, Hélène (2011) "Agents of Translation", in *Handbook of Translation Studies*, vol. 2, Yves Gambier and Luc Van Doorslaer (eds). Amsterdam: Benjamins, 6–12.

Calvet, Louis-Jean (2007) "La mondialisation au filtre des traductions". *Hermès, La Revue* 49(3): 45–57.

Carpenter, Kirsty (1999) *Refugees of the French Revolution: Emigrés in London, 1789–1802*. London: Palgrave Macmillan.

Casanova, Pascale (1999) *La République mondiale des lettres*. Paris: Seuil.

——— (2002) "Consécration et accumulation de capital littéraire". *Actes de la recherche en sciences sociales* 144: 7–20.

Caves, Richard (2000) *Creative Industries: Contracts between Art and Commerce*. Cambridge, MA/London: Harvard University Press.

Chan, Andy Lung Jan (2008) *Information Economics, The Translation Profession and Translation Certification*, PhD dissertation. Universitat Rovira y Virgili, Spain.

Chan, Andy Lung Jan, Anthony Pym, François Grin, and Claudio Sfreddo (2014) *The Status of the Translation Profession in the European Union*. London/New York/Delhi: Anthem.

Chartier, Roger, and Henri-Jean Martin (eds) (1990a) *Histoire de l'édition française: Le livre triomphant, 1660–1830*. Paris: Fayard / Cercle de la Librairie.

——— (1990b) *Histoire de l'édition française: Le temps des éditeurs, 1830–1900*. Paris: Fayard / Cercle de la Librairie.

Chatzis, Konstantinos, Thomas Morel, Thomas Preveraud, and Norbert Verdier (2017) "Traduire des mathématiques 'pour et par des élèves' dans la première moitié du XIXe siècle: Acteurs et pratiques de traduction à travers trois cas d'étude en Europe et aux Etats-Unis". *Mémoires du Livre/Studies in Book Culture* 9(1).

Chesterman, Andrew (2009) "The Name and Nature of Translator Studies". *HERMES – Journal of Language and Communication in Business* 22(42): 13–22.

——— (2021) "View from Left Field: The Curious Case of Douglas Hofstadter", in *Literary Translator Studies*, Klaus Kaindl, Waltraud Kolb, and Daniela Schlager (eds). Amsterdam: Benjamins, 279–92.

Chesterman, Andrew, and Emma Wagner (2002) *Can Theory Help Translators? A Dialogue between the Ivory Tower and the Wordface*. London/New York: Routledge.

Chevrel, Yves, and Jean-Yves Masson (eds) (2012) *Histoire des traductions en langue française: XIXe siècle*. Lagrasse: Verdier.

Choi, Jungwha, and Hyang-Ok Lim (2002) "The Status of Translators and Interpreters in Korea". *Meta* 47(4): 627–35.

Clavel, Marcel (1938) *Fenimore Cooper, sa vie et son œuvre*. Aix-en-Provence: Imprimerie Universitaire de Provence.

Cler, Christian, and Susan Pickford (2009) "Traduction/Édition: État des lieux", in *Vingt-Sixièmes Assises de la Traduction Littéraire*, Alain Fleischer, Nedim Gürsel, and Leslie Kaplan (eds). Arles: ATLAS/Actes Sud, 86–90.

Coase, R. H. (1979) "Payola in Radio and Television Broadcasting". *The Journal of Law and Economics* 22(2): 269–328.

Cointre, Annie, and Anne Rivara (eds) (2006) *Recueil de préfaces de traducteurs de romans anglais (1721–1828)*. Saint-Etienne: Presses Universitaires de Saint-Etienne.

Collectif (2020) *Faut-il se ressembler pour traduire? Légitimité de la traduction, paroles de traductrices et traducteurs*. Joinville-le-Pont: Double Ponctuation.

210 Bibliography

Condette, Jean-François (2006) *Les recteurs d'académie en France de 1808 à 1940: Tome 2. Dictionnaire biographique*. Paris: Institut national de recherche pédagogique.

Cordingley, Anthony, and Céline Frigau Manning (eds) (2016) *Collaborative Translation from the Renaissance to the Digital Age*. London/New York: Bloomsbury Academic.

Cordingley, Anthony, and Chiara Montini (2015a) "Genetic Translation Studies: An Emerging Discipline". *Linguistica Antverpiensia, New Series: Themes in Translation Studies* 14: 1–18.

——— (eds) (2015b) "Towards a Genetics of Translation". Special issue of *Linguistica Antverpiensia* 14.

Cordingley, Anthony, and Patrick Hersant (2021a) "Translation Archives: An Introduction". *Meta* 66(1): 9–27.

——— (eds) (2021b) "Archives de traduction/Translation archives", special issue of *Meta* 66(1).

Crofts, Jennifer (2021) "Why Translators Should be Named on Book Covers". *The Guardian*, 10 September. URL: https://www.theguardian.com/books/2021/sep/10/why-translators-should-be-named-on-book-covers (accessed 9 May 2023).

Cross, Máire (2013) "The French in London during the 1830s: Multidimensional Occupancy", in *A History of the French in London: Liberty, Equality, Opportunity*, Debra Kelly and Martyn Cornick (eds). London: Institute of Historical Research, 129–54.

Cross, Nigel (1985) *The Common Writer: Life in Nineteenth-century Grub Street*. Cambridge/New York: Cambridge University Press.

D'hulst, Lieven (2014) *Avatars de Janus: Essais d'histoire de la traduction*. Paris: Classiques Garnier.

D'hulst, Lieven, and Kaisa Koskinen (2020) *Translating in Town: Local Translation Policies during the European 19th Century*. London/New York: Bloomsbury Academic.

Dam, Helle V., and Karen Korning Zethsen (2008) "Translator Status: A Study of Danish Company Translators". *The Translator* 14(1): 71–96.

——— (2010) "Translator Status: Helpers and Opponents in the Ongoing Battle of an Emerging Profession". *Target* 22(2): 194–211.

Dam, Helle V., and Kaisa Koskinen (eds) (2016) "The Translation Profession: Centres and peripheries", special issue of *JoSTrans*, 25.

Darnton, Robert (1982) "What is the History of Books?". *Daedalus* 111(3): 65–83.

Davis, Elmer (1940) *Some Aspects of the Economics of Authorship*. New York: New York Public Library.

De Groote, Brecht, and Tom Toremans (2014) "From Alexis to Scott and de Quincey: Walladmor and the Irony of Pseudotranslation". *Essays in Romanticism* 21(2): 107–23.

Dehérain, Henri (1925) "Le voyage du consul Joseph Rousseau d'Alep à Bagdad en 1807". *Syria: Revue d'art oriental et archéologie*, vol. 6. Paris: Paul Geuthner, 174–187.

——— (1991 [1922]) "Jeunes de langue et interprètes français en Orient au XVIIIe siècle". *Anatolia Moderna. Yeni Anadolu* 1: 323–35.

Delisle, Jean (1999) *Portraits de traducteurs*. Ottawa/Arras: PUO/APU.

——— (2002) *Portraits de traductrices*. Ottawa: Presses Universitaires d'Ottawa.

——— (2021) *Les traducteurs par eux-mêmes*. Quebec: PUL.

Derome, Amélie (2021) *Les traductions en langue française de Gulliver's Travels de Jonathan Swift (1727–2017): une conquête temporelle entre éternité et fragilité*, PhD dissertation. Université Aix-Marseille, France.

Bibliography 211

Dubuc, M. A. (1959) *Charles-Louis Havas (1783–1858) et son agence internationale de presse*. Paris: Imprimerie nationale.

Eberharter, Markus (2021) "Translator Biographies as a Contribution to Translation Studies: Case Studies from Nineteenth-century Galicia", in *Literary Translator Studies*, Klaus Kaindl, Waltraud Kolb, and Daniela Schlager (eds). Amsterdam: Benjamins, 73–88.

Ehrensberger-Dow, Maureen, and Andrea Hunziker Heeb (2016) "Investigating the Ergonomics of a Technologized Translation Workplace", in *Reembedding Translation Process Research*, Ricardo Muñoz (ed.). Amsterdam: Benjamins, 69–88.

El Ghazi, Omar, and Chakib Bnini (2020) "Arabic Translation from Bait Al-Hikma to Toledo School of Translators: Key Players, Theorization and Major Strategies". *International Journal of Linguistics, Literature and Translation* 3(9): 66–80.

Felkay, Nicole (1987) *Balzac et ses éditeurs, 1822–1837: Essai sur la librairie romantique*. Paris: Promodis/Cercle de la Librairie.

François, Pieter (2012) "If It's 1815, This Must Be Belgium: The Origins of the Modern Travel Guide". *Book History* 15: 71–92.

Frank, Robert H., and Philip J. Cook (2010) *The Winner-Take-All Society: Why The Few At The Top Get So Much More Than The Rest of Us*. London: Virgin.

Freeth, Peter (2022) *Beyond Invisibility: The Position and Role of the Literary Translator in the Digital Paratextual Space*, PhD dissertation. University of Leeds, UK.

Fullerton, Ronald (2015) *The Foundations of Marketing Practice: A History of Book Marketing in Germany*. London/New York: Routledge.

Garnett, Richard (1991) *Constance Garnett: A Heroic Life*. London: Faber and Faber.

Georgiou, Nadia (2020) *The Translator as Reader: The Case of Poetry Translators from Modern Greek into English*, PhD dissertation. University of Surrey, UK.

Ghadie, Heba (2013) *Les traducteurs dans les collections littéraires en France, 1821–1852: Identités réelles et discursives*, PhD dissertation. University of Ottawa, Canada.

Gibbels, Elisabeth (2022) "The Lost Cast of Women Translators, or the Case of the Lost Women Translators?". *Counterpoint* 8: 13–17.

Gillespie, S. (2005) "The Developing Corpus of Literary Translation". In *The Oxford History of Literary Translation in English Vol. 3: 1660–1790*, S. Gillespie and D. Hopkins (eds). Oxford: Oxford University Press, 121–146.

Gillies, Mary Ann (2007) *The Professional Literary Agent in Britain, 1880–1920*. Toronto: University of Toronto Press.

Gilmore, Oisín (2021) "The Working Week in Manufacturing since 1820", in *How Was Life? Volume II: New Perspectives on Well-being and Global Inequality since 1820*. Paris: Éditions OCDE.

Gold, David (2009) *Democracy in Session: A History of the Ohio General Assembly*. Athens: Ohio University Press.

Gomez, Hannelore (2017) "A Closer Look into the Life of Ordinary Translators through Unordinary Sources: The Use of Obituaries as a Microhistory Tool to Study Translators and Translation in Ohio". *New Voices in Translation Studies* 16: 55–83.

Grbić, Nadja, and Pekka Kujamäki (2018) "Professional vs. Non-Professional? How Boundary Work Shapes Research Agendas in Translation and Interpreting Studies", in *Moving Boundaries in Translation Studies*, Helle V. Dam, Matilde Brøgger, and Karen Zethsen (eds). London: Routledge, 113–131.

212 Bibliography

Green, F. C. (1957) "Scott's French Correspondence". *The Modern Language Review* 52(1): 35–49.

Guénette, Marie-France (2020) *Traducteurs et traductions imprimées à la cour anglaise de la reine Henriette-Marie (1625–1642)*, PhD dissertation. Université de Laval, Canada.

Guillon, Olivia (2020) *La Situation socio-économique des traducteurs littéraires*. Paris: ATLF.

Harper, Charles (1903) *Stage-Coach and Mail in Days of Yore*. London: Chapman and Hall.

Havelange, Isabelle (1986) "Burnouf Jean-Louis", in *Les inspecteurs généraux de l'Instruction publique. Dictionnaire biographique 1802–1914*, Isabelle Havelange, Françoise Huguet, and Bernadette Lebedeff-Choppin (eds). Paris: Institut national de recherche pédagogique, 208–209.

Haynes, Christine (2010) *Lost Ilusions: The Politics of Publishing in Nineteenth-Century France*. Cambridge, MA: Harvard University Press.

Heilbron, Johan (1999) "Towards a Sociology of Translation: Book Translations as a Cultural World-System". *European Journal of Social Theory* 2(4): 429–44.

Heilbron, Johan, and Gisèle Sapiro (eds) (2002) "La traduction: les échanges littéraires internationaux". Special issue of *Actes de la recherche en sciences sociales* 144.

Heinich, Nathalie (1984) "Les traducteurs littéraires: l'art et la profession". *Revue française de sociologie* 25(2): 264–80.

Hemmungs Wirtén, Eva (1998) *Global Infatuation: Explorations in Transnational Publishing and Texts. The Case of Harlequin Enterprises and Sweden*. Uppsala: Skrifter utgivna av Avdelningen för litteratursociologi vid Litteraturvetenskapliga institutionen i Uppsala.

Hepburn, James (1968) *The Author's Empty Purse and the Rise of the Literary Agent*. London: Oxford University Press.

Hermetet, Anne-Rachel, and Frédéric Weinmann (2012) "Prose Narrative", in *Histoire des traductions en langue française*, vol. 3, Yves Chevrel, Lieven d'Hulst, and Christine Lombez (eds). Lagrasse: Verdier, 537–663.

Hersant, Patrick (1999) "Defauconprêt, ou le demi-siècle d'Auguste". *Romantisme* 106: 83–88.

Holden, Nigel, and Snejina Michailova (2014) "A More Expansive Perspective on Translation in IB Research: Insights from the Russian Handbook of Knowledge Management". *Journal of International Business Studies* 45(7): 1–13.

Holz-Mänttäri, Justa (1984) *Translatorisches Handeln: Theorie und Methode*. Helsinki: Suomalainen Tiedeakatemia.

Hughes, Helen Sard (1919) "Notes on Eighteenth-Century Fictional Translations". *Modern Philology* 17(4): 225–31.

Ingelbien, Raphael (2020) "An Irish Diasporic Translator: Louise Swanton-Belloc and the Diffusion of Irish Writing in Nineteenth-century France". *Translation Studies* 13(2): 138–52.

Jacob, Margaret (2014) *The First Knowledge Economy: Human Capital and the European Economy, 1750–1850*. Cambridge: Cambridge University Press.

Jalabert, Romain, and Dirk Sacré (2010) "Bibliographie intermédiaire des poètes et versificateurs latins en France au XIXe siècle". *Humanistica Lovaniensia* 59: 223–304.

Jemielity, David (2018) "Translation in Intercultural Business and Economic Environments", in *The Routledge Handbook of Translation and Culture*, Sue-Ann Harding and Ovidi Carbondell Cortés (eds). London/New York: Routledge, 533–57.

Jenn, Ronald (2013) *La pseudo-traduction, de Cervantes à Mark Twain*. Louvain-la-Neuve: Peeters.

Kaindl, Klaus (2021) "Introduction", in *Literary Translator Studies*, Klaus Kaindl, Waltraud Kolb and Daniela Schlager (eds). Amsterdam: Benjamins, 1–38.

Kaindl, Klaus, Waltraud Kolb, and Daniela Schlager (eds) (2021) *Literary Translator Studies*. Amsterdam: John Benjamins.

Kalinowski, Isabelle (2002) "La vocation au travail de traduction". *Actes de la recherche en sciences sociales* 144: 47–54.

Kelly, Debra, and Martyn Cornick (2013) *A History of the French in London. Liberty, Equality, Opportunity*. London: Institute of Historical Research.

Kinane, Vincent (1993) "Printers' Apprentices in 18th- and 19th-century Dublin". *The Linen Hall Review* 10(1): 11–14.

Kinnunen, Tuija, and Kaisa Koskinen (2010) *Translators' Agency*. Tampere: Tampere University Press.

Kleinman, Sylvie (2005) *Translation, the French Language and the United Irishmen 1792–1804*, PhD dissertation. Dublin City University, Ireland.

Kotze, Haidee (2021) "Translation is the Canary in the Coalmine". URL: https://haidee-kotze.medium.com/translation-is-the-canary-in-the-coalmine -c11c75a97660 (accessed 9 May 2023).

Lahire, Bernard (2006) *La Condition littéraire. La double vie des écrivains*. Paris: La Découverte.

Lambert, Joseph, and Callum Walker (2022) "Because We're Worth It: Disentangling Freelance Translation, Status and Rate-Setting in the United Kingdom". *Translation Spaces* 11(2): 277–302.

Larbaud, Valéry (1946) *Sous l'Invocation de Saint-Jérôme*. Paris: Gallimard.

Large, Duncan (2021) "Towards a Literary Translation Studies". URL: https:// www.youtube.com/watch?v=pc_fQh_p8Xg&ab_channel=TrinityCentreforLit erary%26CulturalTranslation (accessed 9 May 2023).

Laviosa, Sara (2014) *Translation and Language Education: Pedagogic Approaches Explored*. London/New York: Routledge.

Lee, Tong King (2020) "Translation and Copyright: Towards a Distributed View of Originality and Authorship". *The Translator* 26(3): 241–56.

Legouis, Emile (1971) "La fortune littéraire de Walter Scott en France". *Etudes anglaises* 24(4): 492–500.

Lemonnier, Léon (1928) *Les Traducteurs d'Edgar Poe en France de 1845 à 1875*. Paris: Presses Universitaires de France.

Lepouchard, Camille (1994) *Louise Swanton-Belloc: Du bon usage des modèles anglais et américains dans les milieux intellectuels français du XIXe siècle*. La Rochelle: La Rumeur des Âges.

Levick, Tiffane, Clíona Ní Ríordáin, and Bruno Poncharal (2021) "Thème/version: quelle influence des concours sur l'enseignement de la traduction en France?", in *Enseigner la traduction dans les contextes francophones*, Tiffane Levick and Susan Pickford (eds). Arras: Artois Presses Université, 27–46.

Liemer, Susan (2011) "On the Origins of le droit moral: How Non-economic Rights Came to be Protected in French IP Law". *Journal of Intellectual Property Law* 19(1): 65–114.

Littau, Karin (2011) "First Steps towards a Media History of Translation". *Translation Studies* 4(3): 261–81.

Lord, William Jackson (1962) *How Authors Make A Living. An Analysis of Freelance Writers' Incomes, 1953–1957*. New York: Scarecrow.

214 Bibliography

MacDonald, Simon (2014) "Les journaux anglophones sous la Révolution française", trans. Laurent Turcot. *Etudes Epistémè: Revue de littérature et de civilisation, XVIe–XVIIIe siècles* 26.

Maclaren, Ian (2011) "In Consideration of the Evolution of Explorers and Travellers into Authors: a Model". *Studies in Travel Writing* 15(3): 221–41.

Malmkjaer, Kirsten (2009) "What is Translation Competence?". *Revue française de linguistique comparée* 1: 121–34.

Marello, Carla (2009) "Bilingual Dictionaries of the Nineteenth and Twentieth Centuries", in *The Oxford History of English Lexicography*, A. P. Cowie (ed.). Oxford: Oxford University Press, 86–104.

Masson, Frédéric (1877) *Le Département des affaires étrangères pendant la Révolution, 1787–1804*. Paris: Plon.

McIntosh-Varjabédian, Fiona (2019) "Henry Thomas Buckle's *The History of Civilization in England* in France (1865–1918): A Transnational Reception Case". *Reception: Texts, Readers, Audiences, History* 11: 40–57.

McMurran, Mary Helen (2009) *The Spread of Novels: Translation and Prose Fiction in the Eighteenth Century*. Princeton: Princeton University Press.

Melnyk, Veronica (2002) *"Half Fashion and Half Passion"*. *The Life of Publisher Henry Colburn*. Unpublished PhD dissertation, University of Birmingham.

Menger, Pierre-Michel (2006) "Artistic Labor Markets: Contingent Work, Excess Supply and Occupational Risk Management", in *Handbook of the Economics of Art and Culture*, David Throsby and Victor Ginsburgh (eds). Amsterdam: Elsevier, 765–811.

Merkle, Denise (2015) "L'exécution de Louis David Riel (16 novembre 1885) et les enjeux de la traduction au Canada", in *L'appel de l'étranger. Traduire en langue française en 1886 (Belgique, France, Québec, Suisse)*, S. Humbert-Mougin, L. Arnoux-Farnoux, and Y. Chevrel (eds). Tours: Presses universitaires François-Rabelais, 301–15.

Messaoudi, Alain (2015) *Les Arabisants et la France coloniale, 1780–1930. Savants, conseillers, médiateurs*. Lyon: ENS.

Meylaerts, Reine (2011) "Habitus and Self-image of Native Literary Author-translators in Diglossic Societies", in *Identity and Status in the Translational Professions*, Rakefet Sela-Sheffy and Miriam Schlesinger (eds). Amsterdam: Benjamins, 135–54.

Mignot, Jean-François (2015) "L'adoption simple en France: le renouveau d'une institution ancienne (1804–2007)". *Revue française de sociologie* 56(3): 525–60.

Milan, Michelle (2021) "Towards a Professional Identity: Translators in the Victorian Publisher's Archive". *Meta* 66(1): 48–72.

Misiou, Vasiliki (2023) *The Renaissance of Women Translators in Nineteenth-Century Greece*. New York: Routledge.

Mollier, Jean-Yves (1988) *L'Argent et les lettres. Histoire du capitalisme d'édition, 1880–1920*. Paris: Fayard.

Mongin, Jean-Louis (2017) "Vous avez dit Olszewicz?". *Bulletin de la Société Jules Verne* 195. URL: http://www.societejulesverne.org/bulletin/195.php (accessed 13 June 2024).

Montagne, Edouard (1889) *Histoire de la Société des gens de lettres*. Paris: Librairie mondaine.

Monteil, Vincent (1961) "Les bureaux arabes au Maghreb". *Esprit* 300(11): 575–606.

Monti, Enrico, and Peter Schnyder (eds) (2018) *Traduire à plusieurs*. Paris: Orizons.

Moorkens, Joss (2020) "A Tiny Cog in a Large Machine: Digital Taylorism in the Translation Industry". *Translation Spaces* 9(1): 12–34.

Bibliography 215

Mortier, Roland (1982) *L'Originalité: Une nouvelle catégorie esthétique au siècle des Lumières*. Genève: Droz.

Munday, Jeremy (2013) "The Role of Archival and Manuscript Research in the Investigation of Translator Decision-making". *Target. International Journal of Translation Studies* 25(1): 125–39.

––––––– (2014) "Using Primary Sources to Produce a Microhistory of Translation and Translators: Theoretical and Methodological Concerns". *The Translator* 20(1): 64–80.

Naugrette, Jean-Pierre (1998) "Paris-Londres ou les Chroniques de M. Stendhal". *Revue des deux mondes* (May): 143–54.

Nunes, Ariadne, Joana Moura and Marta Pacheco Pinto (2020) *Genetic Translation Studies. Conflict and Collaboration in Liminal Spaces*. London: Bloomsbury.

O'Brien, Patrick, and Caglar Keyder (2011) *Economic Growth in Britain and France, 1780–1914*. London/New York: Routledge.

Orr, Leah (2017) *Novel Ventures: Fiction and Print Culture in England, 1690–1730*. Charlottesville: University of Virginia Press.

O'Sullivan, Carol (2012) "Introduction: Rethinking Methods in Translation History". *Translation Studies* 5(2): 131–38.

Paloposki, Outi (2017) "In Search of an Ordinary Translator: Translator Histories, Working Practices and Translator – Publisher Relations in the Light of Archival Documents". *The Translator* 23(1): 31–48.

––––––– (2021) "Translations not in the Making? Rejections, Disruptions and Impasses in Translator – Publisher Correspondence". *Meta* 66(1): 73–91.

Parfait, Claire (2010) *The Publishing History of Uncle Tom's Cabin, 1852–2002*. Aldershot/Burlington, VT: Ashgate.

Park, Jiyoung (2019) "Critical Analysis of Korean Court Rulings on Translators' Copyrights: On the Originality of Translation and Translators' Economic and Moral Rights". *Perspectives* 27(5): 732–46.

Peñarroja, Josep (2013) "Histoire des experts traducteurs et interprètes". *Traduire* 228: 121–34.

Pic, François (1989) "Essai d'inventaire des textes en occitan de la période révolutionnaire (1788–1800)", in *Le Texte occitan de la période révolutionnaire*, Henri Boyer, Georges Fournier, Philippe Gardy, Philippe Martel, René Merle, and François Pic (eds). Montpellier: Section française de l'Association internationale d'études occitanes, 434.

Pickford, Susan (2007) "Between *Version* and *Traduction*: Sterne's Sentimental Journey in Mid-nineteenth Century France". *Translation and Literature* 16(1): 53–65.

––––––– (2011) "Combe and Rowlandson's Dr Syntax, Pierce Egan's Life in London, and the Illustrated Character as a Form of Literary Property", in *Book Practices & Textual Itineraries: Tracing the Contours of Literary Works*, Nathalie Collé-Bak, Monica Latham, and David Ten Eyck (eds). Nancy: Presses Universitaires de Nancy, 45–66.

––––––– (2012a) "Les traducteurs", *Histoire des traductions en langue française vol. III: Le XIXe siècle*, Yves Chevrel, Lieven D'hulst, and Christine Lombez (eds). Lagrasse: Verdier, 149–87.

––––––– (2012b) "Writing with 'manly vigour': Translatorial Agency in Two Early Nineteenth-century English Translations of François Pouqueville's *Voyage en Morée, à Constantinople et en Albanie* (1805)", in *Travel Narratives in Translation: Nationalism, Ideology, Gender*, Alison E. Martin and Susan Pickford (eds). London/New York: Routledge, 197–217.

216 Bibliography

———— (2014) "Les traducteurs littéraires en Europe: une pratique professionnelle?", in *Commerces et traduction*, Sylvaine Hughes (ed.). Paris: Presses Universitaires de Paris Ouest, 297–314.

———— (2018) *Le voyage excentrique: Jeux textuels et paratextuels dans l'anti-récit de voyage (1760–1850)*. Lyon: ENS éditions.

———— (2019) "Translation Competence and Professional Habitus in the 2009 English Retranslation of Simone de Beauvoir's *Le deuxième sexe*", *De Genere: Rivista di studi letterari, postcoloniali e di genere* 5: 27–42.

———— (2021) "Le traducteur et l'archive: considérations historiographiques". *Meta* 66(1): 28–47.

Pollard, Sidney (1965) *The Genesis of Modern Management: A Study of the Industrial Revolution in Great Britain*. Cambridge, MA: Harvard University Press.

Popa, Ioana (2010) *Traduire sous contraintes: Littérature et Communisme, 1947–1989*. Paris: CNRS.

Puren, Christian (1988) *Histoire des méthodologies de l'enseignement des langues vivantes*. Paris: Nathan-Clé International.

Pym, Anthony (2009) "Humanizing Translation History". *HERMES - Journal of Language and Communication in Business* 42: 23–48.

———— (2011) "The Translator as non-author, and I am Sorry about that", in *The Translator as Author: Perspectives on Literary Translation*, Claudia Buffagni, Beatrice Garzelli, and Serenella Zanotti (eds). Berlin: LIT.

———— (2014) *Method in Translation History*. London: Routledge.

Pym, Anthony, Andrea Rizzi, and Birgit Lang (2019) *What is Translation History? A Trust-Based Approach*. Cham: Palgrave Pivot.

Rebolledo-Dhuin, Viera (2017) "Les libraires parisiens au XIXe siècle. Mobilités sociales et spatiales". *Ethnologie française* 47(1): 59–74.

Reboul, Juliette (2014) *French Emigration in Great Britain in Response to the French Revolution: Memories, Integrations, Cultural Transfers*, PhD dissertation. University of Leeds, UK.

Recht, Pierre (1969) *Le droit d'auteur: Une nouvelle forme de propriété, histoire et théorie*. Paris: LGDJ.

Reinert, Sophus (2011) *Translating Empire: Emulation and the Origins of Political Economy*. Cambridge, MA/London: Harvard University Press.

Richter, Julia (2020) *Translationshistoriographie: Perspektiven und Methoden*. Vienna: New Academic Press.

Risku, Hanna, and Angela Dickinson (2017) "Translators as Networkers: The Role of Virtual Communities". *Hermes: Journal of Language and Communication in Business* 22(42): 49–70.

Risku, Hanna, Regina Rogl, and Jelena Milosevic (eds) (2019) *Translation Practice in the Field: Current Research on Socio-cognitive Processes*. Amsterdam/Philadelphia: Benjamins, 25–41.

———— (2020) "Researching Workplaces", in *The Bloomsbury Companion to Language Industry Studies*, E. Angelone, M. Ehrensberger-Dow, and G. Massey (eds.). London: Bloomsbury Publishing, 37–62.

Robinson, Douglas (2023) *The Behavioral Economics of Translation*. New York/Abingdon: Routledge.

Rogers, Pat (2021) *The Poet and the Publisher: The Case of Alexander Pope, Esq., of Twickenham versus Edmund Curll, Bookseller in Grub Street*. London: Reaktion.

Rogers, Pat, and David Hopkins (2005) "The Translator's Trade", in *Oxford History of Literary Translation in English Vol. 3: 1660–1790*, Stuart Gillespie and David Hopkins (eds). Oxford: Oxford University Press, 81–95.

Rundle, Christopher (ed.) (2021) *The Routledge Handbook of Translation History*. London: Routledge.

Rybicki, Jan, and Magda Heydel (2013) "The Stylistics and Stylometry of Collaborative Translation: Woolf's *Night and Day* in Polish". *Literary and Linguistic Computing* 28(4): 708–17.

Saglia, Diego (2013) "'The International Commerce of Genius': Foreign Books in London in Romantic-Period London". *Gramma: Journal of Theory and Criticism* 21.

Salines, Emily (2004) *Alchemy and Amalgam: Translation in the Works of Charles Baudelaire*. Amsterdam/New York: Rodopi.

Sangster, Matthew (2021) *Living as an Author in the Romantic Period*. Basingstoke: Palgrave Macmillan.

Sangsue, Daniel (1987) *Le récit excentrique: Gautier, de Maistre, Nerval*. Paris: José Corti.

Santana López, Belén, and Críspulo Travieso Rodríguez (2021) "Staging the Literary Translator in Bibliographic Catalogs", in *Literary Translator Studies*, Klaus Kaindl, Waltraud Kolb and Daniela Schlager (eds). Amsterdam: Benjamins, 89–104.

Santoyo, Julio César (2006) "Blank Spaces in the History of Translation", in *Charting the Future of Translation History*, Georges L. Bastin and Paul F. Bandia (eds). Ottawa: University of Ottawa Press, 11–43.

Schor, Laura (2022) *Women and Political Activism in France, 1848–1852: First Feminists*. Cham: Palgrave Macmillan.

Schreiber, Michael (2015) "'Citoyens – Ciudadanos – Cittadini': Le travail des traducteurs de la Convention nationale", in *La ciencia como diálogo entre teorías, textos y lenguas*, Jenny Brumme and Carmen López Ferrero (eds). Berlin: Frank & Timme, 145–66.

Sela-Sheffy, Rakefet (2006) "The Pursuit of Symbolic Capital by a Semi-Professional Group: The Case of Literary Translators in Israel", in *Übersetzen – Translating – Traduire: Towards a "social turn"?*, Michaela Wolf (ed.). Vienna/Münster: LIT Verlag, 243–52.

Sela-Sheffy, Rakefet (2011) "Introduction: Identity and Status in the Translational Professions," in *Identity and Status in the Translational Professions*, Rakefet Sela-Sheffy and Miriam Shlesinger (eds.). Amsterdam & Philadelphia: John Benjamins, 1–10.

Sela-Sheffy, Rakefet, and Miriam Schlesinger (2011) *Identity and Status in the Translational Professions*. Amsterdam: Benjamins.

Shaw, David (2002) "French-language Publishing in London to 1900", in *Foreign-language Printing in London, 1500–1900*, Barry Taylor (ed.). Boston Spa & London: The British Library, 101–22.

Shibamoto Smith, Janet (2005) "Translating True Love: Japanese Romance Fiction, Harlequin-style", in *Gender, Sex and Translation: The Manipulation of Identities*, José Santaemilia (ed.). Manchester: St. Jerome, 97–116.

Simeoni, Daniel (1998) "The Pivotal Status of the Translator's Habitus". *Target: International Journal of Translation Studies* 10(1): 1–39.

Simonin, Anne (2013) "La République en ses provinces: la traduction des lois, histoire d'un échec révolutionnaire (1790–1792 et au-delà)", in *La République en voyage: 1770–1830*, Pierre Serna and Gilles Bertrand (eds). Rennes: Presses universitaires de Rennes, 197–218.

Singer Contreras, Nestor (2022) *The Development of Translator Identity: An Interpretative Phenomenological Study of Chilean Translation Students'*

218 Bibliography

Experiences Amid Global and Local Crises, PhD dissertation. University of Manchester, UK.

Smalley, Nichola (2014) *Contemporary Urban Vernaculars in Rap, Literature and in Translation in Sweden and the UK*, PhD dissertation. University College London, UK.

Speller, John (2011) *Bourdieu and Literature*. Cambridge: Open Book.

Stern, Madeleine (1980) "The English Press in Paris and its Successors, 1793–1852". *The Papers of the Bibliographical Society of America* 74(4): 307–59.

Stillinger, Jack (1991) *Multiple Authorship and the Myth of Solitary Genius*. Oxford/New York: Oxford University Press.

Strömholm, Stig (1966) *Le droit moral de l'auteur en droit allemand, français et scandinave, avec un aperçu de l'évolution internationale*, vol. 1. Stockholm: Norstedt.

Strowel, Alain (1993) *Droit d'auteur et copyright. Divergences et convergences: étude de droit comparé*. Paris: LGDJ.

Sullerot, Evelyne (1966) "Journaux féminins et lutte ouvrière, 1848–1849". *Revue d'Histoire du XIXe siècle – 1848* 23: 88–122.

Svahn, Elin, Minna Ruokonen, and Leena Salmi (2018) "Boundaries Around, Boundaries Within: Introduction to the Thematic Section on the Translation Profession", Translator Status and Identity. *HERMES - Journal of Language and Communication in Business* 58: 7–17.

Tekgül, Duygu (2016) "Competition and Cooperation for Recognition and Professional Esteem in the Literary Translation Industry". *Translation Studies* 10(1): 54–68.

Thomas, L. H. C. (1951) "Walladmor: A Pseudo-Translation of Sir Walter Scott". *The Modern Language Review* 46(2): 218–31.

Thompson, John (2010) *Merchants of Culture: The Publishing Business in the Twenty-First Century*. Cambridge: Polity.

Throsby, David, and Victor Ginsburgh (eds) (2006) *Handbook of the Economics of Art and Culture*. Amsterdam: Elsevier.

Thuillier, Guy (1980) *Bureaucrates et bureaucratie en France au XIXe siècle*. Genève: Droz.

Towse, Ruth (ed.) (2003) *A Handbook of Cultural Economics*, first edition. Cheltenham: Edward Elgar.

Trubek, Anne (2016) *The History and Uncertain Future of Handwriting*. New York: Bloomsbury USA.

Van Bolderen, Patricia (2021) *Literary Self-Translation and Self-Translators in Canada (1971–2016): A Large-Scale Study*, PhD dissertation. University of Ottawa, Canada.

Van Tieghem, Paul (1966 [1914]) *L'Année littéraire (1754–1790) comme intermédiaire en France des littératures étrangères*. Genève: Slatkine Reprints.

Vanacker, Beatrijs (2021) "Mediating the Female Transla(u)t(h)orial Posture: Elisabeth Wolff-Becker", in *Literary Translator Studies*, Klaus Kaindl, Waltraud Kolb, and Daniela Schlager (eds). Amsterdam: Benjamins, 215–32.

Venuti, Lawrence (1995a) "Translation, Authorship, Copyright". *The Translator* 1(1): 1–24.

——— (1995b) *The Translator's Invisibility: A History of translation*. London/New York: Routledge.

Vitrac, Julie (2000) "Profession: Traducteur". *Translittérature* 18–19: 70–82.

Walker, Callum (2022) "Translation Pricing with Joseph Lambert and Callum Walker". URL: https://slator.com/translation-pricing-with-joseph-lambert-callum-walker/ (accessed 9 May 2023).

Bibliography 219

—— (2023) *Translation Project Management*. New York/Abingdon: Routledge.

Weissbach, Lee (1977) "Child Labour Legislation in Nineteenth-Century France". *The Journal of Economic History* 37(1): 268–71.

Whitfield, Agnes (2005) *Le métier du double: Portraits de traductrices et traducteurs littéraires*. Montreal: Fides.

Wilfert, Blaise (2012) "Traduction littéraire: Approche bibliométrique", in *Histoire des traductions en langue française: Le XIXe siècle*, Yves Chevrel and Jean-Yves Masson (eds). Lagrasse: Verdier, 255–344.

Willenberg, Jennifer (2008) *Distribution und Übersetzung englischen Schrifttums im Deutschland des 18. Jahrhunderts*. München: Saur.

Williams, Rachel (2010) *Women Translators in Nineteenth-Century France: Genre, Gender and Literary Creativity*, PhD dissertation. Pennsylvania State University, US.

Withers, Charles, Innes Keighren, and Bill Bell (2015) *Travels into Print: Exploration, Writing, and Publishing with John Murray, 1773–1859*. Chicago: University of Chicago Press.

Wolf, Michaela (2015) *The Habsburg Monarchy's Many-Languaged Soul: Translating and Interpreting, 1848–1918*, trans. Kate Sturge. Amsterdam: Benjamins.

Woodmansee, Martha (1984) "The Genius and the Copyright: Economic and Legal Conditions of the Emergence of the 'Author'". *Eighteenth-Century Studies* 17(4): 425–48.

Woodsworth, Judith (2012) *Translators through History*. Amsterdam: Benjamins.

Yu, Pauline (2007) "Your alabaster in this porcelain: Judith Gautier's *Le livre de jade*". *PMLA* 122(2): 464–82.

Zille, Tom (2021) *Christian Felix Weisse the Translator: Cultural Transfer and Literary Entrepreneurship in the Enlightenment*. London: Institute of Germanic Studies, University of London, School of Advanced Study.

Web Links

Albarino, Seyma (2023) "Finland's Audiovisual Translators Win Higher Rates, Paid Leave in Historic Agreement". URL: https://slator.com/finlands-audiovisual -translators-win-higher-rates-paid-leave-historic-agreement/ (accessed 12 May 2023).

ATLF (2020) "Enquête sur la crise sanitaire du coronavirus: Conséquences du confinement sur les revenus des traducteurs littéraires". URL: https://atlf.org/ wp-content/uploads/2020/06/ENQUE%CC%82TE_ATLT_CONFINEMENT _04_2020.pdf (accessed 13 April 2023).

—— (2023) "Code des usages pour la traduction d'une oeuvre de littérature générale" [Standard Practice in French Literary Translation Contracts]. URL: https://atlf.org/wp-content/uploads/2021/10/CODE-DES-USAGES.pdf (accessed 11 May 2023).

Belgraviabooks.com (2019) "Diary of an In-house Translator (Or, 5 Things I've Learned About Translation)". URL: https://belgraviabooks.com/diary-of-an-in -house-translator-or-5-things-ive-learned-about-translation (accessed 21 April 2023).

Bulletin des Bibliothèques de France (1968) "Nécrologie: Jacques Feller". URL: https://bbf.enssib.fr/consulter/bbf-1968-07-0325-001 (accessed 1 May 2023).

Calhanas, Bernardo (2021) "How Many Pages can a Translator Translate per day?". *The Translation Guy*. URL: https://thetranslationguy.net/2021/06/23/ how-many-pages-can-a-translator-translate-per-day/ (accessed 13 June 2024).

220 Bibliography

Cap Magellan (2019). "Les 100 ans de l'enseignement du portugais en France". URL: https://capmagellan.com/les-100-ans-de-lenseignement-du-portugais-en-france/ (accessed 11 June 2024).

Centre National du Livre (2020a) "Bilan du plan d'urgence du CNL au 30 juin". URL: https://fill-livrelecture.org/wp-content/uploads/2021/01/Bilan-plan-durgence-CNL-au-30-juin-2020.pdf (accessed 13 April 2023).

——— (2020b) "L'activité et le statut des traducteurs face à la crise du Covid-19". URL: https://fill-livrelecture.org/wp-content/uploads/2021/05/ENQUETE-CRISE-SANITAIRE-2-copie.pdf (accessed 13 April 2023).

——— (2021) "Bilan des aides 2021". URL: https://centrenationaldulivre.fr/donnees-cles/bilan-des-aides-2021 (accessed 13 April 2023).

Copyrighthistory.org (2023) "Court of Appeal on Translations, Paris (1845)" [Rosa vs. Girardin]. URL: https://www.copyrighthistory.org/cam/tools/request/showRecord.php?id=record_f_1845a (accessed 11 May 2023).

Cousin, Victor (ed.) (2010) *Platon, Oeuvres*. URL: https://www.textesrares.com/pages/philosophie/platon-ouvres-editees-par-v-cousin.html (accessed 11 May 2023).

Doctrine.fr (2021) "E. X. v Editions de l'éclat". URL: https://www.doctrine.fr/d/CA/Paris/2021/CC1D55967454E17764D4D (accessed 11 May 2023).

Familysearch.org (2023a) "Jeanne Florimond". URL: https://www.familysearch.org/ark:/61903/1:1:WR9H-3WZM (accessed 11 May 2023).

——— (2023b) "Louis-Florian Cadiot". URL: https://www.familysearch.org/ark:/61903/3:1:3Q9M-CSRX-MSNL-Q?cc=2840171 (accessed 26 April 2023).

Fédération Interrégionale du Livre et de la Lecture (2022) "Crise sanitaire dans le secteur culturel: Impact de la pandémie de Covid-19 et des mesures de soutien sur l'activité et la situation financière des entreprises culturelles en 2020". URL: https://fill-livrelecture.org/wp-content/uploads/2022/04/CE-2022-1_Crise-sanitaire-dans-le-secteur-culturel-corpus-web.pdf (accessed 13 April 2023).

Hansen, Damien (2021) "Défis et pertinence de la traduction littéraire assistée par ordinateur". *La Main de Thôt* 9. URL: https://interfas.univ-tlse2.fr/lamaindethot/index.php?id=982 (accessed 12 May 2023).

Historicalstatistics.org (2016) "Historical Currency Converter (test version 1.0)". URL: https://www.historicalstatistics.org/Currencyconverter.html (accessed 17 April 2023).

Institut mémoires de l'édition contemporaine (2024) https://www.imec-archives.com/qui-sommes-nous/l-imec-en-quelques-dates (accessed 18 June 2024).

Jeffares, Neil (2021) "Dictionary of pastellists before 1800". URL: http://www.pastellists.com/Articles/FrancoisH.pdf (accessed 10 January 2023).

Légifrance (2023) "Droits moraux". *Code de la propriété intellectuelle*. URL: https://www.legifrance.gouv.fr/codes/section_lc/LEGITEXT000006069414/LEGISCTA000006161636/#:~:text=Chapitre%20Ier%20%3A%20Droits%20moraux%20(Articles,%C3%A0%20L121%2D9)%20%2D%20L%C3%A9gifrance&text=L'auteur%20jouit%20du%20droit,est%20perp%C3%A9tuel%2C%20inali%C3%A9nable%20et%20imprescriptible (accessed 11 May 2023).

Maxted, Ian (2016) "Sir Walter Scott and the Parisian Pirates: A Bibliographical Paddle in Murky Waters". *Exeter Working Papers in Book History*, 17 March. URL: https://bookhistory.blogspot.com/2016/03/sir-walter-scott-and-parisian-pirates.html (accessed 13 June 2024).

Ministère De L'Éducation Nationale et De La Jeunesse (2023) "Loi Générale sur L'Instruction Publique Du 1er Mai 1802 (Floréal An X)". URL: https://www

.education.gouv.fr/loi-generale-sur-l-instruction-publique-du-1er-mai-1802-11
-floreal-x-1646 (accessed 13 June 2024).

Négrier, Emmanuel (2017) "Le ministère de la Culture et la Politique culturelle en France: Exception culturelle ou exception institutionnelle?". URL: https://hal. science/hal-01442310 (accessed 1 May 2023).

OECD (2021) "The Pandemic has not Improved Things for Women". URL: https:// www.oecd.org/coronavirus/en/data-insights/the-pandemic-has-not-improved -things-for-women (accessed 1 May 2023).

Pelletier, Geoffroy (2011) "Les chiffres de la traduction". *Société des gens de Lettres*. URL: https://www.sgdl.org/%20ressource/%20documentation-sgdl/ actes-des-forums/la-traduction-litteraire/1519-les-chiffres-de-la-traduction-par -geoffroy-pelletier (accessed 17 April 2023).

Proceedings of the Old Bailey, 1674–1913 (2018). URL: http://www.oldbaileyonline .org.

Rideau, F. (2008) "Commentary on the Rouen Court of Appeal on Translations (1845)", in *Primary Sources on Copyright (1450–1900)*, L. Bently and M. Kretschmer (eds). URL: http://www.copyrighthistory.org (accessed 11 May 2023).

Schwartz, Ros (2023). URL: https://www.rosschwartz.co.uk/ (accessed 13 June 2024).

Scott, Walter (2005) *Letters*. URL: http://www.walterscott.lib.ed.ac.uk/etexts/ etexts/letters.html (accessed 13 June 2024).

——— (2015) *Peveril of the Peak*. URL: http://www.walterscott.lib.ed.ac.uk/ works/novels/peak.html (accessed 13 June 2024).

Société des Anglicistes de l'Enseignement Supérieur [SAES] (2015) "Agregation Externe d'Anglais". URL: https://saesfrance.org/wp-content/uploads/2014/08/ rapport-agreg-ext-2015.pdf (accessed 13 June 2024).

Société française des traducteurs, "Notre histoire", https://www.sft.fr/fr/notre -histoire-3 (accessed 12 May 2023).

Staniforth, Eleanor (2022). *Twitter*. URL: https://twitter.com/E_Staniforth/status /1480543434268098564 (accessed 13 June 2024).

The Gazette (2023). URL: http://www.thegazette.co.uk (accessed 13 June 2024).

Thompson, Shannon (2022) "Pay-to-Play in Traditional Publishing, and Why We Need to Talk about it", 1 August. URL: https://shannonathompson.com/2022 /08/01/pay-to-play-in-traditional-publishing-and-why-we-need-to-talk-about -it/ (accessed 13 June 2024).

Wikipedia (2022) "Marie-Noémi Cadot". URL: https://en.wikipedia.org/wiki/ Marie-No%C3%A9mi_Cadiot (accessed 28 April 2023).

Wynne, Frank (2023) *Terrible Man*. URL: https://www.terribleman.com/ translations/ (accessed 13 June 2024).

Index

Page numbers in **bold reference tables.

A. P. Watt agency 83
accreditation 35
acquisition rights 68
administrative staff with foreign
  language skills, importance of
  20–22
ALAI *see* Association Littéraire et
  Artistique Internationale
Alceste 148–149
Alexis, Willibald 60–61; *see also*
  Häring, Georg Wilhelm Heinrich
Allen, Esther 49
Allouard, Antoine-Ignace 125
Allouard, Emma 72, 115,
  122–129, 172
Allouard, Pierre 122–123
amateur translators 51–52
Anceaux, J. 172
Anger, Louis-Simon 47n4
Appert, J. 172
Arabic 23, 28
Arbieu, Jacques 70n7
artists 114; stipends 118–120
Association des Traducteurs Littéraires
  de France (ATLF) 83, 112, 166–167
Association Littéraire et Artistique
  Internationale (ALAI) 87, 109
Athenee Polyglotte agency 37–39, 40
ATLF *see* Association des
  TraducteursLittéraires de France
Aubrée, Armand 3, 92
authorial rights 81–92, 95–96; moral
  rights 99–108 *see droit d'auteur*

Babbage, Charles 59
Balzac, Honoré de 40–41

Barba, Gustave 81
Barbier, Auguste 172
Barzilay, Jacques 37
Baudelaire, Charles 51
Beauchène, Mme de 173
Belha[t]te, Germain-Eugène 196–197
Bellaguet, Frédéric 77, 173–174
belles infidèles model 64
Belloc, Jean-Hilaire 115, 118–120
Bennett, Anna Maria 141
Bentzon, Thérèse 72, 174
Bereaud, Jacques 132
Berlay, François 77, 174
Berne Convention 105
Bernofsky, Susan 49
Berthoud, Charles 81, 176
Bétolaud, Victor 75, 77, 176
Béville, Marie-Céleste 134
Bibliothèque nationale 18, 149
Bignon, Jeanne 176
bilingual dictionaries 17–18
bilingualism 17
Billecocq vs. Glandaz (1814) 101
Biot, Edouard 59
Blanc, Etienne 89
Bobée, Auguste 91
Bode, Johann Joachim Christoph 43
Bogé-Rousseau, Patricia 142, 163
Bogne de Faye, Pierre-François-Jean
  26–27
Boisjolin, Jacques de 125
book history approach 148
Borghers, Alphonse 51
Bouillet, Adolphe 77, 176–177
Boyer, Abel 145–146
Bracevich, Auguste 23, 28, 31

Index   223

Bracevich, Louis 23
Braddon, Mary Elizabeth 177
Bret, Patrice 14
broker-interpreters 33–34
Brossollet, Louis-Joseph 75, 177
Brunel, Charles 177–178
"bureau de traduction de Dijon" 14
bureaucratisation of translation
    practice 14
Burée, Mme 178
Burellier, M. 178
Burney, William 145
Burnouf, Jean-Louis 75, 102–103,
    178–179
business of translation 44–45
Buttura, Antonio (Antoine) 29–30

Cadiot, Emma *see* Allouard, Emma
Cadiot, Louis-Florian 122
Cadiot, Marie-Noémi 122
Calmels, Édouard 95
Calvert, Louis-Jean 44
Casanova, Pascale 44
Catlin, George 179
Centre national du Livre 166–167
Challemel-Lacour, Paul 74–75, 77, 179
Chambaud, Lewis 18
characteristics of wages and profits
    114–115
Charleval, M. de 74
Cherbuliez, Victor 70n8, 71, 104
Chevalier de la Petite Rivière,
    Amélie 72
child labour 57
circulation of ideas 90
civil servants 22; *see also* French Civil
    Service
classes 43–44
classical translation 77
Clément, M. 151
Cobet, John Frederick 165
Code de commerce 33
Colburn, Henry 17, 139
collective agreements 168–169
collective translator profile research in
    France 112–115
Collège de France 112
Collège Louis le Grand 13–14
Collins, Wilkie 83, 125, 179–182
colonial language brokers 23
Comédie-Française 100, 112
conducteurs de navire (ship agents) 33

Convention nationale translators 5
copyright 89–99, 96
Corrard, Justin-Charles 75,
    106–107, 180
Coulon de Thevenot, Jean-Félicité 151
counterfeiting 94
Courben, Jean-Jacques 165
Courrouve dit Pold, Léopold 8,
    37–39, 74
court battles 1820s and 1830s 88–99
courtiers-interprètes (combining the
    function of brokers and
    interpreters) 33
Cousin, Victor 103
Covid pandemic 109–110
Crawford, Francis Marion 194
Croft, Jennifer 1–3
Curll, Edmund 45

D'Albert Durade, François 104,
    171–172
Darcy, Mme Jean 83–84, 180
Dauthereau, M. 82
de la Grange, Édouard 58–59
de Lahaye, Marguerite 105–107, 191
de Villers, Elisa 104, 200
Decker, Alice 180–181
Defauconprêt, Auguste-Jean-Baptiste
    81–82, 131–132, 152–153;
    biography of 132–136; launching
    career in translation 136–141;
    translation career 141–153;
    translation of Walter Scott works
    153–164; as tutor 140–141
Defauconprêt, Charles-Auguste 7,
    143–145, 149–153
Defauconprêt, Félicité 134, 136
Defauconprêt, Jean-Baptiste-Ernest 134
Delestre, Pierre-François 77, 181
Delisle, Jean 49
Derosne, Charles Bernard 96, 98,
    174–176, 194
Des Essarts, Alfred 183
Dickens, Charles 181–182
dictation of translation 152
dictionaries 145–146
Dieu, Léon 82, 182
Direction de la Presse 25–26
Disraeli, Benjamin 181–182
distribution of translated languages in
    the IMEC archives **70**
division of labour 52, 58–59

224 *Index*

divorce 123n20
Dousterswivel, Mr. 60–61
droit au respect 101
droit d'auteur legislation, moral rights
99–108
droit de divulgation 99, 100, 102
droit de paternité 99, 105–106
droit de repentir 99, 104–105
droit de respect 99, 100, 104–105
Dubergier, Pierre 54–56
Duca, Jean-Louis-Sébastien 28–29, 32
Duckett, William 8
Dufief, Nicolas Gouin 146
Dugas (first name unknown) 14
Dupuy, Marie 182
Dutton, Thomas 43–44

E. X. 85–87
école de jeunes de langue 13
école des langues orientales 23
economic knowledge 20
economic lives of translators 110–111
economic significance of translation
16–17
Edgeworth, Maria 93–94
Editions de l'éclat 85–87
editorial competence 146–148
eighteenth-century France 13–15,
44–45
Eliot, George 104
Enault, Louis 182–183
English, distribution of translated
languages in the IMEC archives **70**
"enterprise Dugas" (Dugas
enterprise) 14
entrepreneurship 136
exposition universelle of 1855 22
extraduction (translation out of
French) 112

Feller, Jacques 123
financial woes of translators 56;
Defauconprêt, Auguste-Jean-
Baptiste 135–136; Swanton-Belloc,
Louise 115–120
Fiorentino, Pier-Angelo 182
Fix, Théobald 192
Flammarion 67, 69
Flammarion, Ernest 67
Flesch, Maurice-Ernest 22, 27
Fliche, Amélie (née Chevalier de la
Petite-Riviere) 72, 183–184

Florimond, Mlle J. 105–106, 184
Forster, Georg 57
Foucou, Félix 184
Fournier jeune, H. 94
François, Henri-Joseph 136
French Civil Service 22–32
Fréron, Elie 47
Fresneau, Henriette 76, 184–185
Freytag, Gustav 185
full-timers 113

G. T., Mme (E. Guidi) 187 *see also*
Guidi, E
Galignani, Giovanni Antonio 17
Gallic Books 114n13
Garnett, Constance 150
Garve, Christian 45n1
Gaskell, Elizabeth 185–186
Gausseron, Bernard-Henri 42
Gébelin, Jules Baytun 66, 75, 172–173
"Gem" 186
gender of translators, Institut mémoires
de l'édition contemporaine (IMEC)
71–73
genealogy websites 6
Genêt, Edmé-Jacques 14
genres, payment based on literary
genre 75–77
Gentilhommes de la chambre 100
Gerard, Dorothea (a.k.a. Dorothea
Longard de Longgarde) 184, 186
ghostwriter 57n14
Gibbels, Elisabeth 72
Gide, Théophile-Etienne 152, 154
Gillet, Thomas 153–154
Girette, Marcel 187
Gorman, Amanda 1, 168
Gosselin, Charles 81, 92, 152,
154, 162
Götz von Berlichingen (Goethe) 91
Gougenheim, Auguste 165
grammar-translation method 19
Gréard, H. 72, 75, 187
"Grub Street" 47
Guidi, E. 187
Guyton de Morveau, Louis-Bernard 14

Hachette 67, 70n8, 76, 83, 106
Hachette, Louis 67, 79–80, 102
hack translators 45, 48
Hackney, Iscariot (i.e. Richard Savage)
45–46

Index

Hallays-Dabot, Pierre-Victor 187
Halpérine-Kaminsky, Ely 188
handwriting translations 151
Häring, Georg Wilhelm Heinrich 61–62, 161
Hauff, Wilhelm 159, 169
Havas, Charles-Louis 39–42
Heilbron, Johann 44
Hetzel 67, 98–99, 126–128
Hetzel, Pierre-Jules 67, 105
The Hill We Climb (Gorman) 1
Hinstin, Gustave 188
hiring practices of translators 140
Hoefer, Ferdinand 188
Hughes, William 105–107, 188–189
humdrum inputs 113

identity, translatorial identity 48–52
illness, impact on workflow 55–56
IMEC *see* Institut mémoires de l'édition contemporaine
income for translators 74–75, 113; Allouard, Emma 125–128; irregularity of 168
indemnité littéraire 118–120
industrial labour, translation as 52–59
industrial literature 53
Institut mémoires de l'édition contemporaine (IMEC) 67; distribution of translated languages **70**
intellectual property 46, 85–86, 90; infringement of 94–95
international copyright legislation 89–99, 96
intraduction (translation into French) 112
Isoard, Léopold 24–25
Ivanhoe 92

Janin, Jules 79, 189
Jassaud, Adrien de (Vernoy) 189–190
Jaubert, Amédée 31
Jouan, Emile 124
Judicis de Mirandol, Louis 190
Judith Gautier (wife of the poet Catulle Mendès) 73

Kergomard, Jules 66, 190
Kieliasiantuntijat 168
knowledge economy 19
Kropotkin, Peter 68, 191

La Comtesse Gédéon de Clermont-Tonnerre, Mme 179
la littérature industrielle (industrial literature) 53
labour time 74, 117
labour-for-hire model 45
Lacroix, Albert 191
Ladvocat, Pierre-François 91
Lafond, Ernest 191
Lahure, Charles 68, 191–192
Langlès, Louis-Mathieu 8, 148
language flows 70–71
Laroche, Benjamin 192
Larousse 67
Larousse, Pierre 67
L'Athénée polyglotte 8
Lattimore-Clarke, Rose 152
Lauwereyns de Roosendaele, Louis 19
Lavigne, Ernest 78, 192
lawsuits, Billecocq vs. Glandaz (1814) 101
lawsuits 1820s and 1830s, 88–99
Le Comte, Charles 26
Le Dantec, Yves-Gérard 51
Le Play, Frédéric 20–22
Lebas, Philippe 192
Lefebvre, Jean-Pierre 167
legal liabilities 35
legal ownership of intellectual labour of translation 90–91
Lemaire, Pierre-Auguste 192
Leroy, Albert 193
Lesourd, Antoine-Adolphe 193
Lever, Charles 68
Les Jouets du Destin 106
literary capital 44, 77–81
literary entrepreneurship 136
literary piracy 90
loomwork, translation as 60–61
Lorain, Paul 72n12, 75, 103–104, 193
Lord, William Jackson 110
Lortholary, Bernard 167
Lytton, Edward Bulwer 178

MacLeod, John 144, 154
Madgett, Nicholas 7
Mainwaring, Mrs. 53–54, 56
Marchant de Beaumont, François-Marie 35–36
maritime vocabulary, translating **145**
Martin, John 154
Martin, Nicolas 194

226 Index

Masson, Frédéric 3, 7, 14
Materne, Auguste 194
media history approach 151
Méquignon-Marvis, Augustin-Claude-
  François 94–95
Mesnier, Alexandre 94
method of clue 6
Meunier, Isabelle 51
Michaelis, C. F. 162
military interpreters 23
Mirandol, Louis Judicis de 78
mistranslations 146; *see also* shifts
  in translated texts; treatment of
  challenging lexis and cultural
  references
modern translation market, rise of
  16–22
Montémont, Albert de 92, 160
Montgolfier, Adélaïde 94
moral rights 99–108
multilingualism 17
Munier, Roger 166
Murray, Sophia 24–25

Neville, Mr. 155
Niboyet, Eugénie 120–121
Nicolai, Christoph Friedrich 43–44
Nicolas, Henry 29
Nicolle, Henri 152
Nisard, Désiré 106
Nugent, Thomas 146
Nunez Taboada, M. E 36

Oberthal, Emma 123
Oberthal, Marguerite Eliette 123–124
oeuvre de l'esprit 90
Olszewiec, Julien 30
Opie, Amelia 141
Oriental languages 23
Ouida (Maria Louise Ramé) 81,
  194–195
Ovrée, Gustave 199
ownership of manuscripts 101

Pardessus, Jean-Marie 36–37, 89, 101
Pariset, Étienne 94–95
Parisot, Jacques-Théodore 154
Parsons, Anne 17
Paulmier, Adrien-Augustin 70n7, 195
payment 3; based on genre 75–77;
  for broker-interpreters 33; for
  military interpreters 23; for ministry

employment 29–30; translator
  income 74–75; *see also* income of
  translators
Pellecat, M. 33
Perrot d'Etivareilles, M. 25
Picardet, Claudine 14
Pichot, Amédée 77, 151, 162, 195–196
Pillaut, Julien 32
plagiarism 92
playwrights 100
Plumptre, Anne 56
Poe, Edgar Allan 51
Portuguese 24
privilége system 88
production lines 58–59
productivity 159
professional translators 2, 50n5
professionalisation 112
propriété littéraire 100
proto-moral rights 102
pseudonyms 72
publishers, translators in publishing
  chain 81–84
publishing: division of labour 52;
  structuring of the field of translation
  67–70; translators in publishing
  chain 81–84

quality control 15, 19
Quérard, Joseph-Marie 141–142

recruitment to civil service 27–28
Rély, Victor de (or Derély) 196
remuneration 75, 77
Renouard, Augustin-Charles 88–89,
  95–96
reputation 77–81, 114
retranslation theory 163
Rey, Théodore-Albert 196–197
Richelot, Henri 197
right of attribution 99, 103–104 *see
  droit de paternité*
right of disclosure/to decide when and if
  the work is ready for publication 99
right of integrity/not to have one's
  work altered without consent 99
right of withdrawal/to remove a work
  from the public sphere 99
Rignoux, François 92–93
Rijneveld, Marieke Lucas 1
Roberts, M. 144
Rolland, Abraham-Auguste 197

Rolland, Madeleine 197
Rosny, J. H. 124–125
Rothschild, Nathan Meyer 39
Rousseau, Joseph 31n11
Rouvier, Maurice 122
Rovetta, Gerolamo 84

SACD *see Société des auteurs et compositeurs dramatiques*
Saint-Saëns, Camille 69, 128
Sapiro, Gisèle 44
satires 46
Scenes of Clerical Life 104
Scott, John 138
Scott, Sir Walter 60–62, 82, 92, 141–143; translations 153–164
Sebaldus Nothanker 45, 53
Sela-Sheffy, Rakefet 48–49
SGDL *see Société des Gens de Lettres*
shifts in translated texts 144–146
ship agents 33
shorthand 151
Silvestre, Augustin-François de 19–20
slavery 57
Smith, Adam 114, 116
Smith, James 154
social capital 25, 28–29, 31, 73, 77–81, 104
social status 77n18
Société des auteurs et compositeurs dramatiques (SACD) 128
Société des Gens de Lettres (SGDL) 82, 112
Société Françaisedes Traducteurs 83
Soldi, David (or Soldin) 70n9 197–198
Sommer, Édouard 79
Soskice, Juliet 150
Speke, John Hanning 198
Squid Game 1
standardisation in translation process 15
Stapfer, Albert 91
stare decisis 92
Stendhal 163
Sterne, Laurence 43
stipends for artists 118–120
Stone, John Hurford 7, 153
Strömholm, Stig 100
structuring the field of translation for publishing 67–70; language flows 70–71; literary capital 77–81; payment based on literary genre 75–77; social capital 77–81; translator gender 71–73; translator income 74–75; translatorial reputation 77–81; translators in publishing chain 81–84
stylistic authorship attribution 164
subcontracting 72, 153
subtitles 1
Swanton-Belloc, Louise 80–81, 93–94, 115–121, 198–199
sworn translators 22, 31–32, 35
Syndicat des traducteurs de l'édition (Union for translators in the publishing sector) 167

teach-yourself language manuals 18
Teste, Auguste 199
Thackeray, William Makepeace 199
theft of printed works 154–155
Toledo school 13
traducteurs jurés (sworn translators) 22
translating agent 13
translating maritime vocabulary **145**
translation agencies 36–39
translation archives 65–67
translation as a business 44–45
translation as creative act 92
translation as industrial labour 52–59
translation as loomwork 60–61
translation contracts 68
translation criticism 50
translation entrepreneurs 32–42
translation factories 47–48, 132, 159
translation flows, market demand 71
translation market, rise of 16–22
translation pricing model 69–70
translation services with institutional support 19–20
translation speed 149–150
translational labour 57
translation contracts, language flows 70–71
translator gender, Institut mémoires de l'édition contemporaine (IMEC) 71–73
translator income 74–75
translator profile research 112–115
translator visibility 1
translator-editor relationships 158
translatorial identity 48–52
translatorial labour 57

228 *Index*

translatorial moral rights 99–108
translatorial paratext 50
translatorial reputation 77–81
treatment of challenging lexis and cultural references **147**

Übersetzungsfabriken 43
Ulliac-Trémadeure, Sophie 72–73
unionisation of translators 166–169

van Tieghem, Paul 47
Varembey, Achille 199
Vatismenil, Henri de 18
Vergé, M. 25
vérificateur 14
Verrier, Xavier 199–200
Vignon, Claude 122
Voïart, Elise (Elise Petitpain) 200

Von Asten, J. C. 33–34
Voysey, Mary Ellison 134n2, 136

Wailly, Léon de 51, 200
Walker, John 138
Walladmor 61–64
Weisse, Christian Felix 52, 55–56
Westen, Gustavus 165
Whitfield, Agnes 49
Willenberg, Jennifer 6
winner takes all market model 114
women: and their economic experiences 109–130; Covid pandemic 109–110; as interpreters 23; underrepresentation of 71–72
working conditions of translators 26–27
Worth, Charles Frederick 124
Wyzewa, Théodore de 66